Cybersecurity First Principles

Cybersecurity First Principles

A Reboot of Strategy and Tactics

Presented by the cyberwire

Rick Howard

WILEY

Published by John Wiley & Sons, Inc., Hoboken, New Jersey.
Published simultaneously in Canada and the United Kingdom.

ISBN: 978-1-394-17308-2
ISBN: 978-1-394-17309-9 (ebk.)
ISBN: 978-1-394-17339-6 (ebk.)

For general information on our other products and services or for technical support, please contact our Customer Care Department within the United States at (800) 762-2974, outside the United States at (317) 572-3993 or fax (317) 572-4002.

If you believe you've found a mistake in this book, please bring it to our attention by emailing our reader support team at wileysupport@wiley.com with the subject line "Possible Book Errata Submission."

Wiley also publishes its books in a variety of electronic formats. Some content that appears in print may not be available in electronic formats. For more information about Wiley products, visit our web site at www.wiley.com.

Library of Congress Control Number: 2023933118

Cover design: Wiley

SKY10076552_060424

For the people who no one imagines anything of and who will do the things that no one can imagine, it's time to step up.

—Rick Howard, author

To Seneca who has given me the best advice, like: life is very short and anxious for those who forget the past, neglect the present, and fear the future. I would dedicate it to my family, but they will never read this.

—Steve Winterfeld, editor

We wrote this to satisfy mobs,
though me and my friends are all swabs.
So thanks to you hackers,
And bad cyber actors,
Without whom we wouldn't have jobs.

—Brandon Karpf, editor

ABOUT THE AUTHOR

Rick Howard and Steve Winterfeld are best friends, have known each other for more than 20 years, and for the entire time, have argued about everything under the sun, including cybersecurity issues. Brandon Karpf is a colleague of Rick's at The CyberWire where one of his most onerous tasks is to keep Rick straight in terms of facts and clarity. With a nod to Stephen King, these guys are here to keep Rick from turning into a literary gasbag.

Rick is the chief analyst and senior fellow at The CyberWire, the world's largest B2B cybersecurity podcast network, and the chief security officer (CSO) of N2K (The CyberWire's parent company). His prior jobs include CSO for Palo Alto Networks (a commercial cybersecurity vendor), CISO for TASC (a defense contractor), GM for iDefense (a commercial cyber threat intelligence service at VeriSign), global SOC director for Counterpane (one of the original managed security service providers), and commander for the U.S. Army's Computer Emergency Response Team (responsible for coordinating network defense, network intelligence, and network attack operations for the Army's global network). He was one of the founding organizers of the Cyber Threat Alliance (an ISAC for security vendors), and he also created and still participates in the Cybersecurity Canon Project (a Rock & Roll Hall of Fame for cybersecurity books). He has years of experience creating and building organizations from scratch or transforming existing organizations into productive organizations by developing strategy and tactics that were in line with senior leadership. He taught computer science at the United States Military Academy for 5 years and, out of all the jobs he has had in his long 40-year career, considers himself to be a teacher above all things.

ABOUT THE TECHNICAL EDITORS

Steve Winterfeld is the advisory CISO at Akamai where he collaborates on strategy with customers, trains internal Akamai security and sales teams about how to think about the security issues of the day, and helps drive vision for the product line. Before joining Akamai, he built security programs as the CISO for Nordstrom bank, the director of Cybersecurity for Nordstrom Corp, and the director of incident response and threat intelligence at Charles Schwab. He met Rick when he was the senior technical director and cybersecurity and group CTO at Northrop Grumman where he built RCERT South (the U.S. Army's South American Computer Emergency Response Team). He has vast experience in retail, finance, intelligence, and government contracting but has a deep understanding of how to build operational defense and compliance-based programs that will stand up to hackers and auditors. Steve has published two books on cyber warfare (one is a Cybersecurity Canon Hall of Fame candidate), and he holds the CISSP, ITIL, and PMP certifications. Steve is a regular guest at The CyberWire's Hash Table where he provides his expertise on several of Rick's podcasts.

Brandon Karpf is the Executive Director of New Markets at N2K Networks where he oversees the company's multi-market strategy and growth operations. His prior jobs include Technical Editor and Strategy Lead at CyberWire, and as a Cryptologic Warfare Officer in the US Navy. His tours in the Navy included assignments at the National Security Agency office of Computer Network

Operations as a senior watch officer and branch chief, US Cyber Command as an operations chief, the US Naval Academy as an adjunct professor of cyber science, and as the head of Information Warfare onboard USS Boxer where he was the ship's expert in cryptology, signals intelligence, electronic warfare, and information operations. Brandon graduated with honor and distinction from the US Naval Academy with a degree in Robotics and Control Engineering, holds a Masters of Science from Massachusetts Institute of Technology, and is pursuing his Executive Masters of Business Administration from Georgetown University. He is a published writer in the domains of national security and cybersecurity policy, cyberwarfare and operations, technology risk and compliance, advanced network architectures, and the defense technology ecosystem. He is a teacher,
a husband, and one of the world's preeminent podcast-listeners.

ACKNOWLEDGMENTS

Writing a book is way harder than I thought it was going to be. I loved going through the process, but there are so many people who helped me get through it. There's no way I could have done this on my own.

First things first, let me start by thanking my awesome wife, Kathy. Through the process, she kept the household trains on time, directed potential catastrophes away from my purview, and tolerated my brusque and impatient answers to important family questions when I was knee deep in writing. Thanks, honey. You're the best wife I have.

A very special thanks to an old boss of mine, Mark McLaughlin. I've had the honor and pleasure of working for him twice in my career, once at VeriSign and once at Palo Alto Networks. Bar none, he is the best leader I have ever worked for (both in the military and in the commercial sector), and he has been my role model for what an honorable man should be. Thank you for your guidance over the years, Mark. If you ever need anything, just call.

Next is my boss, Peter Kilpe, the CEO of N2K Networks. When I came to him in early 2022 and said "Hey, I think I have enough material for a company sponsored book," he didn't laugh me out of his office. He even pulled some strings with his buddies at Wiley and convinced them this would be a good idea. Peter, I will be ever forever grateful.

To my best friend, Steve Winterfeld, one of the editors. Steve is the guy I'm calling when I need to get out of the country because of. . .reasons. He's the guy that executes with no questions asked. He's also one of the smartest people on the planet when it comes to cybersecurity. My friendship with him and the rollicking back-and-forth debates about cybersecurity issues (and cybersecurity movies) over the years greatly shaped my own thinking in the space. He's also the guy who will call me out on my own nonsense in life and in writing this book. I love you, man.

Thanks to my colleagues at The CyberWire: John Petric, Elliot Peltzman, and Brandon Karpf. A lot of this material in this book came from initial essays that I wrote for my own *CSO Perspectives* podcast. John was the editor of all of that and made it so that I didn't come off sounding like a complete idiot. He is a prolific and efficient writer, and his skill and keen eye have made me a better writer too. Where I have failed, I didn't take John's advice. Elliot has been my sound engineer at The CyberWire since the beginning. His sense of what sounds good and what doesn't has made me a better storyteller. Finally, Brandon, one of the book's editors and a relative newbie compared to the rest of us old-timers, soaks up information like a sponge and is quick to point out errors in language and logic that I would never have found on my own. Thanks to you all.

To my friend and colleague, Jack Freund, thank you for reviewing the chapter on risk forecasting. Jack's Cybersecurity Canon Hall of Fame book, *Measuring and Managing Information Risk: A Fair Approach*, co-authored with Jack Jones, got me started down the path of trying to understand risk forecasting. Every time I have ever asked for help, Jack has always responded. Thank you, sir.

Next is my friend, George Finney, who kindly reviewed the chapter on zero trust. He has written his own book, *Project Zero Trust: A Story about a Strategy for Aligning Security and the Business*, that I highly recommend. George and I met years ago through our mutual appreciation of books and cybersecurity. Thanks for your help, George. Your review soothed my mind that I wasn't living in crazy town.

To my very long-term colleague and friend, Dr. Georgianna (George) Shea. I have bent her arm to help me with my own projects (the Cybersecurity Canon and The CyberWire's Hash Table) and now she has more than returned the favor by reviewing the resilience chapter. You're the best George.

I want to also thank Adam Barlow and Sridevi Joshi who have spent hours with me at the white board working through potential Monte Carlo and other calculations trying to find an easy way to calculate risk. Every time we met, I got one step closer. Their review of the risk forecasting chapter was invaluable.

To my new friend and colleague, John Eiben. He took the stick figures I made with crayons and duct tape and turned them into beautiful illustrations of my ideas. Because of his work, I even understand what I was talking about with more clarity than I had before. I can't thank you enough John.

Lastly, I want to thank my Wiley colleagues for walking me through this editorial process. Their steady hands kept this virgin author on track. This is a formal shout-out to Jim Minatel, Dabian Witherspoon, Pete Gaughan, Melissa Burlock, Magesh Elangovan, and Kim Wimpsett.

CONTENTS

CONTENTS

WHO WE ARE

I didn't want to write a book, even a short one like this, that would leave me feeling like either a literary gasbag or a transcendental asshole. There are enough of those books—and those writers—on the market already, thanks.

—Stephen King, author

Foreword

During my career, I have had the privilege of working as the CEO with some exceptional teams in two great companies, VeriSign and Palo Alto Networks. In some cases, I had the distinct pleasure and good fortune to work with the same people in both companies, Rick Howard being one of them and a standout in both. Back when VeriSign was a significant security player in addition to a leading Internet infrastructure provider, Rick ran a business for me called iDefense. It was in this role that I first got to see Rick at work both as a security practitioner, evangelist, leader, and storyteller, which is a rare combination in any discipline, let alone security. I was very fortunate to benefit from Rick's expertise, advice, and his ability to explain very complicated issues in a down-to-earth and understandable way. Rick has a way of seeing the big picture while never losing sight of the tyranny of the urgent that plagues cybersecurity professionals. Turns out that is a very helpful and valuable skill set in an industry that moves at extremely high speed and where the bad actors are on the bleeding edge. So, it may be no surprise that when I joined the Palo Alto Networks team in 2011 that I was soon trying to recruit Rick to the team as our first CSO. Despite being a pretty small company at the time and my inability to give him a solid job description of the CSO role, Rick joined us on our vision and mission of protecting our digital way of life. He quickly became an integral part of the team and was in high demand with our customers, prospects, and the industry at large. Along the way, he was instrumental in the formation and success of some bedrock organizations like Unit 42 (the company's first public-facing cyber intelligence team), the Cyber Threat Alliance, the first security vendor ISAO, the CyberSecurity Canon Project, and the Joint Service Academy Cyber Summit. Through that journey, Rick demonstrated his amazing ability to summarize all of cybersecurity history, make that history relevant to you now, and give counsel and advice on what the future likely holds. With that kind of ability and passion, it is natural that Rick currently is the CSO, senior fellow, and chief analyst at The CyberWire, and that his writings and podcasts are incredibly popular and eagerly anticipated. I often tell individuals just starting in cyber that if they want to understand what is going on, go listen to Rick. And, when people write books like *The Perfect Weapon* and *This Is How They Tell Me The World Ends*, they call the likes of Rick first. Rick's new book, *Cyber Security First Principles*, is chock full of wisdom, experience, relevant advice, and, above all, the importance of first principles in cyber. I'm sure you will enjoy it and find it valuable reading. And, make sure to check out all of Rick's podcasts at CyberWire. They are all great listening. But if you listen to only one, make it "A CSO's 9/11 Story: CSO Perspective." This one will tell you all you need to know about Rick personally. Back at our common alma mater, West Point, they say the leaders are the ones who run to the sound of the shooting, not away. Rick is that leader.

Happy Reading,

Mark McLaughlin

Former President, CEO, and Chairman of the Board, Palo Alto Networks

Vice Chairman of the Board, Palo Alto Networks

Chairman of the Board, Qualcomm, Inc.

Member and former Chairman, U.S. National Security Telecommunications Advisory Council

INTRODUCTION

Map out your future—but do it in pencil. The road ahead is as long as you make it. Make it worth the trip.

—Jon Bon Jovi, American singer, songwriter, guitarist, and actor

Who Is This Book For?

This is about rethinking cybersecurity from the ground up using the idea of *first principles*. I will explain what I mean by that in Chapter 3, "Zero Trust," but at a high level it's a list of fundamental truths that serves as the foundation for building your cybersecurity program. That said, my intention for writing the book was to target a broad swath of security practitioners in three groups.

The first group consists of security executives. These are my peers, colleagues, and the people who work for them in the cybersecurity industry supporting the commercial sector, government circles (both policy and technical), and academia. With this first principles notion, my intent is to challenge how these network defender veterans think about cybersecurity. I am going to suggest that for the past 25 years, we've all been doing it wrong and that a reexamination of first principles will guide us back to the right path and will help us disrupt our current thinking to pursue defensive postures that have a higher probability of success.

The second group consists of the newbies coming into the field. These would be young and fresh-faced college graduates, government civil servants transitioning into the commercial sector, and career changers who are tired of what they have been doing and look to cybersecurity to be more interesting and lucrative. I am going to give this group a foundational framework based on first principles to build their knowledge, including the first principle historic background so that they can understand the current state of the cybersecurity landscape and an idea of where we all might be heading in the near future.

The last group will consist of teachers and students at the elementary through graduate levels. Within the cybersecurity discipline there exist numerous, valuable, and fascinating by-waters of study that many students and educators feel are loosely connected and, because of the volume, quickly become overwhelming. First principles will be a framework for your curriculum. I will lay out how to tie everything back to cybersecurity first principles that will allow them to chart a course through the volume of material they need to get through.

That said, there are typically three kinds of organizations that network defenders work for: commercial, government, and academia. I can make an argument that there are two different categories of government network defenders too: traditional defense (like their commercial and academia peers) but also offensive cyber for espionage and continuous-low-level-cyber-conflict (cyber warfare purposes). I will discuss the former and not the latter.

Lastly, since the early Internet days, organizations typically fall across a network defense spectrum between the haves and the have-nots, and where they fit within that range normally depends on how big the organization is (not always). On the have-not side, these are organizations that are small (like startups and city/county governments) where they barely have enough resources to keep the lights on. On the have side, these are typically large organizations (like Fortune 500 firms) that have more resources than they know what to do with. I will cover first principle strategies and tactics that any infosec program should consider regardless of size. Fully deploying all of these strategies and concepts would be expensive, something reserved for the have side of the spectrum. That said, these ideas are not checklists. They represent ways to reduce the probability of material impact. Depending on your environment, some will work better than others. Especially for the have-nots, where possible, I highlight where you can pursue these ideas on a shoestring budget.

What the Book Covers

First principles in a designated problem space are so fundamental as to be self-evident; so elementary that no expert in the field can argue against them; so crucial to our understanding that without them, the infrastructure that holds our accepted best practice disintegrates like sandcastles against the watery tide. They are atomic. Experts use them like building blocks to derive everything else that is known in the problem domain. All new knowledge gained in the problem domain is dependent on our previously developed first principles. That means there is an absolute first principle, the principle that starts everything.

The Internet started to become useful to academia, government, and the commercial sector sometime in the early 1990s. As it did so, cyber bad guys discovered that the Internet might be valuable for their chosen activity too: crime, espionage, hacktivism, warfare, and influence operations. Organizations began hiring people like me, network defenders, to prevent these "black hats" from being disruptive. In the early days, the network defender community made a lot of assumptions about how to do that. Twenty-five years later, many of those best practices turned out not to be first principles at all; mostly they were first and best guesses. Twenty-five years later, it's time to reset our thinking and determine what our baseline cybersecurity first principles are and what the ultimate cybersecurity first principle is.

I make the case for the atomic cybersecurity first principle, explains the strategies necessary to achieve it, and consider the required tactics, techniques, and procedures for each.

Writing Conventions

Here are a few conventions I use in the book to aid in your understanding.

Cybersecurity

I use the term cybersecurity as a catchall for the work that practioners do. Over the years, the community has adopted many synonyms that have the same meaning. Here are just a few:

- Digital security
- IT security
- Information technology (IT) security
- Information security (infosec)

For my purposes, they all refer to the same thing and I use them interchangeably.

Cybersecurity Professionals

The same goes for the phrases we all use when we describe each other.

- Infosec practitioners
- Network defenders
- Security practitioners
- Security professionals

For my purposes, I also use them interchangeably.

Organizations

There are generally three types of organizations that invest in the cybersecurity people-process-technology triad: commercial companies, government organizations, and academia. Where I refer to one of the three, assume that I am talking about all of them. When I'm not, I will call it out explicitly.

The Cybersecurity Canon Project

The Canon project (`cybersecuritycanon.com`) is a security professional community effort to identify all the books that cybersecurity professionals should read. I founded the project in 2013, and at the time of this writing, it is sponsored by Ohio State University. I refer to many Hall of Fame and Candidate books that the reader might find useful. On the web page, readers will find book reviews of those books and many others.

Rick's War Stories

I've been working in the cybersecurity industry for more than 30 years. Along the way, I have had experiences that some readers might like to hear about. I call them *war stories*. Many are only loosely connected to the topic at hand, and some may have no connection at all (I just liked them). I've re-told some of them here. That said, I realize that some readers might want to just read the meat of the book (like one of my editors, Steve Winterfeld, who just wants to skip over the war stories). I have color coded the text of my war stories differently (in gray), like this section, to make it easier for the readers who stand with Steve.

Book Website

Whiles doing the background research, I created supplemental materials that helped me organize my thought process. They include the following:

- Agile Manifesto
- Bayes Success Stories (summarized from Sharon McGrayne's book, *The Theory That Would Not Die*)
- Chaos Engineering Historical Timeline
- Referenced Cybersecurity Canon Hall of Fame Books
- Cybersecurity Historical Timeline
- Cybersecurity Intelligence Historical Timeline
- Encryption Historical Timeline
- Equifax Hack Timeline
- Identity and Authentication Historical Timeline
- Kindervag's Nine Rules of Zero Trust
- Red Team, Blue Team Historical Timeline
- RSA Security Hack Timeline
- SDP (Software Defined Perimeter) Historical Timeline
- Research Summary on Why Heat Maps Are Poor Vehicles for Conveying Risk

You don't need these materials to understand my main thesis, but some of them might be useful or at least interesting.

For more information, please visit `thecyberwire.com/CybersecurityFirstPrinciplesBook`.

Road Map

I cover a lot of material. If you find yourself getting lost in the blizzard of ideas and can't remember where you are in relation to the overall thesis, refer to Figure 1. Read it from the bottom up. The

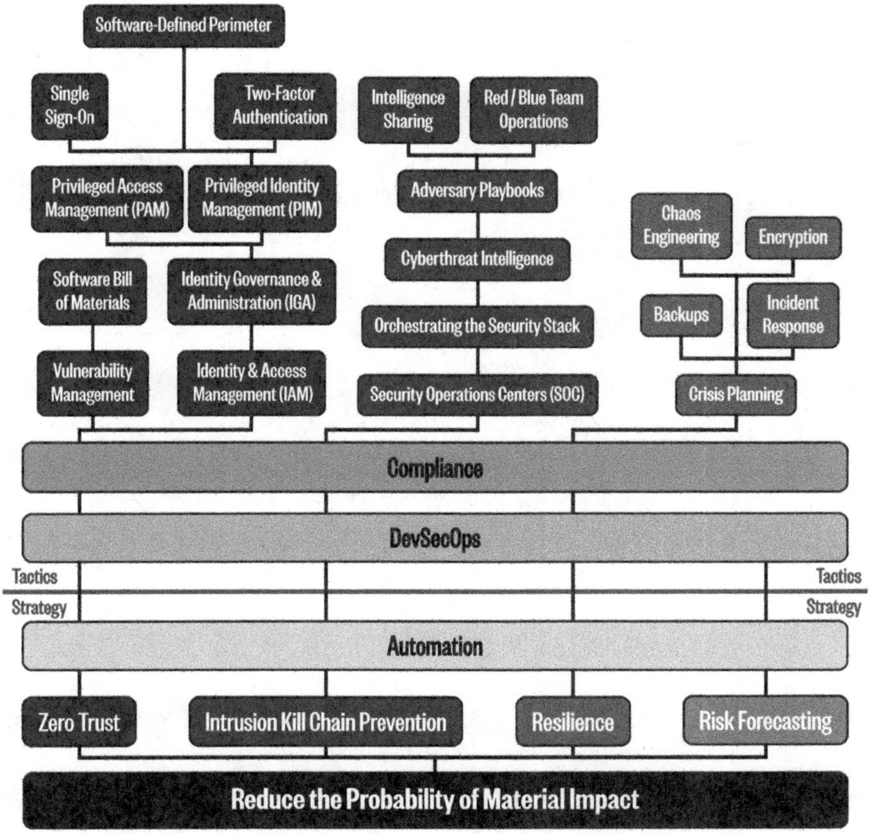

Figure 1 Cybersecurity first principles road map

first box is the foundation and absolute cybersecurity first principle (see Chapter 2). The next two rows are the follow-on first-principle strategies that you might use to pursue the ultimate first principle: zero trust (Chapter 4), intrusion kill chain prevention (Chapter 5), resilience (Chapter 6), risk forecasting (Chapter 7), and automation (Chapter 8). The remaining boxes are the tactics you might use to pursue each strategy. They show up as sections within the chapters. The gray lines show the connections between the strategies and the tactics. Note that the automation strategy and compliance tactic cut across everything. Chapter 8 tells you why.

[illegible]

[illegible]

1 First Principles

First principle thinking is the idea that everything you do is underpinned by a foundational belief, or first principles.

—Reed Hastings, Netflix CEO

. . .in order to study the acquisition of [knowledge], we must commence with the investigation of those first causes which are called Principles.

—Rene Descartes, philosopher

I think it's important to reason from first principles rather than by analogy. . . . [With first principles] you boil things down to the most fundamental truths. . .and then reason up from there.

—Elon Musk, SpaceX founder

Overview

This chapter is for you if you are not familiar with the idea of first principles as a general scientific best practice. It's not just a meme that you heard about on Twitter. Scientists have been using the idea since the world was young to discover the hidden secrets of nature and society. This entire book is my exploration of that concept applied to cybersecurity. There have been discussions of basic cybersecurity fundamentals, sure, but, as you'll see, researchers believed early on (1970s–1980s) that the absolute cybersecurity first principle was to build a completely secure computer. By the early 2020s, practitioners had largely abandoned that idea as impractical. That said, the security community hasn't replaced it with anything substantial except for maybe the concept of the CIA triad (confidentiality, integrity, and availability). Even advocates of the triad don't elevate it to the level of a first principle. They talk about it in terms of general best practices. In this chapter, I explain why the CIA triad—as well as other accepted best practices such as practicing good cyber hygiene (patching), preventing malware infestations, performing incident response operations, following the checklists in security frameworks, and adhering to international compliance law—doesn't qualify as an absolute first principle. After all of that, I propose what the true atomic cybersecurity first principle should be.

What Are First Principles?

The idea of first principles goes all the way back to the great philosopher Aristotle (384–322 BCE) in his published work *Physics*[1] (about 340 BCE), where he established his initial concepts of natural philosophy, the study of nature (*physis*). Before he starts his main thesis, though, he establishes that we can't really understand a concept completely until we understand its essence: "For we do not think that we know a thing until we are acquainted with its primary conditions or first principles, and have carried our analysis as far as its simplest elements."[2] He describes his method for finding these primary conditions by taking what we think we know from casual observation and working our way back to the core of it. He says, "The natural way of doing this is to start from the things which are more knowable and obvious to us and proceed towards those which are clearer and more knowable by nature."[3] He makes it clear, though, that these

[1]Aristotle, 1996. Physics. Oxford University Press, USA.
[2]Aristotle, 1996. Physics. Oxford University Press, USA.
[3]Aristotle, 1996. Physics. Oxford University Press, USA.

atomic ideas known to nature are unique building blocks, and all study starts there. "For first principles must not be derived from one another nor from anything else, while everything has to be derived from them."[4] Once you find these essential concepts, they are the "big bang" to the overall hypothesis. "First principles are eternal and have no ulterior cause."[5,6,7,8]

Although Euclid, the famous Greek mathematician and teacher, never mentions "first principles" in his foundational math book *Elements* (~300 BCE), his sparse presentation of 23 definitions, five assumptions (postulates or axioms), and five common notions has been the underlying bedrock of geometry and other math disciplines for more than 23 centuries.[9] There's no clearer case that first principle thinking will lead to humankind's understanding of the true nature of the world that we all live in.[10,11,12]

In 1644, the greatest philosophical doubter of all time and the father of modern philosophy, Rene Descartes, published his

---

[4]Aristotle, 1996. Physics. Oxford University Press, USA.
[5]Aristotle, 2009. Physics. Neeland Media.
[6]Aristotle, 1999. Encyclopedia Britannica.
[7]Irwin, T., Irwin, T.H., 1990. Aristotle's First Principles. Oxford University Press.
[8]Juma, A., 2017. Aristotle and the Importance of First Principles - The Startup - Medium. The Startup.
[9]Euclides, 2008. Euclid's elements of geometry.
[10]Allen, D., 1997. EUCLID, The Elements [WWW Document]. Texas A&M University. www.math.tamu.edu/~dallen/history/euclid/euclid.html (accessed 10/29/22).
[11]Taisbak, C.M., 1998. Euclid. Encyclopedia Britannica.
[12]Washington, E., 2014. On Euclid, Archimedes and first principles [WWW Document]. RenewAmerica. www.renewamerica.com/columns/washington/140531 (accessed 10/29/22).

"Principles of Philosophy."[13,14,15] He starts "with the most common matters, as, for example, that the word PHILOSOPHY signifies the study of wisdom, and that by wisdom is to be understood not merely prudence in the management of affairs, but a perfect knowledge of all that man can know, as well for the conduct of his life as for the preservation of his health and the discovery of all the arts." Now that is a gigantic research goal. How would you ever pursue it? He says, to procure that understanding, we must infer it from initial sources. "To subserve these ends must necessarily be deduced from first causes; so that in order to study the acquisition of it (which is properly called philosophizing), we must commence with the investigation of those first causes which are called PRINCIPLES." He then says that these first principles must meet two requirements. "In the first place, they must be so clear and evident that the human mind, when it attentively considers them, cannot doubt of their truth; in the second place, the knowledge of other things must be so dependent on them as that though the principles themselves may indeed be known apart from what depends on them." What he means is that all knowledge about the subject comes from these first principles. "It will accordingly be necessary thereafter to endeavor so to deduce from those principles the knowledge of the things that depend on them, as that there may be nothing in the whole series of deductions which is not perfectly manifest."

One thing to note here is that finding first principles for any subject is hard. With his book, Descartes completely upended the current philosophical thinking of the day saying that Aristotle and his contemporaries (Plato and Socrates) never found the first principle of

[13]Descartes, R., 1644a. Principles of Philosophy (Principia Philosophiae): With A Special Introduction. Amazon Kindle.
[14]Descartes, R., 1644b. Principia philosophiae. Google Books.
[15]Descartes, R., n.d. The Principles of Philosophy. Full Text Archive.

philosophy. Ouch! Descartes' approach, by doubting everything, established the ultimate first principle of philosophy: "I think, therefore I am (Cogito, ergo sum).[16]

Two British mathematicians, Alfred Whitehead and Bertrand Russell, published a book, *Principia Mathematica*, in 1910, that attempted to rebuild the language of math from the ground up using a small set of first principles.[17] They recognized some inconsistencies in the current set of rules used by the math community at the time. You could use the same rules to get two different and absolutely correct results, something called the Russell paradox.[18] In a precision engineering world, that was a recipe for disaster. So, they went back to the drawing board, threw everything out, and started from scratch. It took them 80 pages to mathematically prove that 1 + 1 = 2. In a footnote, Whitehead and Russell famously wrote this line: "The above proposition is occasionally useful." And you all thought that math nerds weren't funny. Shame on you.

In our modern day, when asked about how he approached the concepts of economic space flights, Elon Musk didn't say that he looked at what NASA and Boeing had done during the Apollo and Space Shuttle missions in the 1960s and took the next step. Instead, he threw all of that out and started over with first principles—a gutsy move for sure but that is probably why he is a gazillionaire, and I'm not.[19,20,21]

---

[16]Watson, R.A., 1998. Rene Descartes. Encyclopedia Britannica.
[17]Whitehead, A.N., Russell, B., 1910. Principia Mathematica: to *56. Merchant Books.
[18]Irvine, 1995. Russell's Paradox [WWW Document]. Stanford Encyclopedia of Philosophy. plato.stanford.edu/entries/russell-paradox r(accessed 10/29/22).
[19]Contributor, Q., 2015. Does Elon Musk's "First Principles" Learning Style Work? Slate.
[20]Rose, K., 2012. Foundation 20 // Elon Musk. YouTube.
[21]Vance, A., 2015. Elon Musk: Tesla, SpaceX, and the Quest for a Fantastic Future. Ecco.

What Aristotle, Euclid, Descartes, Whitehead and Russel, and Musk are going on about is that to solve any complex problem set, practitioners have to reduce it to its primary essence.

First principles in a designated problem space are so fundamental as to be self-evident; so elementary that no expert in the field can argue against them; so crucial to our understanding that without them, the infrastructure that holds our accepted best practice disintegrates like sand castles against the watery tide. They are atomic. Experts use them like building blocks to derive everything else that is known in the problem domain. All new knowledge gained in the problem domain is dependent on our previously developed first principles.

If that is true, and I believe that it is, the next logical question then is, what are cybersecurity's first principles?

Prior Research on Cybersecurity First Principles

In the modern world, the computer era started in earnest when the mainframe computer became useful to governments, universities, and the commercial world (circa 1960–1981). It took about a decade before the mainframe community realized that they might have a computer security problem, and it started with the U.S. military. Willis Ware's "Security Controls For Computer Systems," published in 1970 when Ware was working for the Rand Corporation, started the process.[22] The paper is not so much a definition of cybersecurity as it is a listing and description of all the ways computers were going to be a problem in the future when they started sharing resources across networks. I would put this in the category of, "the first step in

[22]Ware, W.H., 1970. Security Controls for Computer Systems (U): Report of Defense Science Board Task Force on Computer Security. The Rand Corporation.

solving any problem is recognizing that you have a problem." It hints at the idea that the security community needs to determine how to build a secure system. This idea will be the focus of researchers through the 1990s. In the Cybersecurity Canon Hall of Fame book, *A Vulnerable System: The History of Information Security in the Computer Age*, published in 2021, the author, Andrew Stewart, laments the fact that since the beginning of the digital age, nobody has been able to build a secure system.[23] This idea has largely been abandoned.

The paper "Computer Security Technology Planning Study," published by James Anderson for the U.S. Air Force in 1972, feels like a continuation of thought from the Willis Ware paper.[24] It's an early expression, maybe the first expression, of the idea that security shouldn't be added on after the system is built, something that security professionals still talk about today when you hear them discuss the idea of shifting left or security by design. It mirrors the idea that building a secure system is the ultimate goal but proposes that any secure systems will require a way to monitor that system for defects and intrusions.

The next year, David Bell and Len LaPadula, then working for MITRE, published their paper called "Secure Computer Systems: Mathematical Foundations."[25] In it, they provide the arithmetic proof that would guarantee that a computer system is secure. Unfortunately, they admit up front that even if you could build a system that adheres to the proof, how would system builders guarantee that they implemented everything correctly? Theoretically, you could do it, but

---

[23]Stewart, A.J., 2021. A Vulnerable System: The History of Information Security in the Computer Age. Cornell University Press.

[24]Anderson, J.P., 1972. Computer Security Technology Planning Study (Volume I). Electronics System Division 1.

[25]Bell, D., LaPadula, L., 1973. Secure Computer Systems: Mathematical Foundations. Mitre.

practically, how would you vouch for the veracity? And this is the problem that plagued this kind of research for 30 years.

In 1975, Jerome Saltzer and Michael Schroeder published their paper, "The Protection of Information in Computer Systems," in *Proceedings of the IEEE*.[26] In it, they lay out the early beginnings of the CIA triad, even though they don't use that exact terminology. They also likely make the first case that username/password combinations are a weak form of authentication, and two-factor authentication will be required. Further, they might be the first to champion the reduction of complexity in all things related to security design and, for whatever the design becomes, to not hide it in secrecy. In other words, this may be the first public record of researchers making the argument against security through obscurity. Finally, they promote an idea called *fail-safe defaults*, meaning deny everything first and allow by exception. This idea is possibly the first inklings of perimeter defense: building an outer barrier to the network that could control access. This was about a decade before we had the technology to do it (firewalls).

Dr. Fred Cohen published the first papers in 1991 and 1992 that used defense in depth to describe a common cybersecurity model in the network defender community.[27,28,29] He didn't invent the phrase, but he is most likely the first one to describe it in a paper. Defense in depth is the idea that network architects erect an electronic barrier that sits between the Internet and an organization's digital assets.

[26]Saltzer, J., Schroeder, M., 1975. The Protection of Information in Computer Systems. Proceedings of the IEEE 63, 1278–1308.
[27]Cohen, F., 1989. Models of practical defenses against computer viruses. Computers & Security 8, 149–160. doi.org/10.1016/0167-4048(89)90070-9
[28]Cohen, F., 2016. Defense in Depth.
[29]Cohen, F., 1992. [PDF] Defense-in-depth against computer viruses. Computers and Security 11, 563–579.

To get on the inside of the barrier from the Internet, you had to go through a control point (usually a firewall but sometimes in the early days, with a router). From the 1990s until present day, the common practice has been to add additional control tools behind the firewall to provide more granular functions. In the early days, we added intrusion detection systems and antivirus systems. All of those tools together formed something called the *security stack*, and the idea was that if one of the tools in the stack failed to block an adversary, then the next tool in line would. If that one failed, then the next would take over. That is defense in depth.

In 1998, Donn Parker published his book *Fighting Computer Crime: A New Framework for Protecting Information*, where he strongly condemns the elements in the CIA triad as being inadequate.[30] He never mentions the phrase "CIA triad," though. He proposed adding three other elements (possession or control, authenticity, and utility) that eventually became known as the Parkerian Hexad, but the idea never really caught on for reasons probably only a marketing expert could explain.

During this period, most security practitioners spent time improving the security stack in one form or the other. As cloud environments emerged around 2006, though, the number of digital environments we had to protect exploded. Organizations started storing and processing data in multiple locations that I like to call *data islands* (traditional data centers, mobile devices, cloud environments, and SaaS applications). The security stack idea became more abstract. It wasn't one set of tools physically deployed behind the firewall any longer; it was a series of security stacks deployed for each data island. The security stack became the set of all tools deployed that improved the organization's defensive posture regardless

---

[30]Parker, D.B., 1998. Fighting Computer Crime: A New Framework for Protecting Information. Wiley.

of where they were located, in other words, defense in depth applied abstractly to all of the environments. Most of the research in this period focused on improving our CIA triad capability by building better tools for the security stack (such as application firewalls, identity and access management systems, XDR, etc.) and better models for stopping adversary activity (Kindervag's zero trust "No More Chewy Centers" paper, 2010[31]; Lockheed Martin's intrusion kill chain model, also 2010[32]; the U.S. Department of Defense's Diamond model, 2011[33]; and the MITRE ATT&CK Framework, 2013[34].)

I'm not sure exactly when I heard about the Whitehead and Russel story, but I started thinking and writing about cybersecurity first principles as early as 2016. My thoughts weren't fully formed yet, but even then, I knew that the security practitioner community was going in the wrong direction. We had somehow chosen, in a groupthink kind of way, that securing individual systems with the CIA triad was the way to go. And yet, the number of breaches reported, just in the public, continued to grow. I knew even then that the CIA triad wasn't elemental enough. We didn't need to protect individual computer systems. We needed to prevent material impact to our organizations. It was clear to me that we needed to get back to first principles.

About the same time, the academic community started some preliminary thinking about how to apply the first principle idea to

[31]Kindervag, J., 2010. No More Chewy Centers: Introducing The Zero Trust Model Of Information Security. Forrester.

[32]Hutchins, E., 2010. Intelligence-Driven Computer Network Defense Informed by Analysis of Adversary Campaigns and Intrusion Kill Chains. Lockheed Martin.

[33]Caltagirone, S., Pendergast, A., Betz, C., 2011. The Diamond Model of Intrusion Analysis. Center for Cyber Threat Intelligence and Threat Research.

[34]Strom, B., Applebaum, A., Miller, D., Nickel, K., Pennington, A., Thomas, C., 2020. MITRE ATT&CK: Design and Philosophy. Mitre.

cybersecurity. Buffalo State's Charles Arbutina and Sarbani Banerjee tied what they called *foundational propositions* to the U.S. National Security Agency (NSA) checklist of what makes up a secure system.[35] But the work assumes that building a secure system is the absolute cybersecurity first principle without any discussion. It's the right idea, pursuing cybersecurity first principles, but not atomic enough; it doesn't get to what the actual first principle is. Some of their proposed tasks—such as domain separation, process isolation, and information hiding—might and should be used as a tactic, but the authors don't illustrate exactly what it is they are trying to do. They don't get to the essence of the problem.

In 2017, Dr. Matthew Hale, Dr. Robin Gandhi, and Dr. Briana Morrison covered similar ground using the NSA checklist in its "Introduction to Cybersecurity First Principles" designed for elementary students (K-12).[36] And, in 2021, Dr. John Sands, Susan Sands, and Jaime Mahoney, from Brookdale Community College, cover the same material with more detail but again don't offer any argument about why these are first principles, just that they are.[37]

Shouhuai Xu published his paper "The Cybersecurity Dynamics Way of Thinking and Landscape" at the 7th ACM Workshop on Moving Target Defense in 2020.[38] Xu proposes a three-dimensional axis with first principles modeling analysis (assumption driven), data

---

[35]Sarbani, B., Arbutina, C., n.d. Cybersecurity First Principles.
[36]Hale, M., 2017. Introduction to Cybersecurity First Principles. nebraska-gencyber-modules [WWW Document]. Nebraska-Gencyber-Modules. mlhale.github.io/nebraska-gencyber-modules/intro_to_first_principles/README (accessed 10/29/22).
[37]Sands, J., Sands, S., Mahoney, J., n.d. Cybersecurity Principles [WWW Document]. NCyTE, WA. www.ncyte.net/faculty/cybersecurity-curriculum/college-curriculum/interactive-lessons/cybersecurity-principles
[38]Xu, S., 2020. The Cybersecurity Dynamics Way of Thinking and Landscape, in: Proceedings of the 7th ACM Workshop on Moving Target Defense. ACM, New York, NY, USA.

analytics (experiment driven), and metrics (application and semantics driven). But again, there is no discussion of why his first principles are elemental.

Nicholas Seeley published his master's thesis at the University of Idaho in 2021: "Finding the Beginning to Discover the End: Power System Protection as a Means to Find the First Principles of Cybersecurity."[39] Out of all the papers reviewed here, this is the most complete in terms of first principle thinking. Seeley also reviewed most of them before he drew any conclusions and makes the case that the main ideas that emerge from those papers revolve around the issue of trust. He then questions whether the idea of trust is fundamental enough to be a first principle. He quotes James Coleman and his book *The Foundations of Social Theory* that says "situations that involve trust are a subset of situations that involve risk." Or, as Seeley says, "without risk there is no need for trust." Seeley says that risk is a function of probability, a measure of uncertainty. He believes that uncertainty is more fundamental than the CIA triad or any of the other analytical checklists that the previous authors came up with. Interestingly, the father of decision analysis theory, Dr. Ron Howard, says the same thing in his book *The Foundations of Decision Analysis Revisited.*

Seeley takes an idea from the Luhmann/King/Morgner book *Trust and Power* that trust allows us to reduce complexity in our lives.[40] He then proposes a set of assumptions (postulates or axioms), similar to Euclid, that are his set of cybersecurity first principles.

- Complete knowledge of a system is unobtainable; therefore, uncertainty will always exist in our understanding of that system.

---

[39]Seeley, N., 2021. Finding the Beginning to Discover the End: Power System Protection as a Means to Find the First Principles of Cybersecurity (Degree of Master of Science). University of Idaho.
[40]Luhmann, N., 2018. Trust and Power. John Wiley & Sons.

- The principal of a system must invest trust in one or more agents.
- Known risks can be mitigated using controls, transference, and avoidance, else the risks must be accepted.
- Unknown risks manifest through complexity.

But then he stops short of identifying the absolute cybersecurity first principle and uses his axioms to design a better proof than Bell and LaPadula to decide if one system design over another is more secure using eigenvalue analysis of the associated graphs. In other words, he went back to the traditional well of trying to design secure systems.

The idea of first principle thinking has been around since almost the beginning of enlightened scientific thought. Applying the concept to cybersecurity is a relatively new idea, though.

Although the cybersecurity founding fathers (Ware, Anderson, Bell/LaPadula, Saltzer/Schroeder, and Clark/Wilson) never mentioned first principles, they established two main ideas that were essentially used as first principles for the discipline. The first is that we are all trying to formalize the security of systems. The research community eventually abandoned the idea sometime in the 1990s as unworkable. We discovered that the more secure we made the machines, the less useful they became for general purposes. Secure systems have some application for niche use cases (like government secrets), but for the common Internet user, not so much. The second idea was the concept of the CIA triad. Despite the critic's complaints about the inadequacy of the idea and attempts to make it better, the general meaning of it has been unchanged since the Saltzer/Schroeder paper. With an organization like NIST proclaiming its authenticity as late as 2020, the CIA triad is the de facto cybersecurity first principle.

In the next section, I will make the case for why that's not true and suggest a more robust cybersecurity first principle.

What Is the Atomic Cybersecurity First Principle?

In the previous section, my intent was to give you the sense that the infosec community has made incremental progress in providing digital defenses for our organizations. It's clear that we have come a long way since the early days. But when I heard about Whitehead and Russell, it occurred to me that we are in the middle of our own Russell paradox. We keep adding on to the pile of things we've already done with no thought about whether our previous assumptions were correct. Our defensive systems are much improved, and yet it seems that we are no better at preventing cyberattacks than we were at the beginning. Indeed, with the volume of successful attacks hitting the press headlines every day, we might even conclude that our defenses are worse. This is not true for everybody. Some do quite well. I'm talking about the infosec community as a whole. Like Whitehead and Russell, different groups within the infosec community are using the same established best practices and getting different results.

I came to the conclusion that maybe all the things we do as a community—the defensive people-process-and-technology triad we tell our bosses that we are doing to keep their organizations safe—may not be fundamental enough to have a major impact. Of course, they do have some effect. But the problem is they are just not sufficient if implemented fully, or they are too complicated or too costly to implement fully, and thus have not been successful.

And I reject the notion that cybersecurity is somehow different from all the other problems in the world, so unique that it can't be solved with any certainty. We have put people on the moon for goodness sake, harnessed nuclear energy, and invented the Internet. I fundamentally believe that "solving cybersecurity" is a lesser problem than those and many other complex problems. The issue as I see it is that when I say "solving cybersecurity," we have no consensus about what that means. If you ask any three network defenders to describe what it is that they are trying to do with their infosec program, you will get three fundamentally different ideas.

If the community can't agree on what we are trying to do as a group, it's time to get back to first principles. Indeed, it's time to define the ultimate first principle as the baseline definition of cybersecurity. Still, up to this point, the community uses a collection of terms and phrases as shorthand for cybersecurity or when they define a subset of cybersecurity. Some will say things like the following:

- Implement CIA.
- Establish a robust patching program.
- Stop malware from being successful.
- Detect quickly and eliminate efficiently (incident response).
- Strengthen the deployment of the NIST Cybersecurity Framework (or pick your framework of choice here).
- Maintain a robust compliance program.

There are many more, and some are quite good. But none seems fundamental enough. None gets to the foundational element that we can use to build our programs on. And how is it possible that after 30 years of doing this kind of work, there is no community consensus about what it is that we are all trying to do? That idea is the main thesis of the book.

As I said earlier in the chapter, establishing a set of cybersecurity first principles is the act of reducing the idea of network defense to its core essence. The previous ideas might be on our list somewhere as potential tactics, but they are not atomic enough. We can't use them like building blocks to derive everything else that is known in the problem domain like Bertrand and Russel needing 80 pages, block by block, to prove a simple math concept.

To that end, let's start by showing how the previous ideas in turn are not cybersecurity first principles.

Is CIA an Absolute First Principle?

The CIA triad has endured as the overriding best practice security philosophy from the early days (1970s) throughout the early 2020s. The U.S. National Institute of Standards and Technology (NIST) published "NIST SPECIAL PUBLICATION 1800-25: Data Integrity: Identifying and Protecting Assets Against Ransomware and Other Destructive Events" in 2020 proclaiming that "The CIA triad represents the three pillars of information security." In other words, it is their strategy for protecting government systems.[41]

Jennifer Reed, a 20-year security and technology veteran, in an exchange with me in August 2022, made the case that the Saltzer and Schroeder paper might be the first public statement about the CIA triad: the idea that to make a system secure, architects have to provide confidentiality, integrity, and availability. She says that Saltzer and Schroeder don't use the phrase CIA triad and don't mention the specific terms (confidentiality, integrity, and availability), but they "referred to three types of invasion from the perspectives of security specialists, known as (a) unauthorized information release [or confidentiality], (b) unauthorized information modification [or integrity], and (c) unauthorized denial of use [or availability]."

---

[41]Cawthra, J., Ekstrom, M., Lusty, L., Sexton, J., Sweetnam, J., 2020. NIST SPECIAL PUBLICATION 1800-25: Data Integrity: Identifying and Protecting Assets Against Ransomware and Other Destructive Events. National Institute of Standards and Technology (NIST).

The thing is, it's unclear as to when the CIA triad coalesced into a coherent concept. Many of these early papers (Ware, Anderson, Bell/LaPadula, Saltzer/Schroeder, Clark/Wilson,[42, 43, 44] The DOD Orange Book,[45, 46] Branstad,[47] Lipner[48]) discuss one or more of the CIA triad's elements, but only as a general list of things required or as a description of things that could go wrong, not as a tied-together fundamental security principle. That seems like a subtle distinction, but I think it's important. In those early days, each element of what came to be known as the CIA triad were checklist items that were part of building a secure system. They were lumped together with other things. The triad hadn't materialized yet as a fundamental idea, meaning that security professionals didn't have the "CIA triad" in their vocabulary yet.

Jeroen van der Ham, from the National Cybersecurity Centre in the Netherlands and University of Twente, says that Steve Lipner

---

[42]Wilson, D.D.C. and D.R., 1987. A Comparison of Commercial and Military Computer Security Policies. IEEE Symposium on Security and Privacy 184. doi.org/10.1109/SP.1987.10001

[43]Ben, 2010. CIA Triad [WWW Document]. ElectricFork. blog.electricfork.com/2010/03/cia-triad.html (accessed 10/29/22).

[44]Fruhlinger, J., 2020. The CIA triad: Definition, components and examples [WWW Document]. CSO Online. www.csoonline.com/article/3519908/the-cia-triad-definition-components-and-examples.html (accessed 10/29/22).

[45]Department of Defense, 1985. Trusted Computer System Evaluation Criteria ["Orange Book"].

[46]Rosenberg, J., 2021. How the DoD Orange Book Paved the Way for Modern Cybersecurity [WWW Document]. Dover Microsystems. info.dovermicrosystems.com/blog/department-defense-orange-book (accessed 10/29/22).

[47]Branstad, D.K., 1987. Considerations for security in the OSI architecture. IEEE Network 1, 34–39. doi.org/10.1109/mnet.1987.6434189

[48]Lipner, S., 1982. Non-Discretionary Controls for Commercial Applications. Proceedings of the 1982 IEEE Symposium Security and Privacy.

coined the phrase tying everything together in 1986.[49] In a separate exchange with me (Aug 2022), Lipner says it wasn't him, though.[50]

> You can put Lipner in the same box of cybersecurity founding fathers with Ware, Anderson, Bell/LaPadula, Saltzer/Schroeder, and Clark/Wilson. He is one of the authors of the DOD Orange book (1985) and one of the architects of Microsoft's Trusted Computing Initiative in the 2000s.

Even in the Parker book, where he describes the three elements as a distinct set of ideas that aren't adequate, he doesn't call it the triad. Somewhere between the Saltzer/Schroeder 1975 paper and the 1998 Parker book, the security community started to think about the three CIA elements together as a fundamental principle, a cybersecurity first principle if you will. But, as a concept, the "triad" doesn't emerge until sometime after the Parker book and it's unclear of the exact date. It's strange though that a foundational doctrine so widely accepted and so long lasting by the practitioner community is not claimed by anyone. This is just more evidence that the security community really does believe in "rough consensus," an idea coined by David Clark.

That said, even early on, researchers recognized that the CIA triad has some issues. Read the Parker book for a long argument about why.

For me, though, obvious concerns emerge when you think about confidentiality, integrity, and availability as a first principle. The first

---

[49]Van der Ham, J., 2021. Toward a Better Understanding of "Cybersecurity" [WWW Document]. ACM Digital Library. dl.acm.org/doi/fullHtml/10.1145/3442445#Bib0002 (accessed 10/29/22).

[50]Howard, R., Lipner, S., 2022. Discussion of who created the CIA Triad Concept.

is, do they go far enough back to be a first principle? Are they atomic? For instance, when you think of each of the three elements, do you not have any other clarifying questions? For instance, do you apply these strategies to all data and systems even if they aren't material? Do you apply those principles forever? In other words, do you protect all systems and all data perpetually? That seems extreme. The triad is silent about those kinds of issues. The next concern is, do we only want to have general-purpose defenses with no thought about how the adversary actually operates? I mean, you don't get to an active intrusion kill chain prevention by considering only the passive confidentiality, integrity, and availability. The third concern is from Parker's book. The triad doesn't account for misuse of the system. For example, employees who have legitimate access to company sensitive information don't release it to the public, don't change it, and don't make it unavailable to its customers, but they still manipulate it in some way that is profitable to themselves in some fraudulent way. That doesn't violate the triad rules.

With those concerns in mind, the CIA triad doesn't go far enough to be an atomic first principle.

Is Patching an Absolute First Principle?

In the early days (1990s), one of the very first best practices that emerged from the infosec community was software patching. The idea was that if we could just close the vulnerability holes in all the software as we discovered them and before the bad guys could exploit them, we could keep the criminals, the spies, and the hacktivists out of our networks. To this day, many cybersecurity professionals spend a lot of their limited resources on this one activity alone and refer to it as a community best practice. But according to Caroline Wong, author of the Cybersecurity Canon Hall of Fame book, *Security Metrics, A Beginner's Guide*, she believes that the phrase *best practice* is misapplied by most network defenders.[51] She says, "A best practice should refer to an approach or methodology that is understood to be more effective at delivering a particular outcome than any other technique when applied in a particular situation." She says that many accepted cybersecurity best practices, although good ideas, have not delivered on those outcomes.

From my own experience, software patching is one of those so-called best practices. Don't get me wrong. Systematically upgrading all of our software components whether we wrote the software ourselves, have purchased it from a commercial vendor, or have borrowed it from the open source community, is an important function. The bad guys are always looking for openings in our defensive armor. Exploiting software vulnerabilities is a bad guy go-to move because there are so many vulnerabilities created in software and they seem to grow exponentially every year. The question that comes to mind, though, is whether patching software vulnerabilities is so important that it's a cybersecurity first principle, that we focus on that strategy as foundational and build everything up from there. I'm making the case that it's not.

It's an important tactic that we can use to prevent bad guys from causing damage to our organization, but it's not the most important one. There are a gazillion other tactical things that we might pursue that will have the same impact or better, like installing a robust identity and authorization system to limit employee access to only the absolutely minimum resources they need to get their job done and nothing else, deploying as many prevention controls as possible to your security stack for each step in known adversary attack sequences, or implementing procedures that will allow your organization to recover from a crippling cyberattack quickly.

---

[51]Wong, C., 2011. Security Metrics, A Beginner's Guide. McGraw Hill Professional.

Besides, hackers use code exploitation in only less than ~10 percent of the publicly known breaches.[52, 53] That number is an approximation based on reporting from the UK's IT Governance consulting company and data from Valerii Marchuk's Zero-Day Tracking Project, but even if the percentage is much higher, it's still a low probability relative to all the other actions hackers use to compromise their victims. The point is that basing an infosec program on the premise that preventing software exploits as a best practice will generate positive outcomes is false. The infosec community has been pursuing that strategy for more than two decades and has not abated the volume of successful cyber breaches. Caroline Wong is right. Patching as a best practice has not delivered the outcomes we thought. From my point of view, we therefore can't make it the basis for an infosec program based on first principles.

Is Preventing Malware an Absolute First Principle?

The difference between software exploits and malware is that some hackers use exploits to gain access to a system and use malware to do everything else: search the system for the data they have come to steal or destroy, escalate privilege, move laterally in the victim's network to continue the search, exfiltrate data out the command-and-control channel, etc. Sometimes, hacker malware even includes software exploits as part of the kit. This seems important. If we could stop all malware, then we could eliminate any chance of hackers successfully breaching our networks. Shouldn't that strategy be the basis for our cybersecurity first principle program?

---

[52]Irwin, L., 2022. List of data breaches and cyber attacks in February 2022 [WWW Document]. IT Governance UK Blog. www.itgovernance.co.uk/blog/list-of-data-breaches-and-cyber-attacks-in-february-2022-5-1-million-records-breached (accessed 10/29/22).

[53]Marchuk, V., 2022. Free zero-day vulnerability tracking service - zero-day.cz [WWW Document]. Zer0-Day. www.zero-day.cz (accessed 10/29/22).

Referring to Caroline Wong again, I don't think so. Similar to how the infosec community embraced patching as a best practice, we have also adopted anti-malware as a best practice with similar unfavorable outcomes. Antivirus tools have been around since the beginning (early 1990s) and have recently (mid-2010s) morphed into endpoint detection and response (EDR) tools. These modern tools are way better than the ones we had in the beginning, and most organizations have a version of them running in their networks as a best practice. As a general observation, though, the number of successful cyberattacks has remained relatively steady for the past six years. According to the Identity Theft Resource Center, the average annual number of public breaches from 2015 to 2021 is 1,259 and each year is consistently above 1,000 and below 2,000.[54] If anti-malware solutions offer such good outcomes and most of the infosec community has some version of them deployed, shouldn't the number of public breaches be close to zero?

Again, I'm not saying that anti-malware tools are a bad idea. We should all consider deploying them as a tactic that we can use to reduce our chances of being compromised. But using them is probably not the most important strategy that exists, and the strategy, like patching, is not foundational. It's not something to build an entire infosec program on. From my point of view, we therefore can't use anti-malware as the basis for an infosec program based on first principles.

Is Incident Response an Absolute First Principle?

Sometime in the 2010s, the infosec community started to pursue the idea that cyber defense is too hard and therefore should be abandoned in favor of incident response; in other words, desert

[54]Custom Breach Search [WWW Document], n.d. Identity Theft resource Center. notified.idtheftcenter.org/s/resource#annualReportSection (accessed 10/29/22).

prevention mechanisms in favor of early detection mechanisms and efficient eradication systems. It turns out that this is as hard and expensive to do well as the traditional defensive approach. The tools you need to do prevention are similar, or the same, compared to the first part of detection and response. For the second part, the response piece, you need a highly trained incident response team that can handle the deeply technical aspects of modern-day cyberattacks, understand your organization's digital architecture better than the original designers, and have the social skills to communicate across to business leaders as potential threats turn into real threats. If you think all of that sounds expensive, it is. Regardless if you have the technical and social skills on hand to perform the function, the cost alone eliminates the best practice as a viable option for any small-to-medium-sized organizations. For those groups that can afford it, incident response might be a key and essential capability. For the rest of us, it's off the table and therefore can't be a cybersecurity first principle.

When I'm asked about how to decide to spend my resources (people, process, and technology) between defense and response solutions, I'm reminded of the distinction between fire marshals and firefighters that Steve Winterfeld (the editor of this book) talks about. Fire marshals examine whether the building in question was built to code, the sprinkler system is functioning properly, fire hazards are stored appropriately, signs and fire extinguishers are in place, etc. That said, sometimes fires happen anyway, and you have to have the firefighters to respond. The better you are at prevention, the less likely it will be that you will need the fire department. But the chance is not zero. This is not an either-or question. You need both.

Is Adherence to Security Frameworks an Absolute First Principle?

One of the fantastic phenomena that emerged during the early Internet days, and continues to this day, is the willingness of network and security engineers to volunteer their time to establish standards and frameworks that benefit the entire community. The efforts of the Internet Engineering Task Force (IETF) is one example of this kind of activity. From its website, the IETF's mission is to "make the Internet work better by producing high quality, relevant technical documents that influence the way people design, use, and manage the Internet."[55] Other standards and frameworks are sometimes driven by regulation, business models, industry best practice, governments needing guidelines, and analyst research. Some of the most well-known are as follows:

Regulatory:

- Federal Financial Institutions Examination Council is for US banking.
- General Data Protection Regulation is an EU law for privacy.
- Data Security and Personal Information Protection is China's data residency law.

Business Model:

- HiTrust (implementation guidance for Health Insurance Portability and Accountability Act) and ISO 27000
- ISO 27001 (International Organization for Standards on Information Security Management)
- SOC 2 (Service Organization Control for service provider data protection)

[55]Staff, n.d. Home [WWW Document]. IETF. www.ietf.org (accessed 12.16.22).

Industry Best Practices:

- Confidentiality Integrity and Availability Triad (CIA)
- Open Web Application Security Project (OWASP)
- Center for Internet Security (CIS) critical security controls
- Control Objectives for Information and Related Technologies (COBIT) from Information Systems Audit and Control Association (ISACA)
- Intrusion Kill Chain by Lockheed Martin (see Chapter 6)
- Payment Card Industry Data Security Standard
- Critical Infrastructure Protection (CIP) from North American Electric Reliability Corporation

Government Sponsored:

- Diamond Model (see Chapter 6, Section 3)
- MITRE ATT&CK® (See Chapter 6, Section 3)
- NIST Cybersecurity Framework (The U.S. National Institute of Standards and Technology)

Analyst Firm developed:

- Forester (Zero Trust; see Chapter 5)
- Gartner (SASE; see Chapter 6, Section 10)

There are many others. Some are fabulous collections of security laundry lists for things to consider in deploying an infosec program. I have often been asked by other security practitioners, which one do I recommend? From a purely practical security standpoint (which one provides the best security), it doesn't really matter that much. Pick one that works for you and follow it. In the big picture, the good ones all cover similar ground. But, from a business perspective, one might be more advantageous than the other depending on where your organization resides in the world.

That said, does any collection of security controls or security control ideas represent first principle thinking? Perhaps, but they are not presented that way by the authors. They are road maps or maturity models that security practitioners can use to demonstrate to leadership and outside compliance auditors that the organization does have an infosec program that adheres to a community-recognized body of best practices. Getting certified in one or more of them is a massive undertaking and can be quite expensive and time-consuming. At the end of all of that labor, the result doesn't get you a living and breathing cybersecurity first principle program either. The result is a snapshot in time. It captures what you did during the certification. It has been my experience that these snapshots get printed, placed into fancy binders, filed in a bookshelf somewhere, and are never to be seen again.

But even if infosec leadership decided to not get certified but to just follow the general concepts, the result is most likely an organization that is way better defended in the digital world compared to an organization that doesn't adhere to a framework.

The question that comes to mind after all that work, though, is this: what are you trying to accomplish with this effort? When you're done and in 100 percent compliance with one framework or another, what did you achieve, and how do you measure the effectiveness of it? The answers are typically all over the map.

That's perfectly acceptable. One organization might need framework compliance to solve one business problem. Another organization might need it for a different purpose. That's legitimate. But, it's not first principle thinking. A cybersecurity first principle program might include adherence to a security framework, but that adherence isn't atomic enough to be fundamental to every security program.

Therefore, adherence to a security framework can't be a cybersecurity first principle.

Is Adherence to Compliance Regulations an Absolute First Principle?

Since the early Internet days, lawmakers and commercial vendors from around the world have tried to regulate digital crime, privacy, and infosec standards. The following are some of the more famous efforts:

- The European Parliament's General Data Protection Regulation (GDPR)
- Federal Financial Institutions Examination Council's (FFIEC)
- North American Electric Reliability Corporation standards (NERC)
- Payment Card Industry Data Security Standard (PCI DSS)
- U.S. Computer Fraud and Abuse Act (CFAA)
- U.S. Gramm-Leach-Bliley Act (GLBA)
- U.S. Federal Information Security Management Act (FISMA)
- U.S. Federal Risk and Authorization Management Program (FEDRAMP)
- U.S. Health Insurance Portability and Accountability Act (HIPAA)

From the very beginning, many security practitioners understood compliance regulations for what they are. They are either attempts to establish the parameters of minimum baseline security/privacy programs or an effort to distinguish between digital criminal activity and normal citizens just surfing the Web. These same security practitioners view them as necessary evils to prevent fines (GDPR, for example) or as the price of doing business (FEDRAMP, for example).

But they don't view them as essential to protecting their organizations on the Internet. You have to follow them because they are legal requirements, but most don't consider them fundamental to their security program and therefore can't be the basis for any cybersecurity first principle program. Besides, for some organizations, it's just easier to pay the fines if they get caught as the cost of doing business. That doesn't seem like a cybersecurity first principle.

The Atomic Cybersecurity First Principle

After walking through that analysis, it's clear to me that the previous first principle candidates are all either too simplistic or too tactical. They deal with technical things such as preventing software exploits, stopping malware, detecting and eradicating bad guy tools, following checklists, and following legal rules. But they don't address specifically the overall purpose of any infosec program. When you read them, you immediately say to yourself, "That's a good goal, but what about these other issues? Does it solve all of my cybersecurity problems?" In other words, they are not fundamental enough. They are also technical and not conducive to an explanation that senior leadership can understand. And they are discrete. Either you did it or you didn't. There's no middle ground. There's no nuance, which is vital to a fast-changing threat and business landscape.

Instead of a binary metric, we should be thinking in terms of a sliding scale, something like a probability. We need to build a program that matches leadership's risk appetite. Our first principle program should drive us closer to reducing the probability of a cyber adversary running a successful attack campaign against us. That gives us some planning room. For example, we can tell the boss that because we spend X amount of dollars on a new security tool or a new security function, we reduced the probability of an adversary group running a successful cyber campaign against us from 20 percent to 15 percent. When we present the infosec program in that manner, then leadership can evaluate whether the spend for the project was worth the effort.

And if it does happen, an adversary successfully steals our intellectual property or encrypts our data, the program is not an instant failure. We didn't tell the board that we would stop all adversary campaigns. We told them that we would reduce the probability of a successful one.

That is getting closer to our absolute first principle. It's no longer a binary question because we couched it in terms of probabilities for the leadership to consider. But it's still missing something. It's still too broad and will cause us to spend resources on things that are not important.

What's missing is a discussion of materiality. Face it, not everything on your network is essential. If the bad guys compromise Luigi's laptop and steal the menu for the lunch special in the company cafeteria, maybe we don't need to call in the FBI for that one. You might be a little embarrassed, but the exfiltration of the lunch menu to the APT's command-and-control server in Tajikistan will not cause the company much heartburn. So, why then would we spend a lot of resources trying to protect it?

I don't know about you, but the volume of resources that I typically get to spend on cybersecurity has never been infinite. If you try to spread that volume thinly over everything, you run out of resources before you run out of things to do anyway. The projects that you did funnel money to are likely not funded completely enough to solve the entire problem. That's like trying to feed a platoon of neighborhood teenagers with one spoonful of Jif peanut butter, extra crunchy of course, and a loaf of bread. Nobody is going to be satisfied at the conclusion of that exercise. In other words, focus only on what is material to the business. Everything else is nice to have.

The risk management team at Datamaran defines materiality this way: "A material issue can have a major impact on the financial, economic, reputational, and legal aspects of a company, as well as on the system of internal and external stakeholders of that company."[56] In the financial world, there are more specific definitions regarding the disclosure of information prior to investments, but in the cyber world, the Datamaran definition is the best and most compact definition of materiality that I have come across.

The thing is, what's material and what isn't is different for every organization. It's based on many factors such as risk tolerance, size of the organization, and type (commercial, academic, or government), to name three. And it changes over time. What's material today for a startup won't be what's material when the startup becomes a Silicon Valley giant. That said, business leaders know what materiality means to their business. It behooves security professionals to have a complete understanding of it too. I want to spend my finite resources on protecting material things, not protecting Luigi's lunch menu.

So far then, we have "reducing the probability of material impact of a cyber event" shaping up as our ultimate first cybersecurity principle, but it's still missing something; it's still not precise enough. The last element that is needed is to bound it by time. Calculating the probability of material impact to an organization any time in the future (say the next 100 years) is a lot different than calculating the probability over the next three years. Will cyber adversaries successfully breach our digital environments sometime in the future? That's likely if the question is open-ended like that, if there's no end date. But, will they have success in the next three years? That probability likely will drop off precipitously if you time bound the question. It also has the added benefit of giving senior leadership something to focus on. Instead of using fear, uncertainty, and doubt (FUD) to get your infosec program funded—as

[56]Materiality definition: the ultimate guide [WWW Document], n.d. Datamaran. www.datamaran.com/materiality-definition (accessed 10/29/22).

in, "OMG, this is a really scary thing and I need a gazillion dollars to fix it"—you could inform the senior leadership team of the potential risk over the next phase of the business. Let's not try to boil the ocean here.

With that said, our foundational first principle, our cybersecurity cornerstone that we will build the entire infosec program on must address three elements: probability, materiality, and time. If that's true, then here is my proposal for the ultimate cybersecurity first principle and the thesis for this book:

> "Reduce the probability of material impact due to a cyber event over the next three years."

That's it. Nothing else matters. We can quibble about the amount of time (1 year, 3 years, 5 years). Just pick a bounded time that makes sense to your organization. But, this simple statement is atomic. You don't read it and say to yourself, "I like it but there are three other things I have to do too." Compared to the other first principle candidates discussed earlier, it states precisely and clearly what we are trying to accomplish. It also gives you a measuring stick to evaluate your program. If you are spending resources on projects that don't have a direct impact on this first principle, you're wasting resources.

Conclusion

In this chapter, I assumed you weren't familiar with the idea of first principles. I explained what they are and told the stories of some of the big thinkers in human history (such as Euclid, Aristotle, Descarte, Whitehead & Russell, and Elon Musk) who have used them to solve some of the thorniest problems known to humankind. I then noted that although in the early digital age, many big thinker computer scientists, such as James Anderson, Willis Ware, Bell and LaPadula, Saltzer and Schroeder, Dr. Fred Cohen, and Donn Parker, tried to find the edges of what cybersecurity meant but didn't quite get there. The closest they came was something called the CIA triad, which is not really a first principle idea at all. I then made the case that other cybersecurity first principle candidates don't really meet the bill either. Efficient patching, malware prevention, rapid detection and eradication, framework checklists like NIST or ISO, and even compliance law all fall short of what a first principle is supposed to be. They're all good tactics that we might find useful, but they are not a coherent first principle strategy.

I then made my case for what I claim is the absolute cybersecurity first principle:

> "Reduce the probability of material impact due to a cyber event over the next three years."

There you have it. I've been thinking, debating, and writing about this idea for almost a decade, and it has gone through many versions. But I think this current iteration is as close as I've ever been to clearly stating what it is we are all trying to accomplish with our infosec programs.

That begs the question, what's next? If reducing the probability of material impact to my organization over time due to a cyber event is the thing we are trying to do, what are the follow-on first principle building blocks that we will install that will help us do that? Just like Whitehead and Russell, what are the essential concepts that will allow us to uniquely prove the equivalent of 1 + 1 = 2 in our network defender world?

The rest of the book is a discussion of the first principle strategies and tactics that could drive the probability of material impact down over a discrete amount of time. In the next chapter, I will provide a high-level overview of the logical follow-on strategies that flow from this cybersecurity first principle.

2 Strategies

Without a goal [maneuvering is] aimless. You might be a master tactician, but you'll have no sense of strategy.

—Garry Kasparov, former World Chess Champion

However beautiful the strategy, you should occasionally look at the results.

—Sir Winston Churchill,
Prime Minister of Britain during WWII

Overview

This chapter is an executive summary for the rest of the book, Chapters 3–8. In Chapter 1, I explained what first principles are and made the case for the ultimate cybersecurity first principle: reduce the probability of material impact due to a cyber event over a finite set of time. In this chapter, I outline the five follow-on strategies that logically flow from this idea. Consider it a primer to get you warmed up for the concepts, the tactics, and the implementation strategies that you will read about in subsequent chapters. Here I want to give you a flavor for what is to come before I bury you in the details. These strategies and tactics are complicated. If you're not careful as you read through the book, you could easily lose your sense of direction. Use this chapter and Chapter 1 to remember where you are and why we are taking this journey.

One final thing as you read through the strategies: I'm not advocating that network defenders from all organizations (government, commercial, and academia) have to implement every single one of them to implement a cybersecurity first principle infosec program. What I'm arguing is that these strategies logically flow from my stated absolute first principle. If we are trying to reduce the probability of material impact, these are the strategies to consider, not others that don't flow from the atomic first principle candidates that I mentioned and rejected in the previous chapter.

Security professionals can use each one of these first principle strategies by themselves, completely or in part, or they can use a combination of one or more. The tactics you use to do that will reduce the probability of material impact to some degree. Which strategies you choose will be dependent on how big your organization is, the risk tolerance of the senior leadership team, and the resource budget you have at your disposal in terms of people, process, and technology. It's also dependent on your ability to measure that probability with enough accuracy to present it meaningfully to the leadership team. That last piece is so important that the subject gets an entire chapter (Chapter 6, "Risk Forecasting").

Strategies vs. Tactics

In Chapter 1, I made the case that the atomic cybersecurity first principle that we all should adhere to is reducing the probability of material impact due to a cyber event over a finite set of time. That's a concise statement of what we are trying to do. In other words, it's a strategy. In our case, it's the first principle strategy, the most important strategy. But it doesn't tell us how to do it. The "how" is a collection of tactics, or discrete steps, that we might take that will bring us closer to achieving the goals of our strategy.

In the Cybersecurity Canon Hall of Fame book, *Cyber War: The Next Threat to National Security and What to Do about It*, by Richard Clarke and Robert Knake, the authors describe the folly of pursuing tactics without a well-developed strategy.[1] Their example is the creation of the U.S. Cyber Command in 2009, a tactic. Their criticism is that the U.S. government created an entire organization without a full understanding of the strategy it would be pursuing. One of the reasons I'm writing a book about cybersecurity first principles is that in my experience, many in the infosec community do the same thing; they pursue a collection of tactics without an overarching strategy.

In *Cyber Warfare: Techniques, Tactics and Tools for Security Practitioners*, by Jason Andress and Steve Winterfeld (one of the editors of this book), the authors describe a middle layer, the operational intermediate objective layer, that connects the strategy (the what) to the tactics (the how).[2] For example, a first principle strategy might be to stop all known adversary behavior. An intermediate objective might be to identify any activity on our network associated with the hacktivist group Killnet. The tactic might be to deploy all prevention and detection controls associated with the tactics, techniques, and procedures of Killnet that reside in the MITRE ATT&CK wiki.[3]

The point is that both strategy and tactics are inextricably linked. A strategy without tactics means that you are good at writing goal

---

[1]Clarke, R.A., Knake, R., 2012. Cyber War: The Next Threat to National Security and What to Do About It. Ecco.
[2]Andress, J., Winterfeld, S., 2011. Cyber Warfare: Techniques, Tactics and Tools for Security Practitioners. Elsevier.
[3]Staff, n.d. MITRE ATT&CK® [WWW Document]. attack.mitre.org (accessed 12/16/22).

statements but have no idea how to actually achieve the goals. Tactics without strategy means that you are flailing about doing things with no clear purpose or direction in mind.

What Are the Essential Strategies Required for a First Principle Infosec Program?

If you've gotten this far in the book and have yet to slam it closed as being preposterous or misguided, you're at least curious about what the first principle strategies might be. Recall from Chapter 1 that first principles in any problem domain are atomic, and we use them like building blocks to identify everything essential. If our overall first principle strategy is reducing the probability of material impact due to a cyber event, then the supporting strategies must logically follow. They are not stand-alone strategies. They don't exist in a vacuum. Framed that way, I believe that we must pursue some combination of five sub-strategies (the what) that can directly support this goal with a collection of tactics for each (the how).

In the following chapters, I'll provide a much more detailed description of each of the sub-strategies and their accompanying tactics, but let me provide a brief overview here. Following directly from our absolute first principle, two of the five sub-strategies immediately present themselves. We can shore up our defensive posture with passive cyber hygiene kinds of things; general-purpose tactics that might thwart any adversary (read about the zero trust strategy in Chapter 3). We can also design more active defenses based on known adversary attack sequences, designing defensive campaigns with specific cyber adversaries in mind (the intrusion kill chain prevention strategy is covered in Chapter 4). The third sub-strategy is resilience (Chapter 5). Resilience is how we can still reduce the probability of material impact even when the inevitable happens and some cyber adversary breaches our defenses. It's how we limit the damage and reduce the material impact after the fact. The fourth sub-strategy is risk forecasting (Chapter 6). If our entire infosec program is based on reducing the probability of material impact, how do we actually calculate that probability and the amount of material impact? Finally, the last sub-strategy is automation (Chapter 7). In a world where infrastructure as code is king, automating our first principle tactics becomes essential.

Zero Trust Strategy Overview

Before 2010, the most common defensive strategy was something called *perimeter defense*. The idea was that you built a strong electronic fence around your digital assets and allowed only authorized users and devices inside. The problem with that strategy is that it works fine until some bad guy gets inside the fence. Once in, they have access to everything (see the case study on Edward Snowden in Chapter 3). Our thinking about that started to change with an original white paper in 2010 from John Kindervag: "No More Chewy Centers: Introducing The Zero Trust Model Of Information Security."[4]

In the paper, Kindervag tells network architects to make the assumption that cyber adversaries are already operating within your digital environments. If that assumption is true, what design decisions would they make to reduce the chances of a material cyberattack?

The first step is to lock all the windows and doors to our digital environments to make it harder for cyber adversaries to operate. Some might call this *cyber hygiene* as Vint Cerf coined the phrase back in 2000,[5] but it's much more than that. We would also absolutely have to know who (employees and contractors) and what (devices and software modules) have permission to access our digital environments,

---

[4]Kindervag, J., 2019. No More Chewy Centers: Introducing The Zero Trust Model Of Information Security. Forrester.
[5]Cerf, V., 2000. Vint Cerf on Cyber Hygiene at the Joint Economic Committee.

specifically what permissions they have when they do it, and some kind of monitoring capability to ensure that the rules are being followed. Obvious tactics like vulnerability management and identity and access management (IAM) come to mind, but there are perhaps many others that might help here (see Chapter 3).

From Kindervag, "In Zero Trust, all network traffic is untrusted. Thus, security professionals must verify and secure all resources, limit and strictly enforce access control, and inspect and log all network traffic." According to NIST (the U.S. National Institute of Standards and Technology), zero trust "assumes there is no implicit trust granted to assets or user accounts based solely on their physical or network location (i.e., local area networks versus the internet) or based on asset ownership (enterprise or personally owned)."[6]

When I was the chief security officer for Palo Alto Networks (a security vendor most famous for its application layer firewalls), the leadership team wanted a way to demonstrate to external customers how the internal Palo Alto Networks security team used the firewall to pursue the zero trust journey. It turns out that application layer firewalls (and all of the firewall vendors, not just Palo Alto Networks, have a version of them) are ready-made to facilitate zero trust functionality. Application firewall administrators create firewall rules based on the application it sees running tied to the authenticated user. In that world, everything's an application. Using any SaaS app is a monitored application, browsing the Internet is an application, printing across the network is an application, pinging a host is an

[6]Rose, S.W., Borchert, O., Mitchell, S., Connelly, S., 2020. Zero Trust Architecture [WWW Document]. NIST. URL www.nist.gov/publications/zero-trust-architecture (accessed 10/29/22).

application, literally anything and everything that a user or device or software component does that generates network traffic that crosses the firewall is a monitored application. We discovered quickly that by just using the security tool we already had in place (our own application firewall), we could get a long way down the zero trust journey without having to buy and deploy another complete set of technology. All we needed were people and processes. And since we used the same firewall for all of our data islands (cloud, SaaS, mobile, and data center), we had to create the rule set only once as policy and the system would propagate the rule to all of the data islands for us. The end result was our new zero trust mindset.

These are some big ideas. In this book, zero trust is a cybersecurity first principle strategy, but it's also a mindset, a philosophy. You don't achieve a zero trust environment; you inch your way toward it with hundreds and thousands of everyday network design decisions that improve your posture. It's a journey with no final destination. In Chapter 3, I will go into detail and discuss some of the tactics to consider to deploy a zero trust strategy.

But the zero trust strategy is passive, meaning that the implemented design parameters are configuration decisions and best practices that everybody should follow regardless of the threat environment. To be more active, to deploy prevention controls based on known adversary behavior, you need a different strategy: intrusion kill chain prevention.

Intrusion Kill Chain Prevention Strategy Overview

We know from experience that when cyber adversaries attack their victims, they don't simply do one thing. They have to accomplish a series of things to achieve their goals. We didn't always know this. It took a research team from Lockheed Martin in 2010 to explain it. From the original white paper, "Intelligence-Driven Computer Network Defense Informed by Analysis of Adversary Campaigns and Intrusion Kill Chains," by Hutchins, Clopper, and Amin, "Intelligence-driven computer network defense is a risk management strategy that addresses the threat component of risk, incorporating analysis of adversaries, their capabilities, objectives, doctrine and limitations. It requires a new understanding of the intrusions themselves, not as singular events, but rather as phased progressions."[7]

From almost the beginning of infosec history, the community has been tracking cyber adversary behavior. Back in 1998, the Defense Information Systems Agency discovered Russian hacker activity against several U.S. government networks (code name: Moonlight Maze).[8] Fast-forward to the 2020s, the MITRE ATT&CK framework has probably the most comprehensive and free collection of tactics, techniques, and procedures for known adversary attack sequences across the intrusion kill chain.

We have also learned through experience that cyber adversaries don't invent completely new attack campaigns for each individually targeted victim. They reuse the same attack sequences over and over again until some network defender thwarts them. Even then, they don't throw the entire campaign out. They change the specific step that has been blocked. Since we know most of the attack sequences, it makes sense that we would design and deploy prevention and detection controls for whatever security stack we have deployed based on this intelligence. Even the most junior cybersecurity analyst has

---

[7]Hutchins, Clopper, Amin, 2010. Intelligence-Driven Computer Network Defense Informed by Analysis of Adversary Campaigns and Intrusion Kill Chains. Lockheed Martin Corporation.

[8]Staff, 2004. A Bunch of Hacks [WWW Document]. CSO Online. www.csoonline.com/article/2117332/a-bunch-of-hacks.html (accessed 10/29/22).

heard the old myth, "Defenders have to get it right 100 percent of the time. An attacker has to get it right only once." Well, intrusion kill chain prevention turns that idea on its head. Now the attacker needs to get it right every step of the way, and the defender needs to get it right only once. Thinking in terms of the intrusion kill chain totally flips the offense-defense balance in favor of the defender.

As the Palo Alto Networks CSO, I was visiting customers and potential customers in France. I had a meeting with the colonel in charge of the C3N cybercrime unit at the French Gendarmerie. He immediately blew me off and handed me over to one of his captains who was clearly annoyed that his boss gave him the onerous task of babysitting an American. Five minutes into the conversation, I could tell that he was barely listening to me (although his English was quite good; my French is nonexistent, which probably annoyed him even more). About 30 minutes in, he stopped the conversation abruptly and exclaimed that he needed actionable intelligence about French cybercrime, not American explanations regarding next-generation firewalls. He needed to be able to arrest criminals, not block bad guy traffic. While the sales guy I was with tried to settle the captain down, I texted my intelligence director (Unit 42's Ryan Olson) and told him that I needed French IP addresses associated with cybercrime command-and-control nodes (see Chapter 4 and the Lockheed Martin kill chain diagram). Ten minutes later, Ryan texted me four IP addresses. The captain's eye lit up when I gave him the list, and he abruptly ran out of the room. I guessed that the meeting was over. A few days later, I learned from the sales guy that the captain immediately got permission to search the physical addresses associated with the French C2 IP addresses and closed down those command-and-control nodes.

As I said, if the zero trust strategy is passive, the intrusion kill chain strategy is active. These two strategies flow directly from the primary first principle. You lock down the environment as much as possible in a zero trust kind of way, and then you specifically deploy detection and prevention controls across the intrusion kill chain for all known adversary attack sequences. In Chapter 4, I will go into detail and discuss some of the tactics to consider to deploy an intrusion kill chain prevention strategy.

With these two strategies, you can reduce the probability of material impact significantly. But, when that inevitable day comes and the cyber adversary still breaks in—after all, we just reduced the probability; we didn't prevent all successful attacks completely—what is the plan? That's where the resilience strategy comes into play.

Resilience Strategy Overview

As a concept, ASIS International coined the phrase as early as 2009, but it was really describing what turned out to be business continuity. The World Economic Forum formalized *resilience* in 2012:

". . .the ability of systems and organizations to withstand cyber events. . ."[9]

Since then, other thought leaders have refined it. U.S. President Obama even signed a presidential policy directive dictating resilience for the country's critical infrastructure in 2013.

In 2017, the International Standards Organization (ISO) defined it as follows:

---

[9]The World Economic Forum, 2012. Partnering for Cyber Resilience. N.d. . MITRE ATT&CK®. attack.mitre.org (accessed 10/29/22).

"...the ability of an organization to absorb and adapt in a changing environment to enable it to deliver its objectives and to survive and prosper."[10]

But the definition I like best comes from Stockholm University in 2015. Fredrik Björck, Martin Henkel, Janis Stirna, and Jelena Zdravkovic, in their paper "Cyber Resilience – Fundamentals for a Definition," explain it this way:

". . .the ability to continuously deliver the intended outcome despite adverse cyber events."[11]

In other words, assume that the bad guys will be successful negotiating the intrusion kill chain at some point or find a chink in your zero trust armor, or, just in general, assume that there will be a massive IT failure sometime in the future. I had an old Army boss who always said that the bad guy gets a vote and is actively trying to destroy your strategy and tactics. If that is the case, then devise a strategy that will ensure that your organization's essential services will still function. That's resilience.

Organizations that are good at this are the big cloud providers like Google, Amazon, and Microsoft. You know that they have thousands of computers, if not millions of computers, running their internal infrastructures. Assuming that the mean time to failure (MTTF) for each individual unit is between 3 and 5 years, you know that each of these vendors has machines that fail all of the time. They have to just by looking at the sheer volume of computers they each have and doing some simple math with MTTF variables. As a

---

[10]ASIS International, 2009. Organizational Resilience: Security, Preparedness, and Continuity Management Systems -- Requirements with Guidance for Use, ASIS SPC.1-2009.

[11]Björck, F., Henkel, M., Stirna, J., Zdravkovic, J., 2015. Cyber Resilience – Fundamentals for a Definition, New Contributions in Information Systems and Technologies. Springer International Publishing, Cham.

consumer of those services, though, do you ever notice the failures? No, not really, because each of those vendors has built resilient systems that can accommodate those failures and continue to deliver service.

In Chapter 5, I will go into detail about the differences and overlap between business continuity, disaster recovery, and resilience and discuss some of the tactics to consider deploying a resilience strategy such as adherence to compliance regulation, crisis planning, backup and restore operations, encryption at rest and in motion, and incident response.

Risk Forecasting Strategy Overview

Since the atomic cybersecurity first principle is reducing the probability of material impact, the obvious strategy that immediately flows from that statement (more obvious than zero trust, intrusion kill chain prevention, and resilience) is that we had better have a good way of forecasting probabilities. If we can't measure our current likelihood of a material impact due to some cyber event in the near future, we definitely can't measure the reduction of that probability after we have implemented one or more of our first principle strategies.

To be charitable, network defenders struggle with this idea. To be brutally honest, we just don't know how to do it at all. I included myself in that set until just recently. I have read all of the Cybersecurity Canon Hall of Fame books on the subject (and there are plenty), and I have even presented a paper at the annual RSA Conference with one of the co-authors, Richard Seiersen ("How to Measure Anything in Cybersecurity Risk"[12]). But in all of those efforts, I was just basically finding the edges of the problem. In the

[12]Hubbard, D.W., Seiersen, R., 2016. How to Measure Anything in Cybersecurity Risk. John Wiley & Sons.

books, I kept expecting a chapter at the end that explained how to do it completely, top to bottom. That chapter doesn't exist. I realized that I had to figure it out myself. After years of trying, I finally have the answer.

The problem, as I see it, is that all of us have tried to make the problem more complicated than it really is. We thought that because it involved math, we needed a highly precise calculation that involves counting all of the things in our networks, accounting for all the known and unknown variables, and plugging everything into some kind of Monte Carlo algorithm. After years of trying this, I realized that was the wrong approach. Security practitioners don't need precise answers to make resource decisions in terms of people, process, and technology. We need good-enough answers, ballpark answers, that will allow us to make decisions quickly, evaluate where we are currently almost instantaneously, and give us the ability to convey that thought process to senior leadership.

Risk forecasting involves using a combination of super forecasting techniques (made famous by Dr. Philip Tetlock and Dan Gardner),[13] Fermi estimates (named after the world famous physicist Enrico Fermi), the Bayes' rule (invented by statistician Thomas Bayes), outside-in back-of-the-envelope calculations using public data, and inside-out back-of-the-envelope calculations using how well we have deployed our first principle strategies.

I know that sounds like a lot, but I will explain each of those things in Chapter 6, and more important, I will show you how to combine it all in two different case studies. In other words, in this book, I'm inserting the chapter at the end that explains how to do it top to bottom.

That leaves us with the last first principle strategy: automation.

---

[13]Tetlock, P.E., Gardner, D., 2015. Superforecasting: The Art and Science of Prediction. Crown.

Automation Strategy Overview

Since the Internet began to be useful to the general populace, say in the early 1990s, automation was key. In those incipient days, we would build programs to perform simple tasks to make our lives easier, such as word processing, antivirus, and email programs. We would run programs for entertainment such as *Doom*, *Half-Life*, and *Golden-Eye 007*. But even back then, future Silicon Valley giants like Amazon and Google were already beginning to understand that they could automate entire ecosystems to provide consistency, scale, fast repairs, and mistake centralization. Their insights led eventually to AWS and Google Cloud by adopting the infrastructure-as-code mantra and embracing the Agile and DevOps programming philosophies. As the authors say in their Cybersecurity Canon Hall of Fame book, *Site Reliability Engineering: How Google Runs Production Systems*, "Automate ALL the Things!"[14]

But as the IT world embraced these new ideas, the infosec world has been slow to join the fray. This is a mistake. It goes without saying that if we want any edge in our efforts to prevent cyber adversary groups from being successful against our digital environments, we as a group have to be more agile than they are. It doesn't matter if you have robust deployments of zero trust, intrusion kill chain prevention, and resilience strategies. If it takes your organization days to weeks to never to implement changes to your first principle infrastructure as the threat picture changes, because you're mired in a tar pit of manual toil, your chances of material impact will still be quite high. We know that the adversaries have automated their infrastructure. If the infosec world continues to operate in manual mode, it's similar to what Sean Connery said in the 1987 movie *The Untouchables*. We're bringing a knife to a gunfight.

---

[14]Beyer, B., Jones, C., Petoff, J., Murphy, N.R., 2016. Site Reliability Engineering: How Google Runs Production Systems. O'Reilly Media.

Viewed through that lens, automation is not merely a nice-to-have feature, something that we will do when we get the time. Automation becomes the lynch pin to the entire first principle strategy deployment.

In Chapter 7, I will talk about the history of automation from the waterfall method to agile and to DevOps. I will cover what it means to secure your own internally developed code and highly recommend that your organization adopts the philosophy of site reliability engineering. I will conclude by lamenting how slow the security community has been to plug themselves into their own organization's DevOps process to create DevSecOps and will use a case study to show the way: Netlfix's Chaos Monkey.

Conclusion

This was the warm-up—the executive summary chapter. Before we get started with the details in the follow-on chapters, I wanted to make sure that you had a clear understanding of where I was coming from in terms of our atomic first principles and the strategies that directly support it. Remember, the strategies are the things we want to accomplish. The collection of tactics (that I will cover in the rest of the book) are how we might accomplish each strategic goal.
I explained at a high level what each of the strategies are.

- Zero trust
- Intrusion kill chain prevention
- Resilience
- Risk forecasting
- Automation

But I also explained that network defenders don't have to implement every strategy to the fullest extent to have a cybersecurity first principle infosec program. The goal of our program is to reduce the probability of material impact. Each of these strategies will have a reduction effect on that probability. How much depends on how well you deploy the tactics. Which of the strategies you choose to implement will depend on the size of your organization, the culture, and the desires of the senior leadership team.

With all of that as the background summary, the next chapter will cover a deep dive of the cybersecurity first principle strategy of zero trust.

3 Zero Trust

Zero Trust is not a project but a new way of thinking about information security.

— John Kindervag, author of the founding zero trust paper, "No More Chewy Centers"

Transitioning to ZTA [zero trust architecture] is a journey concerning how an organization evaluates risk in its mission and cannot simply be accomplished with a wholesale replacement of technology.

—National Institute of Standards and Technology (NIST) Special Publication 800-207

Overview

Remember from Chapter 2 the difference between strategy and tactics? Strategy is what we want to get done. Tactics are how we might go about it. In this chapter, the strategy we are talking about is zero trust, and there are several tactics to consider to help accomplish this goal. I will describe the details, or the tactics, to consider to implement a zero trust strategy. I use the Edward Snowden insider threat case as the poster child for why zero trust is necessary and explain why pursuing it is more of an ongoing journey than an end state. I talk about how you can travel a long distance down that journey with tools and equipment you likely are already using. I explain why vulnerability management is an important zero trust tactic and not a stand-alone strategy. I make the case that you should be organizing your internal systems right now to use software bill of materials (SBOMs) and that a software-defined perimeter (SDP) is a better security architecture for zero trust than the current models. I conclude with a description of the current state of identity and access management (IAM), single sign-on (SSO), and multifactor authentication (MFA).

The Use Case for Zero Trust: Edward Snowden

When you think about the kinds of threats that you need a zero trust strategy for, normally the one that most people think of first is the insider threat case. These threats don't originate from some highly advanced nation-state hacking group. They come from within. They're your employees and contractors who you entrust to run your business or your government operations. Some have access to sensitive information. And some, for many different reasons, decide that they want to take action and cause the organization harm.

Over the years, there have been many examples in the news. Here are three that are infamous:

- *2010*: Chelsea Manning, while a U.S. army soldier, released 500,000 government documents to WikiLeaks.
- *2018*: A disgruntled Tesla employee elevated his privilege, made code changes to the Tesla Manufacturing Operating System, and exfiltrated large amounts of highly sensitive Tesla data to unknown third parties.
- *2019*: A disgruntled Capital One employee exfiltrated 100 million customers accounts and credit card applications to GitHub.

There are many more, but the poster child for why zero trust is required as a first principle strategy is arguably the National Security Agency's (NSA's) classic insider threat case: Edward Snowden. While he was working as a government IT administrator contractor supporting the NSA's classified networks, Snowden began collecting and removing documents regarding what he claimed to think demonstrated government overreach in terms of domestic intelligence collection and secret surveillance programs. In 2013, he released as many as a million of those classified documents to the press.[1]

Regardless of what you think about the guy (traitor or hero), his profile is what the cybersecurity industry means when they talk about insider threats. As an IT administrator, once he logged in to any of the NSA's networks, he had access to almost every data repository stored there. The U.S. government maintains a handful of not-directly-connected-to-the-Internet networks. The names most of us have heard of are the Non-classified Internet Protocol (NIPRNET, essentially the U.S. government's Internet), the Secret Internet Protocol Router Network (SIPRNET, the place where the government can store, share, and communicate SECRET information), and the Joint Worldwide Intelligence Communications System (JWICS, where the U.S. intelligence community stores top-secret information commonly referred to as the *high-side network*).

Snowden purchased a web crawler from the Dark Web for about $100 and turned it loose on JWICS. He collected more than a million highly classified documents, walked out the door with them, and, well, let's just say, created quite an international incident with what he subsequently did with those documents. He didn't run a

[1]Kerr, O., 2015. Edward Snowden's impact. The Washington Post.

Mark-Zuckerberg-level hack that we saw in the movie *The Social Network* to get into JWICS. He basically web-surfed to see what he could find. I guess it didn't hurt that he had system administrator credentials for many of those systems either.[2]

At the time, the JWICS network engineers had no concept of a zero trust network. It wasn't a thing yet. But, the irony doesn't escape me that John Kindervag based his zero trust thesis (see the next section) on how the intelligence community typically compartmentalizes its secrets; essentially it's based on need to know. You don't get access to the information unless it's part of your job, except for system administrators because those people have to maintain the system, right? To be fair, in 2013, nobody anticipated that a highly vetted contractor would do such a thing on a super-secret network. In hindsight, it seems obvious that this could happen, but back then, the controls that the NSA had in place to vet these workers seemed adequate and were better than what most of the rest of us have in place today.

Zero Trust: Overhyped in the Market but. . .

Before I get started, let me clarify the distinction between security vendor marketing hype and internal first principle strategies. I know that the phrase *zero trust* causes a sour taste in the mouth of most network defenders these days. In 2022, the phrase is market saturated, and vendors use it so often that after a while it begins to lose its meaning. Practitioners are tired of hearing about it, and some have even rejected the idea behind the hype as being just marketing spin. But this is a common phenomenon in the tech industry, not just for zero trust but for any promising new concept.

---

[2]Ray, M., 2013. Edward Snowden. Encyclopedia Britannica.

It starts by somebody having a good idea, like John Kindervag in 2010 with his founding zero trust white paper, "No More Chewy Centers: Introducing the Zero Trust Model of Information Security." Slowly but surely, everybody gets excited about how it will solve all of the world's problems including world peace. At some point, though, the crowd turns on the idea because it dawns on them that a practical solution to deploy this great idea is really hard to do and the commercial offerings that claim they've solved it fall a bit short.

These changes to expectations are captured beautifully by the famous Gartner Hype Cycle.[3] According to the Challenging Coder website, Gartner's Jackie Fenn created the concept in 1995. She noticed a repeated pattern of expectation attitudes from consumers of tech and security goods and services as new and innovative products emerged in the marketplace. The expectation starts with a product announcement and then rises through the "peak of inflated expectations" as consumers realize the potential of the new idea. From there, expectations begin to diminish through the "trough of disillusionment" as these same people begin to realize that the new tech is not quite ready for prime time. From there, expectations rise again through a much gentler "slope of enlightenment." Finally, once the product has matured, it reaches the "plateau of productivity." Fenn published a book on the concept in 2008.[4]

Even though many network defenders would put the idea of zero trust squarely in the "trough of disillusionment," at the time of this writing (2022), Gartner analysts see a change. According to the September 2021 Hype Cycle (see Figure 3.1), products that promise

---

[3]Pal, V., 2020. Gartner Hype Cycle: Everything You Need To Know. [WWW Document]. Challenging Coder. challengingcoder.com/gartner-hype-cycle (accessed 11/6/22).

[4]Fenn, J., Raskino, M., 2008. Mastering the Hype Cycle: How to Choose the Right Innovation at the Right Time. Harvard Business Press.

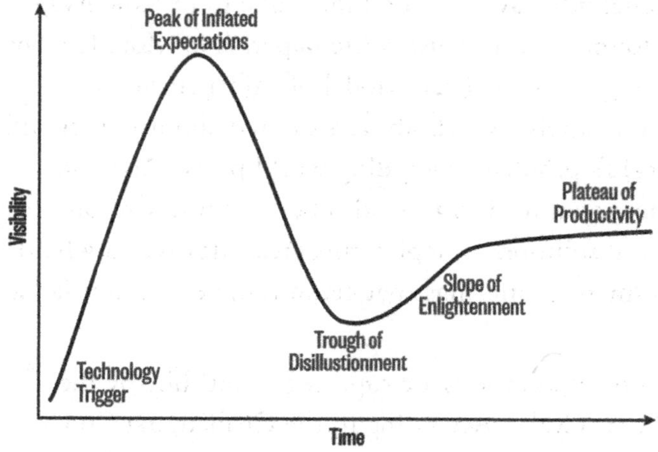

Figure 3.1 An example of a Gartner Hype Chart

zero trust features have just moved out of the trough and have begun their slow climb up the "slope of enlightenment."

But I would say that the capabilities these zero trust products offer generally land in the bucket of restricting access to resources based on need to know. And that's a good thing. But, I want to elevate this conversation a bit and consider zero trust as a first principle strategy, not as a feature to a security product.

Cyber Hygiene, Defense in Depth, and Perimeter Defense: Zero Trust Before We Had Zero Trust

Internet founding father Vint Cerf created *cyber hygiene*. Well, at least he coined the phrase when he testified to the U.S. Congress Joint Economic Committee back in 2000.[5] Cerf is one of the guys who helped create the original TCP/IP stack in the 1970s, and he gets credit for naming this cyber hygiene best practice that most network defenders had been following previously for more than a decade.

[5]Cerf, V., 2000. Vint Cerf on Cyber Hygiene at the Joint Economic Committee.

It began by just trying to keep all the software patched. Think of it like trying to protect your house from common thieves. You could spend a lot of money and time installing, maintaining, and monitoring expensive surveillance equipment. If you forgot to close and lock the doors and windows when you went out for the evening, though, the thieves would have a much easier time breaking in than if you had. In this metaphor, keeping your software patched is equivalent to locking the windows and doors in your house.

Eventually, though, the cyber hygiene strategy evolved into a perimeter defense model where we installed big electronic barriers, usually with firewalls, that created an outside zone, the Internet, and an inside zone, where we all worked. The first commercial stateful inspection firewalls came out around 1994.[6, 7, 8] Organizational material assets resided behind the firewall. To get work done, systems and people operated behind that barrier.

Slowly, perimeter defense morphed into needing more tools designed for specific detection and prevention tasks. We started seeing deployments of intrusion detection systems (IDSs) and antivirus (AV) systems. Dorothy Denning invented the modern-day IDS in 1986,[9] and we started seeing the first AV systems around the same time.[10] We eventually started referring to the multiple tools in the security stack phenomenon as *defense in depth*. Fred Cohen

---

[6]Illumio (2015) The Firewall, a Brief History of Network Security [Online]. www.illumio.com/blog/firewall-network-security (accessed 2022)
[7]Higgins, K.J. (2008). Who Invented the Firewall? [Online]. www.darkreading .com/analytics/who-invented-the-firewall- (accessed 2022)
[8]Cisco (2002). Evolution of the Firewall Industry [Online]. docstore.mik.ua/ univercd/cc/td/doc/product/iaabu/centri4/user/scf4ch3.htm (accessed 2022)
[9]Denning, D.E. (1986). 'An Intrusion Detection Model.' Proceedings of the Seventh IEEE Symposium on Security and Privacy, pages 119–131. users.ece .cmu.edu/~adrian/731-sp04/readings/denning-ids.pdf
[10]Staff, 2020. What was the very first antivirus package? Top Ten Reviews.

coined the phrase in a paper he published in 1992.[11,12,13] We also started calling the set of security tools that we had deployed as the *security stack*.

The idea was that if the first tool failed to prevent that bad actor from getting in, then the second one would have more success. If that one failed, then the third one would, and so on. As the little old lady said to the math scientist, Bertrand Russell, explaining the existence of God, "[Everyone knows that] it's turtles all the way down!" The number of turtles that you had in your security stack depended on how big your budget was. Today, in 2023, with businesses operating on multiple data islands (data centers, mobile devices, SaaS services, and multiple cloud deployments), it's not uncommon for any organization to have between 15 and 300 tools deployed in the security stack depending on how big the organization is.

Perimeter defense and defense in depth, in practice, were essentially cyber hygiene. In other words, once you established the perimeter, you kept all your systems up-to-date with the latest patches, and you kept your security stack current with the latest defensive signatures.

Zero Trust Is Born

Perimeter defense and defense in depth were the dominant security models of the 2000s. Then, in 2010, three gigantic cybersecurity shockwaves reverberated simultaneously around the Internet that changed everything. The first event was the publication of the

[11]Cohen, F., 1989. Models of practical defenses against computer viruses. Computers & Security 8, 149–160. doi.org/10.1016/0167-4048(89)90070-9

[12]Cohen, F., 2016. Defense in Depth.

[13]Cohen, F., 1992. [PDF] Defense-in-depth against computer viruses. Computers and Security 11, 563–579.

Lockheed Martin kill chain paper.[14] The second was the "very" public Chinese cyberattack against Google (Operation Aurora).[15] Finally, the third was the publication of the Forrester white paper on zero trust.[16] Intrusion kill chain prevention is not related to zero trust, but the fact that the Lockheed Martin researchers published it the same year as the Forrester researchers published the zero trust paper is extraordinary. These two ideas dominate this book (this chapter and Chapter 4).

The Google attacks and the Forrester white paper are only slightly related in that the Forrester white paper outlined the zero trust strategy, while the Chinese attacks started the Google engineers on redesigning their own internal networks and deploying one of the first workable zero trust implementations. This eventually led to a commercial offering called Beyond Trust. The feeling in the industry was that if a silicon giant like Google decided to adopt a new idea for security like zero trust, then perhaps the concept was more legitimate than just another theory from an analyst company like Forrester.

Notions associated with zero trust had been bouncing around the industry since the early 2000s. But when John Kindervag published the essential paper, he solidified the philosophy. He called it "No More Chewy Centers: Introducing The Zero Trust Model Of Information Security." It's an unfortunate name because, without studying the paper, the name implies an oxymoron. How can you run a network if you don't trust anything or anybody? But that's not what Mr. Kindervag was saying.

He based his thesis on how the military and intelligence communities think about protecting secrets: treat all information as

---

[14]Hutchins, E., Cloppert, M., Amin, R., 2010. Intelligence-Driven Computer Network Defense Informed by Analysis of Adversary Campaigns and Intrusion Kill Chains, Lockheed Martin.

[15]Schwartz, M.J., 2013. Google Aurora Hack Was Chinese Counterespionage Operation. Dark Reading.

[16]Kindervag, J., 2010. No More Chewy Centers: Introducing The Zero Trust Model Of Information Security, Palo Alto Networks. Forrester.

"need to know." In other words, if you don't require the information to do your job, you shouldn't have access to it. To achieve a zero trust posture then, network architects make the assumption that their digital environments are already compromised and design them to reduce the probability of material impact if it turns out to be true.

That's a powerful concept and completely radical to the prevailing perimeter defense idea at the time.

With perimeter defense, we built a strong outer protection barrier. Once the attackers got in, though, they had access to everything. All transactions on the inside were automatically trusted (see "The Use Case for Zero Trust: Edward Snowden"). From the original paper, John thinks that idea is ludicrous. Just look at the title: "No More Chewy Centers." I like to call it the Tao of M&M network design—hard candy shell on the outside but a scrumptious chocolatey center in the middle. That is perimeter defense.

The Snowden incident caused the NSA and many network defenders elsewhere to rethink their network designs. For the infosec community, it moved Kindervag's theoretical paper from an interesting idea to a key design principle that we're all attempting to adhere to. This was how we were going to build networks moving forward. And then. . .nothing significant happened. Most of us didn't build them. It turns out that even though Kindervag's thesis is brilliant, the practical "how-to" section is sparse. This is why, 10+ years later, we are all still talking about starting it. The rest of this chapter is that how-to section.

Zero Trust Is a Philosophy, Not a Product

It's important to note, as Kindervag originally explained, that zero trust is not a product. It's a philosophy, a strategy, a way to think about security, and it can always be improved. In that way, it's not about the destination. You're never going to get to the end. You're never going to brief your boss saying, "Well, we did it. We have zero trust." It's more about the journey.

Zero trust as a strategy means that even if a person, a device, or a piece of software, let's call them *network entities* for short, are legitimately working in our digital environments, we don't necessarily trust anything they do. And because we don't trust them, we need to limit what they can do to the bare minimum so that they can accomplish their task and not a bit more. In other words, why would we give the fry chef Luigi, down in the cafeteria, permission to access the company's mergers and acquisition database? We want him to order food for the next day, not interact with a potential company acquisition. Why would we give Snowden administrator access to systems he wasn't responsible for? We also need to watch all the network entities like a hawk to make sure that they are not stepping out of their well-defined lane. Why would Luigi have admin permissions on the cafeteria's point of sale system? We further want to continuously validate that these network entities are who they say they are. We don't let Luigi log in on Monday and forget about him until he has to reboot for some reason weeks later. We validate him at every turn, every system he has to connect to, and every time he initiates some kind of transaction. As Kindervag says, every time we confirm Luigi's identity, we are increasing our confidence that he is who he says he is.

We want to reduce the attack surface of everything in our digital space by limiting access to workloads (services and data) for network entities on all of our data islands (mobile devices, data centers, SaaS applications, and cloud deployments). This is 180 degrees opposite of what we used to do with perimeter defense and defense in depth. With that model, once you were in, you were in and likely had access to most things.

Today, the perimeter has disappeared in the traditional sense. We no longer have a single perimeter. Our data and our automated processes are scattered across multiple data islands. Thinking about perimeter defense was hard enough when we had only one perimeter. Now that we have multiple data islands, zero trust seems exponentially hard.

But, zero trust as a strategy tells us what we want to do regardless of how hard it is to accomplish. How we do it, the tactics, is something we adjust on a continuous basis, and we can start with the tools we already have deployed in the security stack. You can buy products to help, but zero trust is a strategic mindset that you can start deploying tactically with systems you already have on your network. Yes, you read that right. You probably already have tools on your system that can get you a long way down the path of zero trust.

There are a million things you can do technically and process-wise that will improve your zero trust posture, that will lock the digital doors and windows that need to be secured, and that will make sure that somebody wandering around the digital hallways of our networks will not find a door ajar and wander in to find something they shouldn't have access to. Or, even if they do, what they discover through that open door will not significantly impact the company. I call that *meat-and-potatoes zero trust.*

Meat-and-Potatoes Zero Trust

Next-generation firewalls became commercially available in 2007, and all the major firewall vendor products do next-generation things.[17] If you're a medium- to large-scale business, you probably already have a boatload of them deployed in your networks.

The firewall has been a staple of the generic security stack since the first commercial offerings back in the early 1990s. But when I say

---

[17]Illumio (2015) The Firewall, a Brief History of Network Security [Online]. www.illumio.com/blog/firewall-network-security (accessed 2022)

firewall, most of us are thinking about the old stateful inspection firewalls invented around that same time. These were basically fancy routers that allowed us to block incoming and outgoing traffic based on ports, protocols, and IP addresses. We deployed them at the boundary between our digital organizations and the Internet. We used them to build our perimeter defense.

But next-generation firewalls are completely different. Security architects use them to block network traffic based on applications tied to the authenticated user, not IP addresses. Let that sink in for a second.

Instead of a layer 3 firewall that operates on ports, protocols, and IP addresses, it's a layer 7 firewall that operates on applications. If you're concerned about your employees visiting Facebook during the workday, you could try to block their access at layer 3 by not allowing them access to a raft of IP addresses that Facebook manages and continuously changes. That's a never-ending task, by the way. Or you could write a next-generation firewall rule, a layer 7 firewall rule, that says the marketing department can go to Facebook but nobody else can. Done. And you never have to touch it again.

In a next-generation firewall world, everything is an application. Using Salesforce? That's an application. Have an internally deployed exchange server? Use of that is an application. Accessing the development code library? That's an application. Pinging a host in your network? That's an application. Reading the *Washington Post*? That's an application. Being able to block applications based on the employee groups that use them provides the infosec team a means to start down the zero trust journey without having to completely redesign their network. They may have to supplement it a bit, but they don't have to start from scratch.

Logical and Micro Segmentation

There are two approaches we can take: logical segmentation and micro segmentation. Logical segmentation is the relatively easier one.

I love it when people tell me that things will be easy. I had an old army boss who loved a Latin phrase that he put on all plaques for departing soldiers: "Nihil Facile Est." His translation: "Nothing is easy." Words to live by.

Logical segmentation is creating layer 7 firewall rules for the big muscle movement functions in your company such as marketing, legal, software development, etc. This is where a lot of network defenders get tripped up. Since we create next-generation firewall rules by tying applications to authenticated users, it's tempting to create rules for individuals in the company. Kevin can go to Facebook, but Luigi can't. In any sizable organization, that quickly becomes a managerial nightmare. Trying to administer the inevitable change with individual employees moving around the organization over time will quickly cause your system to crumble under its own weight. Instead, focus on the 10 to 15 big functional areas. Create rules for what applications they can use and which ones they can't, and you've just moved a long way down the zero trust path. You still have to manage employee movement, but their access permissions are not specific to each employee. They're based on a handful of important company functions.

The other more difficult approach is micro segmentation. This uses the same idea of building functional groups and writing rules for them, but it focuses on the devices used by those functional groups. The marketing team can access the internal cafeteria website from their iPhone to order lunch, but the group does not have access to the financial department's M&A database server. The reason this is harder is that the infosec team has to do the additional work of installing some sort of public key infrastructure on every device in the organization that the next-generation firewall can interrogate. For small- to medium-sized companies, this is probably a bridge too far.

But for larger organizations, they most likely already have this deployed. They just need to decide to use it to its full potential.

The point is that, at least for organizations that already have them, network defenders can use next-generation firewalls to begin their zero trust journey.

Vulnerability Management: A Zero Trust Tactic

In the early 1990s, vulnerability management was more about understanding the bugs and exploits discovered in the software that we all used and then eventually getting around to patching the issues. Exploits didn't happen that often, and we didn't have the armies of nation-states, criminals, kids, and hacktivists attacking us around the clock like we do today. We would patch the issue when it was convenient.

Back then, most of us were running some version of Windows on the desktop and some flavor of Unix on the servers. When issues popped up, we were more concerned about how to prioritize all the things. Do I install the new printer in the lab today, or do I roll out the patch for my Digital UNIX 4.0 system that prevents local users from gaining root privileges via a long command-line argument (buffer overflow)?

In 1995, Dan Farmer created the first vulnerability scanner called Security Administrator Tool for Analyzing Networks (SATAN) that used the network to scan Unix hosts looking for well-known security vulnerabilities.[18] But it was a network and CPU resource hog. It could cripple the network if you weren't careful.

We didn't even have a common language around vulnerabilities and exploits to compare notes with peers and pundits. According to

---

[18]Editor, 2019. Security Administrator Tool for Analyzing Networks (SATAN). Network Encyclopedia. networkencyclopedia.com/security-administrator-tool-for-analyzing-networks-satan (accessed 12/16/22).

Tripwire, back then, every software vendor had their proprietary method of tracking vulnerabilities in their own products.[19] Security professionals had no way to know if vendor A's vulnerability was the same as vendor B's or if they were two separate issues. We were kind of on our own. Let's call that phase 1 of vulnerability management: confusion (early 1990s to 1999).

That started to change in 1999 when MITRE's David Mann and Steven Christey wrote the white paper "Towards a Common Enumeration of Vulnerabilities."[20] The same year, NIST's Computer Security Division created the Internet – Categorization of Attacks Toolkit (ICAT), the first integrated exploitation and vulnerability list.[21] It's ironic that an effort to reduce complexity and confusion added more acronyms to the process than you can throw a stick at: NIST, CVE, ICAT, NVD, CVSS, SCAP, and E-I-E-I-O.

I made E-I-E-I-O up, but it feels like after reading that list of acronyms you should sing E-I-E-I-O in the tune of that classic "Old MacDonald Had a Farm" song.

Mann and Christey proposed creating a Common Vulnerabilities and Exposures (CVE) list that the entire community could use, and the idea quickly gained traction. The very first CVE list they published contained 321 vulnerabilities chosen after careful

---

[19]Staff, 2020. The History of Common Vulnerabilities and Exposures (CVE) [WWW Document]. Tripwire. www.tripwire.com/state-of-security/history-common-vulnerabilities-exposures-cve (accessed 11/6/22).

[20]Mann, D.E., Christey, S.M., 1999. CVE - Towards a Common Enumeration of Vulnerabilities [WWW Document]. CVE. cve.mitre.org/docs/docs-2000/cerias.html (accessed 11/6/22).

[21]Staff, n.d. NVD - Categorization of Attacks Toolkit or ICAT [WWW Document]. General. nvd.nist.gov/General (accessed 12/16/22).

deliberation and consideration of duplicates. By 2002, the CVE list contained more than 2,000 software vulnerabilities, and NIST recommended that the U.S. government use only software that used CVE identifiers.

By 2005, ICAT had morphed into the National Vulnerability Database (NVD) designed to enrich the CVE list with risk and impact scoring using the Common Vulnerability Scoring System (CVSS) and provided other references such as patch information, affected products, and Security Content Automation Protocol (SCAP) mappings.[22] The SCAP scanner compares a target computer or application's configuration and/or patch level against that of the SCAP content baseline. Both CISA and NIST sponsor the NVD today.

I know this sounds complicated, but this was just phase 2. Call it the easy phase (1999 to 2005) because compared to the next phase, phase 2 was relatively simple. It was easier because, for the most part, not many were using their personal laptops and mobile devices for official work and cloud deployments hadn't transformed the industry yet. The "cloud" hadn't been invented yet. Vulnerability management was still relatively contained to devices residing behind the perimeter.

When Concur released the first SaaS service in 2005[23] and Amazon released AWS in 2006[24,25], that started to change. Now we had data sitting on data islands that were not in the traditional data

---

[22]Staff, n.d. A Brief History of NVD [WWW Document]. NIST. nvd.nist.gov/general/brief-history (accessed 12/16/22l).
[23]Tunguz, T., 2015. A SaaS History Lesson – The First SaaS Company's Exceptional Journey by @ttunguz [WWW Document]. Tomasz Tunguz. tomtunguz.com/the-first-saas-company (accessed 12/16/22).
[24]Staff, n.d. History of AWS [WWW Document]. Javatpoint. www.javatpoint.com/history-of-aws (accessed 12/16/22m).
[25]Miller, R., 2016. How AWS came to be • TechCrunch [WWW Document]. TechCrunch. techcrunch.com/2016/07/02/andy-jassys-brief-history-of-the-genesis-of-aws (accessed 12/16/22).

center behind the perimeter. Around 2014, organizations started to allow their employees to use their personal devices (phones, pads, laptops) to do work. That's not a precise date. Some organizations were doing it sooner, and others did later. Governments did it much later, and some still aren't there today. But the complexity of vulnerability management in phase 3, call it the complexity phase (2005 to today), is exponential compared to phase 2. For example, NIST in 2021 tabulated a record fifth straight year of newly discovered vulnerabilities: 18,378.[26] When you consider that these vulnerabilities are scattered across multiple data islands, it's no wonder that young CISOs look like their 107 years old. It ages you.

As the management difficuty skyrocketed, as with most things in the security space, network defenders reached a point where they couldn't manage organizational software vulnerabilities with a spreadsheet anymore. The situation became complex and resource intensive, and most organizations are always behind. It's akin to the painters who work on the Golden Gate Bridge in San Francisco. They paint the bridge from one end to the other. When they are finished, they immediately go back and start over. The job is never done.

Vulnerability Management as an Intelligence Task

According to the Cybersecurity Canon Hall of Fame book *Practical Vulnerability Management*, by Andrew Magnusson, vulnerability management is not simply patch management. Managing patches within an organization is a subset; it's a key and essential piece but not the whole thing. Consider that, as of this writing, of the discovered 18,378 vulnerabilities in 2021, the U.S. Cybersecurity and Infrastructure Security Agency (CISA) had observed only 812 being

---

[26]Greig, J., 2021. With 18,378 vulnerabilities reported in 2021, NIST records fifth straight year of record numbers. ZDNET.

exploited in the wild.[27] Google's Project Zero in 2021 reported 58 zero day exploits in 2021, more than double from the previous year, but still, 58 is a small number compared to 18,000 discovered vulnerabilities.[28]

Many years ago, a salesperson explained to me his analogy for understanding the difference between software vulnerabilities, exploits, and malware. I thought it was brilliant. He said to consider your house in terms of protecting it from burglars. You have some standard security features: doors that lock and windows that latch. But, that system may have some vulnerabilities. You installed a cheap lock on the front door, the window latch can be easily manipulated from the outside, and you installed a doggy door inside the kitchen door leading to the backyard. Nothing bad has happened yet, but these are potential avenues that burglars might explore to break into your house. That's the same for software. When you hear of a software vulnerability, somebody has discovered a potential flaw in a piece of code that a hacker might try to leverage. When burglars showed up at the house one night while you were away and jimmied the front door lock, manipulated the window latch, or crawled through the doggy door, that's an exploit. The burglars leveraged a discovered vulnerability in the system that allows them access to your house. That's the same for code. Hackers write their own code (exploit code) to

[27]Staff, n.d. Known Exploited Vulnerabilities Catalog [WWW Document]. CISA. www.cisa.gov/known-exploited-vulnerabilities-catalog (accessed 12/16/22).

[28]Stone, M., 2022. The More You Know, The More You Know You Don't Know [WWW Document]. Project Zero.googleprojectzero.blogspot.com/2022/04/the-more-you-know-more-you-know-you.html (accessed 11/6/22).

leverage a discovered software vulnerability that allows them access to the computer, like the infamous EternalBlue exploit developed by the NSA, stolen and leaked to the public by the Shadow Brokers hactivist group, used by the North Koreans in the WannaCry ransomware attack, and used by the Russians in the notPetya attack. Once the burglars are in the house, they steal the silverware from the kitchen and the jewelry from the nightstand and exit out the front door. That's akin to malware. Once hackers are on your computer, the code that they use to automate their attack sequence across the kill chain (see Chapter 4) is malware.

When you look at it that way, patch management for the sake of patch management is probably not a good allocation of resources. In other words, patching everything isn't a great strategy. You have to put some thought into how you go about it. There is another entire set of activities that must happen before we can even think about applying patches:

- Continuously monitor all of the software assets running on the network in terms of version control, nested libraries for open source packages, current configuration (who and what can access the asset, what can the asset access itself), the history of who and what have accessed the asset in the past, and exposure to newly discovered vulnerabilities and exploits.
- Using the zero trust strategy as a guide, regularly check and recheck that all of the software assets have access only to what they absolutely need to get the job done.
- Prioritize the most material software assets (the software that would cripple the business if it stopped functioning for even a second or if customer data is exposed because of it).

When new vulnerabilities and exploits pop up, do the following:

- Determine if the organization is exposed.
- Forecast the probability that some bad guy will leverage it.
- Forecast the probability that if it is leveraged, it will be material.
- Determine if there is a reliable patch or other workaround that will mitigate it.
- Decide which actions to take to mitigate the risk (this could be many things or nothing depending on the risk forecast).

Once all of that is done, then you have to implement whatever you decided to do (the risk mitigation plan). Every single bullet listed previously is a critical information requirement to aid in that decision for a newly discovered vulnerability or exploit. Over time, that collection of intelligence will enable you to achieve some success in a vulnerability management program.

I referred to "intelligence collection" on purpose. I will talk in more detail about cyber threat intelligence in Chapter 5, but this is a perfect task for your intelligence team to own, regardless of whether you have a robust team, just two guys and a dog in the broom closet who do this part time, a contractor that does the work for you, or anything in between. The task lends itself to the intelligence life cycle (see Chapter 4).

But for startups, small businesses, and even some medium-sized businesses, this might be a bridge too far. Those organizations don't have the resources to keep the printers working and the coffee brewing, let alone dedicate resources to patch management. Other zero trust strategies might be more worth their time (see below). Still, as you grow and you start to have a few more resources, automating big chunks of the vulnerability management program will save you in the long run (see Chapter 7).

To reduce the probability of material impact, zero trust is a key strategy to pursue. Tactically, there are many direct ways that will improve the zero trust posture, and they mostly deal with identity and authorization. Indirectly, the tactic that most have not associated with zero trust is vulnerability management. But that's where it sits in my mind. Vulnerability management is not some independent set of activity that exists by itself that all network defenders need to do. I don't consider it as a first principle strategy. It's not atomic enough. That said, it's an important first principle tactic that supports zero trust.

Software Bill of Materials: A Zero Trust Tactic

Before I describe what an SBOM is, let me first tell the story of why an SBOM is necessary. As Snowden was the poster child for zero trust, Log4j is the poster child for SBOMs.

The Log4j module first appeared as a logging framework in 1999. The Apache Software Foundation released the general availability of the Log4j module, version 1, in July 2014. The next year, the Apache Logging Services Project Management Committee announced Log4j 2 as a replacement.[29] Fast-forward to November 2021, six years later, Alibaba Cloud Security Team's Chen Zhao Zhin disclosed to the Apache Software Foundation a vulnerability in the module.[30] By December 9, Apache announced exploitation in the wild of the Chen Zhao Zhin vulnerability and named it Log4shell. By the next day,

---

[29]Sally, 2015. Apache™ Logging Services™ Project Announces Log4j™ 1 End-Of-Life; Recommends Upgrade to Log4j 2 [WWW Document]. The Apache Software Foundation Blog. news.apache.org/foundation/entry/apache_logging_services_project_announces (accessed 12/16/22).

[30]Greig, J., 2021b. Chinese regulators suspend Alibaba Cloud over failure to report Log4j vulnerability. ZDNET.

NIST classified the vulnerability as a critical issue in its National Vulnerability Database (NVD).[31]

The reason for the severity is the ubiquity of the Log4j code module and the simplicity of the Log4shell exploitation code. Its ubiquity stems from the fact that the code for the Apache open-source, cross-platform web server is the most popular web server software on the planet. If you're running web services somewhere, there's a good chance that you're running Apache and the Log4j code module. The simplicity results because, at the time, any unauthenticated user of the Log4j service can send a 12-character code segment and take control of the server.

As of this writing, Log4shell leverages the third highest software vulnerability type from the OWASP Top 10, a reference document describing the most critical security concerns for web applications, in this case, injection.[32] In other words, the unpatched Log4j module doesn't isolate its code from its data. It interprets log messages (data) as instructions (code). When hackers send a URL to the module, the service grabs the URL, fetches the data located there, and runs the executable payload with the full privileges of the Log4j main program.

And don't think that the Log4j situation is isolated or unique. It represents a tiny software module in the open-source galaxy of software reuse. According to Microsoft's Jon Douglas, as of November 2021, the percentage of public software repositories that use open source software is north of 80 percent.[33] Based on a report by

---

[31]Hill, M., 2022. The Apache Log4j vulnerabilities: A timeline [WWW Document]. CSO Online. www.csoonline.com/article/3645431/the-apache-log4j-vulnerabilities-a-timeline.html (accessed 12/16/22).

[32]Staff, n.d. OWASP Top 10:2021 [WWW Document]. owasp.org/Top10 (accessed 12/16/22).

[33]Douglas, J., 2022. Best practices for a secure software supply chain [WWW Document]. Microsoft Learn. learn.microsoft.com/en-us/nuget/concepts/security-best-practices (accessed 12/16/22).

Synopsys in 2022, 97 percent of commercial code has an open-source component. And that's not all. Within that 97 percent, the bulk of that code base consists of open-source software (78 percent).[34] Douglas says that means that "thousands of strangers can effectively contribute directly to your production code. Your product, through your software supply chain, is affected by unpatched vulnerabilities, innocent mistakes, or even malicious attacks against dependencies." Most security professionals have no idea what code libraries their organization is using directly and absolutely no clue what code libraries the original open source developers nested within their open source software.

Automobile Manufacturing Is Similar to DevOps

In the Cybersecurity Canon Hall of Fame novel about DevOps, *The Phoenix Project*, the authors explain that how we build software today should be similar to how Toyota reimagined the car manufacturing process after World War II into its famous Toyota Production System (TPS).[35] It's a fantastic metaphor, but one nitpick I had with that idea is that although comparing software development to an automobile production line is all true at a macro level, it breaks down at the micro level. What I mean is that the Toyota Production System applied to software development is the DevOps movement, and I'm a big believer in adopting its philosophy (see Chapter 7). It gets you away from the old waterfall software development method of producing one new working piece of code every couple of years, if

---

[34]Bals, F., 2022. 2022 OSSRA discovers 88 percent of organizations still behind in keeping open source updated [WWW Document]. Synopsys. www.synopsys.com/blogs/software-security/open-source-trends-ossra-report (accessed 12/16/22).

[35]Kim, G., Behr, K., Spafford, G., 2014b. The Phoenix Project: A Novel about IT, DevOps, and Helping Your Business Win. It Revolution Press.

ever, and adopting the Agile methodology to produce potentially dozens of new deploys in a day. That's the macro level, and that works.

At the micro level, though, the day-to-day operational level, the TPS metaphor breaks down. Each part (and I'm talking about hardware parts here, not parts that have a software component) comes from the same trusted contractor or you build it yourself. Once built, the parts don't change that much. There are exceptions to this, of course, but that's the norm. The point is, these hardware parts come from the same place every time you make an order. You mostly know who those people are and how they operate. That's not true in software development.

Commercial Code Is Open-Source Code

Almost all commercial software is more than three-quarters open source. That means, unlike the hardware parts that feed the Toyota Production System, we have no idea where our software parts are coming from, who built them, and whether the people who built them are maintaining them. The problem is even more insidious than you might think. If most software developers are using open-source software, there is a good chance that whoever built a specific open-source component also used a different open source module to create it. The whole idea spirals exponentially in a fractal kind of way. That's not even mentioning that hardware manufacturers don't have to contend with armies of researchers that routinely find ways to exploit those parts for criminal, espionage, and continuous low-level, cyber-conflict purposes. The use of open-source software provides these adversary groups with a wide-open attack pathway that we all call the *software supply chain*. Compared to car manufacturers, DevOps people have to operate at an entirely different level.

Software Supply Chain and Cybersecurity First Principles

We've seen a handful of these software supply chain attacks in the past 20 years, but between 2010 and 2020, the bad guys rediscovered this attack strategy and doubled down on it. Between 2015 and 2020, we observed highly impactful supply chain attacks against third parties like MEDoc, Solarwinds, Asus, CCleaner, Kaseya, Accellion, and Codecov, just to name a few.[36,37] These kinds of attacks are even more Machiavellian than a straight-up frontal assault against our own cyber defenses that we designed, deployed, and spent considerable resources on. With a supply chain attack, it doesn't matter how mature those programs are. The hacker's initial compromise in their attack sequence comes right in through a wide-open back door to our data island defenses, propped open with a chair to make entry even easier. In essence, we install the malware for the bad guys. Cyber adversary groups know this and, as Dmitry Raidman (the CTO at Cybeats) says, "The bad guys are on the hunt for vulnerable open source software (OSS) supply chain components so that they can trojanize other legit commercial and open source products."[38] When Log4j-type problems emerge, though, 80 percent of the mitigation work (besides patching) is just finding all the running instances of the software.

But if we're pursuing zero trust as one of our first principle strategies, it's ludicrous to think that we, as a community, don't have a handle on supply chain defenses yet. We have been busily running

---

[36]Roberts, P., 2022. A (Partial) History of Software Supply Chain Attacks. Reversing Labs. blog.reversinglabs.com/blog/a-partial-history-of-software-supply-chain-attacks (accessed 12/17/22).
[37]Staff, n.d. A Timeline of SSC Attacks, Curated by Sonatype [WWW Document]. Sonatype. www.sonatype.com/resources/vulnerability-timeline (accessed 12/17/22p).
[38]Raidman, D., 2020. Why We Need a Software Bill of Materials Industry Standard [WWW Document]. DevOps.com. devops.com/why-we-need-a-software-bill-of-materials-industry-standard (accessed 12/16/22).

around trying to identify all of our employees, contractors, and devices, and then prescriptively authorizing the workloads they have access to (as covered in this chapter). In parallel, we have mostly turned a blind eye to new software coming in through the delivery door to update our production systems. Even the cybersecurity leaders who do monitor and manage this situation rely on manual, homegrown, and incomplete tooling to get this done.

One solution to that problem is the incorporation of a software bill of materials. An SBOM is a formal record containing the details and supply chain relationships of various components used in building software. SBOMs are lists of nested software components designed to enable supply chain transparency. So, if my business runs a software application called Fortnite, an SBOM will list all of the component pieces to the software, all of the original code written by the developers at Epic (Fortnite's owner), all the open-source components they used to make it run, plus all the fractal subcomponents built by other open-source developers.

According to Dmitry, when thinking about this, it's good to distinguish between SBOM *producers* (upstream, focused on their products) and SBOM *consumers* (downstream, focused on the upstream vendor's products). Both sides would use tools that follow a formal specification of a standard. Unfortunately, as of this writing, we don't really have a standard SBOM platform yet. What we do have is a bunch of developing standards and requirements for tools that will help us reduce the risk of software supply chain exposure. Although vendors are starting to sell SBOM platforms, the idea of an SBOM is, at this point, still more of a concept than a reality.

Pertinent SBOM Standards

Spearheaded by the Linux Foundation in 2010, the Software Package Data Exchange (SPDX), also known as ISO/IEC 5962, became the international open standard for security, license compliance, and other software supply chain artifacts in August 2021.[39] In other words, they became the official SBOM standards body. Despite only being internationally recognized for a short while, companies like Intel, Microsoft, Sony, and VMware are already using the SPDX standards to communicate SBOM information. SPDX was not an overnight sensation, though. It was the result of 10 years of collaboration from vendors across the Software Composition Analysis (SCA) space that created tools that assess open-source software, code libraries, and containers; provide a unified view of risks and remediations; and offer strategies to keep this kind of software up-to-date.[40,41,42]

In 2015, the International Organization for Standardization (ISO) released ISO/IEC 19770-2 for Software identification tags (SWID).[43] This format creates a template in XML format to identify and describe software components and relevant patches. Then, in 2017, the Open Web Application Security Project Foundation (OWASP) designed CycloneDX, a lightweight standard with features of both SPDX and SWID.[44]

---

[39]Staff, 2021. ISO/IEC 5962:2021 [WWW Document]. ISO.www.iso.org/standard/81870.html (accessed 12/17/22).

[40]Staff, 2018. The Evolution of Software Composition Analysis(SCA). E-SPIN. www.e-spincorp.com/the-evolution-of-software-composition-analysissca (accessed 12/17/22).

[41]Staff, 2021. SPDX Becomes Internationally Recognized Standard for Software Bill of Materials. Associated Press.

[42]Ingalls, S., 2021. SBOMs: Securing the Software Supply Chain [WWW Document]. eSecurityPlanet. www.esecurityplanet.com/compliance/sbom (accessed 12/17/22).

[43]Staff, n.d. ISO/IEC 19770-2:2015 [WWW Document]. ISO. www.iso.org/standard/65666.html (accessed 12/17/22q).

[44]Staff, 2022. SPDX vs CycloneDX - A Detailed Comparison [WWW Document]. ERP Information. www.erp-information.com/spdx-vs-cyclonedx (accessed 12/17/22).

Presidential Directive

As I said, an SBOM today is a collection of emerging standards that are not quite there yet, but the community is very close to having something usable. The SBOM concept got a big push in 2021 when U.S. President Joe Biden signed an executive order on cybersecurity, EO 14028,[45] that mandates all Federal Civilian Executive Branch Agencies (FCEBs) and key players meet or exceed specific cybersecurity requirements including the development of an SBOM program. FCEBs are the following:

- Administrator of General Services
- Assistant to the President and National Security Advisor (APNSA)
- Cloud service providers (CSPs)
- Director of the Cybersecurity and Infrastructure Security Agency (CISA)
- Director of the Office of Management and Budget (OMB)
- Federal Acquisition Regulation (FAR) Council
- Secretary of Homeland Security
- Secretary of Defense

Dr. Georgianna Shea, one of the world's experts on the SBOM concept, tracks the progress of all the FCEBs in relation to the presidential directive and says that, for the most part, the government is meeting its deadlines. But she caveats that a bit by saying, "The requirements weren't to be operationally executable. So, the actual

---

[45]Staff, 2021. Executive Order on Improving the Nation's Cybersecurity [WWW Document]. The White House. www.whitehouse.gov/briefing-room/presidential-actions/2021/05/12/executive-order-on-improving-the-nations-cybersecurity (accessed 12/17/22).

requirements were easy to meet. There were two specific SBOM requirements in the EO: to identify the minimum elements and to provide guidance addressing an SBOM."[46,47] The government met both of those. So, all the FCEBs are on track, but there is still a lot of work to do.

Three Tools for Supply-Chain Risk Reduction

It turns out that an SBOM is not the only tool that we need. Once we have a handle on all of our software components with an SBOM, it would be nice if there was a place that was the authoritative source for automatically discovering vulnerabilities and exploits in component software. This would be an upgrade to the Common Vulnerability Scoring System. Instead of me reading reports on software vulnerabilities and trying to determine if they apply to the data in my SBOM, the upgraded CVSS would be machine readable and allow another system, an asset management system, to review my SBOM information and compare it to this upgraded CVSS. We don't really have that yet either.

But what we do have is a standard way to articulate vulnerability information in component software. It's called a Vulnerability Exploitability Exchange (VEX) document.[48,49,50] According to

[46]Howard, R., 2021b. Why it's time for cybersecurity to go mainstream. The CyberWire.
[47]Shea, G., 2021. A Software Bill of Materials Is Critical for Comprehensive Risk Management [WWW Document]. The Foundation for Defense of Democracies. www.fdd.org/analysis/2021/09/29/a-software-bill-of-materials-is-critical-for-comprehensive-risk-management (accessed 12/17/22).
[48]Kruszewsk, D., 2021. Understanding Vulnerability Exploitability eXchange (VEX). aDolus Technology.
[49]Kruszewski, D., 2021. What is VEX and What Does it Have to Do with SBOMs? [WWW Document]. Adolus. blog.adolus.com/what-is-vex-and-what-does-it-have-to-do-with-sboms (accessed 12/17/22).
[50]Kautz, F., 2021. What is VEX? It's the Vulnerability Exploitability eXchange! [WWW Document]. zt.dev. zt.dev/posts/what-is-vex (accessed 12/17/22).

Dmitry, "VEX is a result of the work by the continuation of the NTIA Working group that created the SBOM standard" and is managed by CISA. The NTIA is the National Telecommunications and Information Administration, and their working group created this format that we can use to store vulnerability and exploit information about software components. Dmitry says that OASIS has published a draft standard in the Common Security Advisory Framework (CSAF) to describe VEX in machine-readable format similar to CycloneDX. Currently, both CSAF and CycloneDX support the encapsulation of VEX information in their object structure.

What VEX isn't is a system that stores that information in any automated way. The bottom line is that if we are going to reduce the risk of software supply chains, we need an SBOM system and an asset management system that checks SBOM information against the upgraded CVSS system that stores information in the VEX format.

A Bright Future for SBOMs

In fairness, the concept of an SBOM has been around for many years, but there wasn't a lot of incentive out there for a massive push to get it done. So, quietly in the background, volunteers organized by the NTIA, the Linux foundation, OWASP, and others, began to establish some standards. When supply chain attacks started to rise these past few years coupled with several hugely impactful ones (Solarwinds, MeDoc, and Accellion), somebody convinced President Biden to include SBOMs as part of a presidential directive. That's the good news.

Progress on SBOM development is happening. It helps that the U.S. government, at some point, will mandate that all software suppliers provide SBOM information as part of their contract. I believe that will tip the dominoes and the rest of the industry will follow that lead. But I'm guessing that we are still five years away from the SBOM transitioning from a concept to a real thing. Dmitry disagrees and is more of an optimist. He points to the fact that he has witnessed extensive efforts from organizations "ranging from startups to Fortune 500 companies, and surprisingly most of them have already figured out how to generate SBOMs." He says they fundamentally understand the return on investment of managing SBOMs at scale.

Identity Management: A Tactic for Zero Trust

The concept of identity is fascinating. What are the things that we value about ourselves that show others who we are? Name, address, professional title, hacker alias, political affiliation, volunteer committees, recreation, favorite *Dungeons & Dragons* character alignment, entertainment venue memberships, and many, many other activities and things we belong to or support that make up our personal identity. And that doesn't even cover personas. I have my business persona, my family persona, my neighborhood persona, and my gaming persona. I share my identity personas with the communities that I belong to, but I might not like to share them with my other communities. For example, I may not want to share the persona for my level 20 chaotic neutral Tiefling warlock named Abigail with my CEO. He might not understand.

In a transactional world, though, we need to find things to attach to our identity so that we can authenticate who we are. Once that's done, then the receiving end of the transaction can determine if we are authorized to conduct business. It's one thing to get on Twitter and broadcast to the world about how much you love the Cincinnati Reds. You can't use that baseball love to get money out of an ATM machine, though. So, we find ways to prove to our transactional partners that we are who we say we are, and not some AI bot impersonating us.

In the 1850s, the British started using birth certificates to authenticate citizenship.[51] People could present their birth certificate to a bank to get a loan, for example. In 1903, Missouri and Massachusetts became the first states to require a driver's license to operate a car.[52] After WWI, the League of Nations championed the use of passports for international travel. In 1935, the U.S. Congress passed the U.S. Social Security Act that assigned exclusive numbers to citizens.[53] Social Security numbers became the de facto attribute for many years to uniquely distinguish the John Smith who lived in Albuquerque compared to the John Smith who lived in Fresno.

In the 1960s, when computers started to become an essential tool for big business and government, the late great Fernando Corbató, one of computing's founding fathers, introduced the idea of using passwords to gain access.[54] Unbeknownst to him, Corbató provided a long list of cyber ne'er-do-wells a never-ending attack vector to break into computer systems. In fairness, though, passwords didn't start to really break down as an authentication system until the Internet started humming for online transactions circa the mid-1990s. As the Internet scaled, passwords just didn't cut it anymore. Astonishingly, passwords are still the thing that most people use to authenticate themselves, a technique that's now more than 50 years old.

---

[51]Pines, G., 2017. The Contentious History of the Passport. National Geographic.
[52]Nix, E., 2016. When was the first U.S. driver's license issued? HISTORY.
[53]Staff, n.d. The Social Security Act of 1935 [WWW Document]. US House of Representatives: History, Art & Archives. history.house.gov/Historical-Highlights/1901-1950/The-Social-Security-Act-of-1935 (accessed 12/17/22).
[54]McMillan, R., 2012. The World's First Computer Password? It Was Useless Too. WIRED.

Fun fact: Corbató stored the passwords in a text file, which probably provoked one of the first computer hacks ever. Allan Scherr, working on his PHD at the time, found the unprotected text file, stole passwords from the other students, and was able to grant himself more computer time. You have to love those MIT nerds.

In 1993, Tim Howes, Steve Kille, and Wengyik Yeong collaborated to invent the Lightweight Directory Access Protocol (LDAP).[55] According to Juliet Kemp at ServerWatch, LDAP lets administrators organize information on the network and provide users access to it. Howes and team designed LDAP to facilitate authentication over a distributed TCP/IP network.[56] By 2000, Microsoft included LDAP into its backbone authentication system called Active Directory that uses both LDAP, for user lookup, and Kerberos, for authentication.[57] Kerberos was created at MIT in its Athena project in 1988.

In 2002, the U.S. Congress passed the famous Sarbanes–Oxley law, which, among many other things, held companies liable for bad access control.[58] By 2006, we started seeing the first managed services for identity management, and by 2010, we started seeing the first SaaS identity management services.[59] By 2014, organizational data started to be distributed across multiple data islands: traditional perimeters, private data centers, personal devices, SaaS providers, and

[55]Staff, n.d. History of LDAP [WWW Document]. Ldapwiki. ldapwiki.com/wiki/HistoryofLDAP (accessed 12/17/22).
[56]Kemp, J., 2010. LDAP and Kerberos, So Happy Together. ServerWatch.
[57]Broeckelmann, R., 2018. Kerberos and Windows Security: History. Medium.
[58]Rep. Oxley, M., 2002. Sarbanes-Oxley Act of 2002.
[59]Paula, J., 2019. The Evolution Of IAM (Identity Access Management). Solutions Review.

cloud providers (IaaS and PaaS). It was clear that on-prem identity solutions were on their way out in favor of SaaS identity services.

One of the problems with digital identity and authentication is that our current systems are site-centric. Users of systems have to present credential information to multiple digital silos like Amazon, Netflix, eBay, and the like, and these silos don't talk to each other for the most part. Single sign-on, which I will cover in "Single Sign On: A Zero Trust Tactic," gets close to solving that problem in that not every silo maintains a set of your credentials. But still, some silo holds your credentials, not you.

If Fernando Corbató invented the beta version of identity and authentication in the 1960s, Dick Hardt, an Internet identity evangelist, says that by the mid-2000s we had finally reached identity and authentication version 1.0 with our site-centric systems. When identity federation emerged some time after, that probably moved us to identity and authentication version 1.5.[60]

According to Helen Patton, the former Ohio State University CISO, federation is the idea that if two partners trust each other, they trust each other's users. If Helen traveled to her trusted partner's campus, say the University of Michigan, she is able to log on to the campus Wi-Fi network without any coordination hassles. From my perspective, federation is the associative property of trust. If the University of Michigan trusts Ohio State University and Ohio State University trusts Helen, then the University of Michigan trusts Helen too. That doesn't mean the University of Michigan authorizes Helen to do much. That's an entirely different step, an authorization step. But federation makes authentication easier for one-off partnerships.[61]

---

[60]Lewis, D., 2006b. Identity 2.0 Keynote. YouTube.

[61]Howard, R., 2020b. Identity management around the Hash Table, with Rick Howard, Helen Patton, Suzie Smibert, and Rick Doten. The CyberWire.

That's fine, but it's not yet a perfect solution. One-off partnerships between Ohio State University and University of Michigan don't scale well. Again, single sign-on solutions from the likes of Google, Facebook, Apple, and several others, offer the scale but still require transaction partners to trust a third party as the true credential source for one or both sides of the transaction.

What we need is identity and authentication version 2.0 where we move away from site-centric solutions to a user-centric solution. I become the broker myself. When I want to log into Netflix and Amazon, they interrogate my mobile device for the credentials. I own the credentials, not Amazon. They come to me, not the other way around.

In the early 2000s, two technologies emerged that would move us closer to that goal: SAML and OpenID/OAuth. SAML (pronounced "sam-el") stands for Security Assertion Markup Language and refers to a heavy-weight XML variant language that facilitates one computer to perform both authentication and authorization on behalf of other computers. The OpenID/OAuth pair is a set of competing technologies to SAML that have a crazy and confusing history of Internet drama.[62]

Don't worry if this all sounds confusing. It is. For example, OAuth stands for open authentication. The crazy thing is that OAuth doesn't authenticate anything. It simply authorizes a machine to log in to another machine on behalf of a human. OpenID does the authentication. By 2014, this had all settled down. Today, according to *CSO Magazine*, most network operators use SAML for enterprise applications and OAuth for open Internet situations.[63,64]

---

[62]Staff, 2007. History of SAML [WWW Document]. SAML XML.org. saml .xml.org/history (accessed 12/17/22).
[63]Broeckelmann, R., 2019. SAML2 vs JWT: Understanding OAuth2 - Robert Broeckelmann. Medium.
[64]Broeckelmann, R., 2017. SAML2 vs JWT: Understanding OpenID Connect Part 1 - Robert Broeckelmann. Medium.

At this point, with SAML and OpenID/OAuth, we have probably reached identity and authentication version 1.7, up from version 1.5 that we got with federation, but still not quite at 2.0. To get to 2.0, a user-centric solution, I would direct your attention to a paper written by Kim Cameron in 2005 called "The Laws of Identity."[65] That might be a good place to start. He lists seven characteristics that any modern identity system should have.

1. *User control and consent*: The user is in charge.
2. *Minimal disclosure for a constrained use*: Zero trust for data exchanged.
3. *Justifiable parties*: Zero trust for exchanging parties.
4. *Directed identity*: Omni-directional and one way.
5. *Pluralism of operators and technologies*: Can operate with multiple technologies and multiple entities.
6. *Human integration*: Conducive to humans interacting securely.
7. *Consistent experience across contexts*: As the great Marvel Comics editor-in-chief, Stan Lee, always proclaimed, "'Nuff said."

The bottom line is that the concept of identity is probably the most important thing to get right for the future of transactional Internet business. We can have all of the first principle strategies in place that you want, but being able to know precisely that Abigail, the level 20 chaotic neutral Tiefling warlock, is really Rick Howard and not the owner of a Russian influence operation run out of Novosibirsk, Siberia, is key to everything. Without it, we will not have confidence in any future system such as online voting, census taking, or really any transactional interactions with our governments, commercial business, or academic institutions.

---

[65]Cameron, K., 2005. The Laws of Identity, Kim Cameron's Identity Weblog.

You'd be right to point out that the way we do identity and authentication today, the version 1.7 that I have described, kind of works. And it does. I am able to watch Netflix, buy books from Amazon, and order hamburgers from my local Five Guys all relatively hassle free. But these site-centric systems were designed by commercial firms for the purpose of making money, which I am not against, but maybe there's a loftier design goal that the security community should pursue. Maybe we should design our identity and authentication systems so that users are in control of their own credentials.

That said, for enterprise security, you absolutely can't pursue the zero trust first principle strategy until you have a robust identity management system in place. It can't be done. Unless you know for sure who all the humans are that connect to your network, all the hardware devices that request access to resources, and all the software components (from in-house development to commercial tools to open-source software modules), you can't possibly restrict access on a need-to-know basis. The reason this is so important is because of the way that most cyber adversaries infiltrate and maneuver inside their victim's networks.

In Chapter 4, I discuss the idea of the intrusion kill chain in detail, but in general, once hackers compromise victim zero, they try to move laterally within the network looking for the data they've come to steal or destroy. Along the way, they seek to elevate their privilege wherever possible. A case in point is the Cozy Bear supply chain attacks that targeted the SolarWinds Orion product late in 2020.[66]

Cozy Bear hackers compromised the SolarWinds network first and inserted a backdoor trojan into the Orion software update package. Once Orion customers installed the package, the Cozy Bear team could log in remotely. From this initial beachhead, they moved

[66]Baker, P., 2021. The SolarWinds hack timeline: Who knew what, and when? [WWW Document]. CSO Online. www.csoonline.com/article/3613571/the-solarwinds-hack-timeline-who-knew-what-and-when.html (accessed 12/17/22).

laterally within the victim's networks seeking administrator accounts. According to the Microsoft Security Response Center, the Cozy Bear hackers went after the SAML system that I discussed earlier: "Once in the network, the intruder then uses the administrative permissions acquired through the on-premises compromise to gain access to the organization's global administrator account and/or trusted SAML token signing certificate. This enables the actor to forge SAML tokens that impersonate any of the organization's existing users and accounts, including highly privileged accounts."

The Cozy Bear attacks on the SolarWinds Orion platform highlight a key point. Especially in the infrastructure-as-code era that we're all in now, there are certain legitimate DevOps mechanisms within the code that should require elevated permissions to run, like the creation of SAML tokens. In other words, you don't want Luigi, who updates the menu for the company cafeteria website every day, to have permission to create SAML tokens. That would go against the very nature of our zero trust strategy. You don't want some random software module, which nobody is watching, to have permission to elevate privilege and make changes to the system either.

Now, I'm not picking on SAML. There are probably hundreds of infrastructure transactions within your environment that should require some sort of elevated permission to execute. The point I'm making here is that, as security practitioners, we should know what each of them are and deploy specific rules for which network entities can perform those functions.

According to Gartner, "IAM is the discipline that enables the right individuals to access the right resources at the right times for the right reasons."[67] NIST has a similar definition: "[The process, and

---

[67]Staff, n.d. Definition of Identity and Access Management (IAM) - Gartner Information Technology Glossary [WWW Document]. Gartner. www.gartner.com/en/information-technology/glossary/identity-and-access-management-iam (accessed 12/17/22).

technology required] to ensure the right people and things have the right access to the right resources at the right time."[68]

IAM: IGA and PIM and PAM, Oh My!

Thinking in terms of first principles in general and zero trust specifically as a strategy, the IAM program consists of three parts.[69,70]

- *Identity governance and administration (IGA)*: The internal group of IT, security, and business leaders who define the policy
- *Privileged identity management (PIM)*: The system that dynamically manages all the identities and what they are allowed to access
- *Privileged access management (PAM)*: The system that enforces the rules created by the IGA against the identities in the PIM

Network defenders can buy these services from vendors, build and deploy them in-house, or use some combination of both. The IGA can be formal or loose, the PIM can be managed within a spreadsheet or in a giant database, and the PAM can be manual controls that administrators configure in their Microsoft Active Directory deployments or can be managed in a software-defined perimeter scheme (see the Software-Defined Perimeter: A Tactic for Zero Trust section below). Regardless, some collection of these tactics for all three parts must be present for any true IAM program.

---

[68]Grassi, P.A., Garcia, M.E., Fenton, J.L., 2017. Digital identity guidelines: revision 3. National Institute of Standards and Technology, Gaithersburg, MD.
[69]Staff, n.d. IAM vs PAM vs PIM: The Difference Explained [WWW Document]. MSP360. www.msp360.com/resources/blog/iam-vs-pam-vs-pim (accessed 12/17/22).
[70]Soare, B., 2021. PIM vs PAM vs IAM: What's The Difference? Heimdal Security.

One last thing to consider is that the systems and data inside the IAM program are the keys to the city. In other words, the zero trust IAM system network defenders design and deploy in order to reduce the probability of material impact has itself become a material system on its own because of the information contained within and has to be protected in the same manner I protect all the other material systems to the business. How's that for some recursive security logic? If hackers take control of my IAM system, they can bypass all the zero trust security controls. We have to protect the IAM system of systems with the same strategies that we use to protect the entire organization: zero trust, intrusion kill chain prevention, resilience, risk forecasting, and automation.

Single Sign-On: A Zero Trust Tactic

Before single sign-on (SSO, pre-2000s), identity and access management was simply the handshake process of a user or application sending credentials to a workload in order to gain access. The workload would verify the persona by checking that the user ID and password stored locally matched what the network entity presented and grant access. Users repeated this process for every application and network that they wanted to access. That meant that these same users were expected to keep track of many different passwords. Security leadership blamed them if they couldn't come up with good ones or used the same ones over and over and over again. We still publicly shame those users in annual reports of the most common and lame passwords used by everybody on the Internet, mostly some combination of "12345" and "password." This is essentially victim blaming and faults people for being exceptionally bad at using a stop-gap identity system invented in the early 1960s. That doesn't seem right.

At a conceptual level, SSO is the idea that a user or application can assert their identity once to a trusted source. When that same user needs access to some other workload elsewhere, the user directs the workload and the trusted source to work out if the request is valid. The good news is that users have to remember only one password. The bad news is that they can still use an easily guessable password like "12345." Two-factor authentication can improve that situation, and we will talk about that in the next section. But SSO greatly simplifies the identity and access management process, although it has taken us 50 years to get here since Doctor Corbató invented the idea of passwords in the early 1960s.

OAuth Process

It turns out that to do single sign-on, we use our old friends OAuth and SAML. Remember, OAuth is normally used for the general Internet user. According to Michael Bissell[71] at NWEA, three parties are involved: the user (like raceBannon99, an Internet troll), the identity provider (the authoritative source of some user's identity and roles, like Google), and the service provider (the application raceBannon99 is trying to get access to, like Twitter). raceBannon99 is a regular user of Google's products (Gmail, Google Drive, etc.) and logs in to Google every day. But now, he wants to troll people on Twitter. Instead of logging in to Twitter with a different set of credentials, raceBannon99 surfs over to Twitter and begins the process (see Figure 3.2) to sign in.

1: raceBannon99 asks Twitter if he can use single sign-on to log in.

2: Twitter says to go get an asymmetric key from the identity provider (Google).

3: Race then asks Google for a key to let Twitter validate his credentials.

4: Google packages and sends a key back to him.

[71]Bissell, M., 2017. What is SSO. YouTube.

5: Race then sends that key over to Twitter.

6: Twitter sends the key to Google and asks, "Hey, is this guy legit?"

7: Google responds with, "Why yes, raceBannon99 is a fine fellow," but you know, probably in 1337speak, a language that only computers understand.

In this OAuth transaction, none of the three parties exchanged passwords. They simply passed asymmetric keys to each other. See Figure 3.2.

According to Ben Lutkevich at TechTarget, Google is not the only tech giant that offers authoritative source services.[72] As of this writing, these are some of the more popular companies that offer identity provider services:

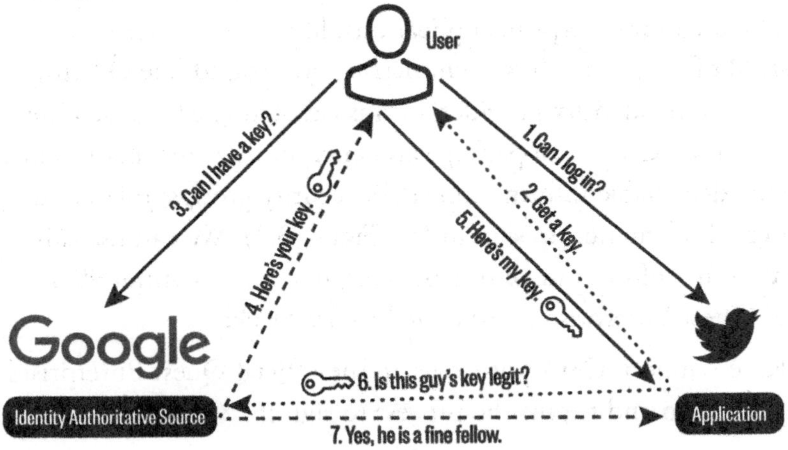

Figure 3.2 Single sign-on via OAuth

- Google
- Facebook
- Apple

[72]Lutkevich, B., 2021. identity provider. TechTarget.

- Fitbit
- Microsoft
- Box
- Amazon Web Services (AWS)

The bottom line is that for general Internet transactions, users pick a company that they trust, allow that company to store their credentials, and then use the credentials as the authoritative source when requesting access to other Internet properties.

SAML Process

For SAML, the process is similar but more robust. Remember, SAML is typically used for enterprise applications, like Quest Enterprises, and instead of simply sending asymmetric keys around like OAuth, SAML allows the identity provider, in this case Google because Quest Enterprises used GSuite, to package and encrypt user information like personally identifiable information (PII), security groups, roles, and other useful information to sign in (see Figure 3.3). We can use this information to enforce our zero trust rules, like is raceBannon99 (CSO of Quest Enterprises) authorized to use Slack?

1: Race Bannon, CSO, surfs over to the official Quest Enterprises Slack application and begins the process to sign in.

2: Slack tells Race to retrieve a PII package from the identity provider (Google).

3: Race then asks Google for his Slack PII package.

4: To verify that Slack is who they say they are, the identity provider (Google) asks Slack for its key.

5: Slack sends Google its public key.

6: Google encrypts Race's PII information with Slack's key and sends it to Race.

7: Race sends the encrypted PII package to Slack.

8: Slack opens Race's PII package with its private key.

There are two things to note here. First, Race can't view the contents of his PII package because Google encrypted it with the Slack public key. Second, after Slack opens the package, it can make decisions about what Race has access to within the Slack application. See Figure 3.3.

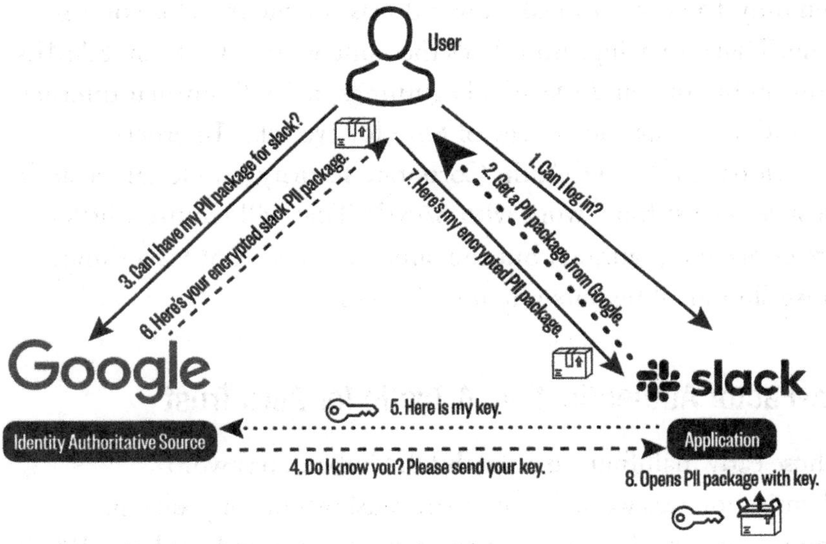

Figure 3.3 Single sign-on via SAML

As in OAuth, the SAML identity provider is essential, and there are many ways to implement it. According to Bissell, here are a few of the common systems that identity and access management programs can use (there are many others):

- Active Directory
- Lightweight Directory Access Protocol

- PingFederate
- SharePoint

SSO has taken a long time in terms of Internet years to come close to something that is usable. In terms of normal years, though, the transition has been phenomenally fast. What I mean by that is that Internet time flies by. We are impatient that it has taken 15 years from the time we got the iPhone (2007) to the time that we could reliably stream *Moon Knight* on it from Disney+. That's Internet time. And it feels like it took forever. But, in human years, OMG! It has taken only 15 years to stream a world-class movie franchise on my phone. That's amazing. And that's the same with SSO. From SAML's inception in 2002 and OAuth's beginnings in 2010, normal Internet users today can take advantage of SSO for everyday Internet interactions thanks to OAuth. Corporate security people can create a robust zero trust framework with SAML. That will require a little more effort and planning, but the bones are there. SSO is a thing, and we should all be pursuing it with vigor.

Two-Factor Authentication: A Tactic for Zero Trust

In those early mainframe days with Dr. Corbató, password authentication was weak, but it wasn't causing a major problem. Computer use was limited to government projects and academic R&D. There weren't a lot of people using networked computers back then. But by the 1980s, with the ARPANet slowly morphing into the Internet, the computer user population started to grow, the community needed more robust authentication methods for business critical systems.

In the mid-1980s, Security Dynamics Technologies was the first company to create a hardware token device that created one-time passwords (OTPs) for authentication.[73] By 1995, AT&T patented the

---

[73]Staff, 2020. A Developer's History of Authentication. WorkOS [WWW Document]. WorkOS. workos.com/blog/a-developers-history-of-authentication (accessed 12/17/22).

idea of two-factor authentication.[74] They said that to identify an authorized user, a system needed to check at least two of three factors: something they have, like a smartphone; something they are, like a fingerprint; or something they know, like a password. But the early systems were clunky, hard to manage, and used only in environments that needed the most security. But, when the smartphone started to emerge in the mid-2000s, that started to change. All of a sudden everybody had a second factor in their pocket. That led to all kinds of innovation.

Types of Two-Factor Authentication

Back in 2017, Chris Hoffman wrote an excellent piece for the How-To Geek website regarding the various forms of two-factor authentication.[75] Let me just summarize how they work here, and then we can talk about how secure they are.

SMS Verification

Internet troll raceBannon99 wants to log in to Audible.com. The website sends a text message with the code into the Audible.com website to gain access to his account.

Email Verification

This is similar to the SMS verification method except that the second factor is email and not the text messaging system.

---

[74]Daragiu, A., 2019. A review of the evolution of multifactor authentication (MFA) [WWW Document]. Typing. blog.typingdna.com/evolution-of-multifactor-authentication

[75]Hoffman, C., 2017. The Different Forms of Two-Factor Authentication: SMS, Authenticator Apps, and More [WWW Document]. How-To Geek. www.howtogeek.com/232598/5-different-two-step-authentication-methods-to-secure-your-online-accounts/

Authenticator Soft Tokens (Like Google Authenticator, ID.me, Blizzard's Battlenet, and LastPass)

Authenticators use an Internet Engineering Task Force (IETF) algorithm to generate one-time codes called *time-based one-time passwords* (TOTPs). Race Bannon, Quest Enterprises CSO, wants to log into his Google G-Suite account. G-Suite asks for a one-time code. Race opens his Google Authenticator application on his smartphone and looks up the listing for Google. He has several listings to choose from like LastPass and Quest Enterprise's HR application. The algorithm is standard, so Google's authenticator application can be used to log into other company's apps like Microsoft or Amazon. He notices that for each listing there is a countdown. Every 30 seconds, the Google Authenticator app generates a different code to use. Race tries to remember the six-digit code and enters it into the Google login screen before the timer winds down.

Push Authentication (from Google, Apple, Microsoft, and Twitter)

Unlike SMS verification, Google's push authentication system uses no codes. Race Bannon is summoned to his mother-in-law's house to fix some tech issue with the iPad. While there, he needs to log into his Gmail account to retrieve some information. Google doesn't recognize the mother-in-law's iPad as a registered device and pushes a notification to him via the Google Application on his iPhone. Race opens the Google Application on his smartphone and pushes a button that says, "Yes, I am indeed Race Bannon." That all takes way more time to explain than it does to do, but in the end, Race gets access to his Gmail account on his mother-in-law's iPad. Apple's version is similar, but it's not tied to an application. It uses the operating system.

Universal 2nd Factor Authentication

Universal 2nd Factor (U2F) authentication is an open standard that improves and simplifies 2FA by using Universal Serial Bus (USB) or near-field communication (NFC) devices. Race Bannon wants to log in to the LastPass Password Manager to access the corporate passwords. He enters his user ID and password, and then LastPass asks Race to insert his physical authentication USB key into the laptop (in this case, Yubico's Yubikey). He touches the button on the outside of the physical key, and LastPass grants access.

The way this works is that the USB key creates a public/private key pair for each website like LastPass. The user's browser verifies those keys to allow the user to gain access. This eliminates the possibility of bad guys using spoofed websites to steal credentials.

There are versions of this that can work wirelessly over either Bluetooth or NFC. NFC is a protocol that helps two devices communicate wirelessly when they are placed right next to each other (the range is about 4 inches) like using your mobile device to validate your boarding pass in airports. Devices with NFC hardware can establish communications with other NFC-equipped devices as well as NFC "tags." NFC tags are unpowered NFC chips that draw power from nearby NFC-capable devices. See Figure 3.4.

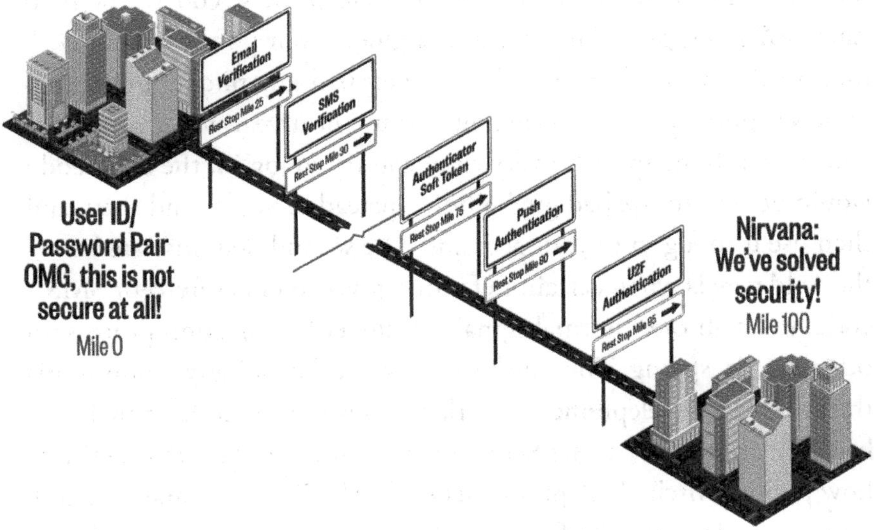

Figure 3.4 Two-factor authentication tools on the road to Nirvana

How Secure Is Two Factor Authentication?

On a simple linear scale, using 2FA is way better than simply using user ID/password pairs. If I were to put all the authentication methods in this section as rest stops on a 100-mile road between the two great cities of "OMG, this is not secure at all" to "Nirvana! We've solved security," the user ID/password pair rest stop would be just a mile out of OMG, just slightly better than having no credentials at all. All the rest of the methods would be rest stops down the road toward, but never quite reaching, Nirvana.

The email verification rest stop would be about 25 miles out on this journey. It's 75 miles away from Nirvana because it doesn't exactly qualify as a second factor. An email account is unique to a user (like a password), but you can access it from anywhere. It's not something you have on your person or some kind of biometric. So, having two password-like factors is better than one, but not by much.

The SMS verification rest stop would be about 30 miles down the road toward Nirvana. It's slightly better than email verification because it's tied to a second factor, but bad guys have demonstrated in the real world three different ways to intercept these codes. The first is called *SIM swapping*. They socially engineer your phone company into moving your phone number to their bad-guy phone; this is the same swapping process you're going to use next year when you buy your new iPhone model. Every time you try to log in, the SMS code would be sent to the bad guy's phone instead of yours, and they could then use it to log in to your account. The second demonstrated-in-the-wild way is when certain nefarious governments intercept SMS codes through their normal signal's intelligence collection process, in other words, spying. The third way is when the bad guys compromise the victim's SS7 telephone network and reroute the code to their bad-guy phone. SS7 is the Signaling System 7 standard that defines how public switched telephone networks (PSTNs) exchange control signals. Having said all of that, SMS verification is way better than parking at the rest stop of user ID/password pairs but still many miles from Nirvana. It's probably fine for run-of-the-mill Internet use, like logging into the library. But if you have material information to protect or if you're a spy, steer clear of SMS authentication.

The Authenticator Soft Token rest stop is located about 75 miles down the road. It's pretty good, a long way away from OMG but close enough to Nirvana that you can see the great city in the distance. It's still susceptible to man-in-the-middle attacks if the user is tricked into entering the code into a bad guy–controlled phishing site. The attack sequence is easier to do than, say, compromising the victim's SS7 network, but definitely in the skill set of the modern day cybercriminal. For it to be reliable, the attacker has to grab the code and log into the account before the authenticator changes it. Timing is critical but doesn't make the attack impossible, just more difficult.

You will find the push authentication rest stop at the 80 mile marker slightly closer to Nirvana than the authenticator's rest stop. Still, victims have observed bad guys sending notification flooding attacks to their phones. If potential victims are busy or are not paying attention, they might click the button to verify their identity just to clear the message, never realizing that they just authorized a bad guy into one of their accounts.

The U2F authentication rest stop is the last waystation before the Nirvana exit ramp (mile marker 95). If you have serious security requirements compared to just surfing the 'Net, this is the way to go. The downside to the USB security key solution, though, is the likelihood of somebody like me losing the key, which I will absolutely do because I'm an idiot. I'm more excited about the future possibilities of the NFC solutions. I'm less likely to lose my phone than I am to lose a USB key. The problem today, though, is that the solution is not widely adopted yet and still maturing. Fast Identity Online (FIDO) is the standards body that is pushing U2F authentication technologies. In the 2021 Hype Cycle Chart for

Identity and Access Management technologies, Gartner puts the FIDO Alliance's efforts as still traveling down the trough of disillusionment and estimates 2 to 5 years before it reaches the plateau of productivity.

The Future of Two-Factor Authentication

Call me crazy, but I don't think that the number of passwords that LastPass will be managing for me in the next decade will shrink. With the Internet of Things growing wildly and 5G networks just over the horizon for common use, the volume of accounts we will all have to manage in our personal and professional lives will just continue to grow. Authenticator soft tokens, push authentication, and U2F will be in our lives for the foreseeable future. And maybe, somewhere along that road between OMG and Nirvana, we might just get rid of Dr. Corbató's stop measure from the 1960s altogether.

Software-Defined Perimeter: A Tactic for Zero Trust

As I've said, perimeter defense and defense in depth were the go-to security models in the early days (mid-1990s). We used the security stack to create a barrier between the Wild Wild West that was the Internet and our bastion of commercial and personal activity (see Figure 3.5). That was great if you worked inside the perimeter all day long and didn't have to go to the Internet for anything. But what happened immediately were all these exceptions. Our stated security policy was that we were going to block everything at the firewall that we didn't trust. But for all kinds of good business reasons, we had to punch holes through the firewall to allow contractors, partners, and employees who operated outside of the firewall to access the things they needed inside the firewall. Sometimes, we would just open up the firewall with specific rules for each exception. By the 2000s, though, we would just give them access to those resources via a virtual private network (VPN) connection. See Figure 3.5.

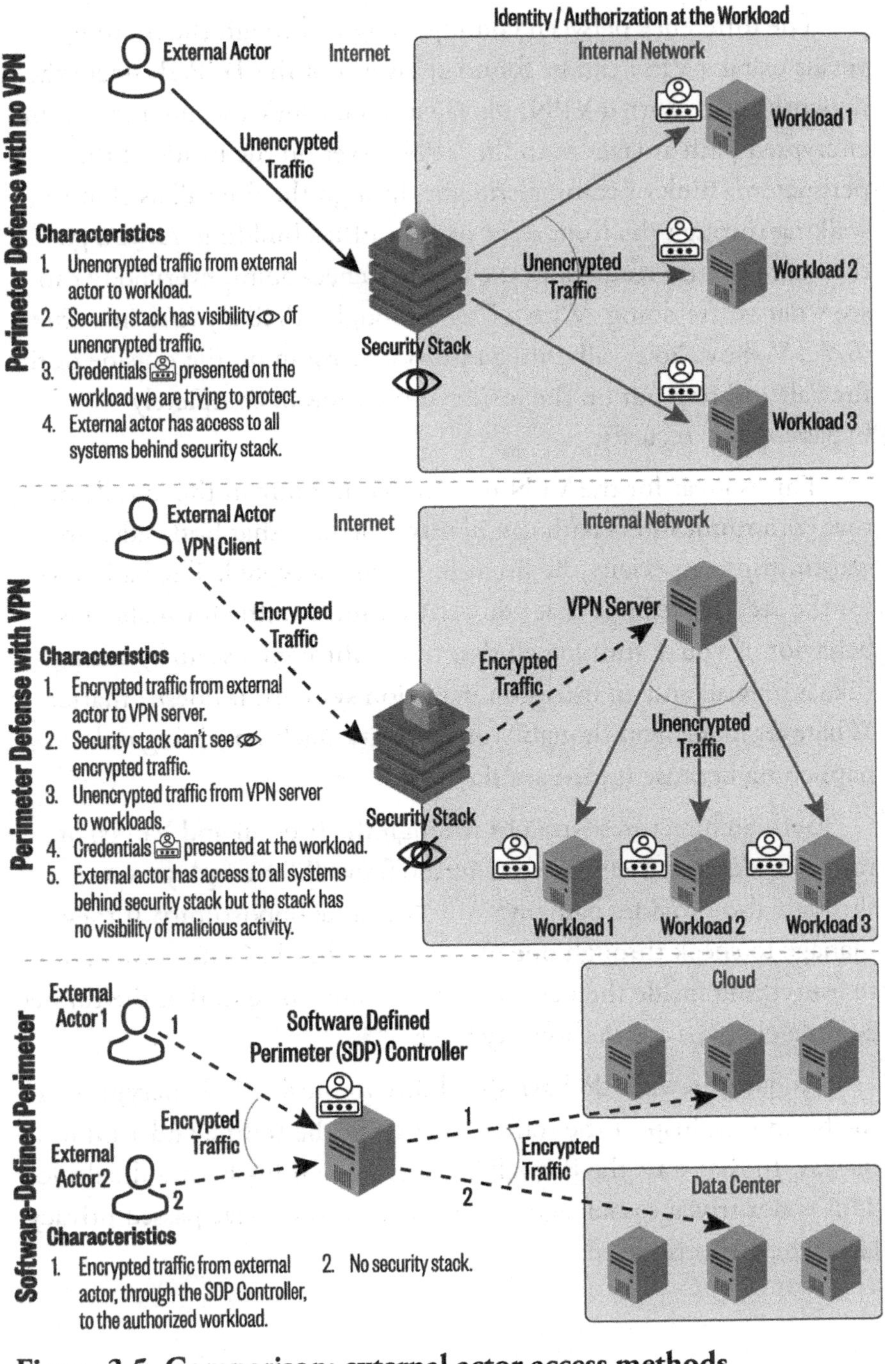

Figure 3.5 Comparison: external actor access methods

The difference between coming straight through the firewall versus using a VPN can be found at layer 3 of the TCP/IP stack: the network layer. With a VPN, the client establishes a secure tunnel, an encrypted path at layer 3, to the VPN server on the inside of the perimeter. Think of coming straight through the firewall as akin to walking through the front door of your office building. As you go through the card reader and the security checkpoint, everybody can see what you're doing. With a VPN, though, it's like you're in a *Star Trek* TV show. You walk into a transporter room on the outside of the firewall and pop out on the inside of the firewall completely bypassing any security.

This is great for the VPN user in that nobody in the middle of that communications path can observe the data that both sides are transmitting, especially the firewall. It's all encrypted. The bad news for the security team is that you can't monitor traffic for malicious behavior. If you're running all that traffic through a security stack (like a firewall and an intrusion detection system), it doesn't matter. Whatever magic you thought your security stack was doing isn't happening because it can't see the data.

Both architectures (straight through the firewall and VPNs) are just poor designs. Leaving holes in the firewall for employees to get through also provides bad guys with the same opportunity. If they manage to sneak through one of the holes, they basically have access to everything inside the perimeter. VPNs are worse in that the tunnel completely bypasses the security stack.

Modern firewalls do have the ability to break VPN encryption at the boundary, inspect the traffic, re-encrypt the traffic, and send it on its way. In that way, the firewall becomes a man-in-the-middle device. This is not trivial to manage, and some countries have passed privacy laws where this is illegal.

Software-Defined Perimeter Becomes a New Model

In the early 2000s, the U.S. military started experimenting with a different architecture called *de-perimeterization* under the project name the Jericho Forum.[76] The idea was to decouple the identification and authorization functions away from the sensitive workload. In other words, you wouldn't connect to a system by going through the firewall or through a VPN tunnel and then try to log in to it. Instead, you connect to a separate system, a software-defined perimeter (SDP) controller outside the firewall, that verifies your identity and validates that you have a need to know and a need to access. If you're authorized, then the SDP controller establishes a VPN-like tunnel connection between you and the workload, but to nothing else. That kind of system hides the workload, and all the workloads, in a kind of "black cloud" as the DOD called it. In other words, any random bad guy on the Internet couldn't easily see or find the sensitive workloads protected behind the perimeter. All they could see is the SDP controller handling the identity and authorization function. Also, even if bad guys corrupted that process and were able to get access to that workload, they wouldn't have access to any other workload. And that is the essence of zero trust, reducing the attack surface to the bare minimum. Unfortunately, the DOD never built it.

In 2010, Google along with a number of commercial and defense contractors announced that they had been breached by a massive Chinese cyber-espionage attack, Operation Aurora.[77] In the weeks that followed, we learned that there wasn't just one Chinese government entity operating inside the Google network. There were two: the People's Liberation Army (PLA) that stole intellectual

---

[76]Staff, 2007. Jericho Forum™ Commandments. The Open Group.
[77]Perlroth, N., 2021. This Is How They Tell Me the World Ends: The Cyberweapons Arms Race. Bloomsbury Publishing.

property, specifically source code from tech companies, and the Ministry of State Security (MSS), who targeted political dissidents like the Dalai Lama, Uighur, and Tibetan ethnic minorities. And in a nod to government bureaucracies everywhere, they each didn't know the other was in there until Google went public with the information.

> Fun fact: In the early days of tracking cyber spies (2000s), one of the indicators of Chinese government involvement was the time when the attacks occurred, mostly between 9 a.m. and 5 p.m. Shanghai time. It was as if the Chinese hackers were clocking in like a regular job. I remember back in those days when we all thought how significant time zones were in attribution. If the attacks occurred between 9 a.m. and 5 p.m. Moscow time, then of course the Russians did it. In hindsight, that seems a bit naive. Today, if I'm planning an offensive cyber operation, there would always be a false flag component to emulate some known adversary and leave behind time zone traces that match. I'm just saying.

In response to the Aurora attack, Google's site reliability engineers (SREs) redesigned their internal security architecture from the ground up using the concepts of de-perimeterization and the zero trust philosophy.[78] A few years later, they released a commercial product called BeyondCorp that incorporated many of the ideas they developed internally.

In 2013, the nonprofit Cloud Security Alliance announced its SDP Initiative and released their 1.0 specification a year later.[79] In

[78]Beyer, B., Jones, C., Petoff, J., Murphy, N.R., 2016. Site Reliability Engineering: How Google Runs Production Systems. "O'Reilly Media, Inc."
[79]Staff, 2013. CSA Announces Software Defined Perimeter (SDP) Initiative [WWW Document]. Cloud Security Alliance. cloudsecurityalliance.org/press-releases/2013/11/13/csa-announces-software-defined-perimeter-sdp-initiative (accessed 12/17/22).

2020, NIST released its zero trust architecture document that outlined some of the early discussions of software-defined perimeter.[80] Finally in 2022, the Cloud Security Alliance announced version 2.0 of its specification document.[81]

Somewhere between the DOD's Jericho Forum and the Cloud Security Alliance's SDP, de-perimeterization became known in the industry as SDP; this is an unfortunate name because it has absolutely nothing to do with perimeter defense at all. It completely decouples the login process from the workload and essentially eliminates the 1990s perimeter as we knew it back then.

If I were in marketing, I would call this de-perimeterization architecture something like the following:

- Software Defined Wormhole
- Black Hole Identity and Authorization
- Identity and Authorization Ducts
- Transporter Room Identity and Authorization (for the *Star Trek* fans)

Maybe I should just stick to cybersecurity.

To my mind, SDP is by far a superior cybersecurity first principle design tactic and is better suited to help us accomplish our zero trust initiatives. It comes built in with an identity and authorization

---

[80] Rose, S., Borchert, O., Mitchell, S., Connelly, S., 2020b. SP 800-207, Zero Trust Architecture [WWW Document]. NIST. csrc.nist.gov/publications/detail/sp/800-207/final (accessed 12/17/22).

[81] Staff, Cloud Security Alliance Issues Expanded Specification for the [WWW Document]. CSA. cloudsecurityalliance.org/press-releases/2022/03/10/cloud-security-alliance-issues-expanded-specification-for-the-software-defined-perimeter-sdp (accessed 12/17/22).

function and keeps access to workloads limited to a need to know. Unfortunately, the architecture is not widely known despite the best efforts of the Cloud Security Alliance and NIST. In a survey done by the Cloud Security Alliance in 2020, only a quarter of the respondents had even heard about it.[82] For those that did, they said the number-one reason that prevented adoption is that it was too hard to rip and replace existing security technologies to do so. That is unfortunate. If zero trust is indeed a cybersecurity first principle, SDP is most likely the long-term path to get there.

One note, though: SDP slides right into your IAM program as mentioned in "Identity Management: A Tactic for Zero Trust." It replaces other architectures or makes existing ones better. This is a reminder that any deployed SDP program is by its very nature a material system to the organization and needs to be protected as such with our cybersecurity first principle strategies. If the bad guys compromise the SDP, it's game over.

Why Zero Trust Projects Fail

When Kindervag published his seminal paper on zero trust in 2010, most of the security community thought it was a good idea—one of a million ideas that we probably were never going to get around to implementing. But, when the Snowden incident happened, that made it real by highlighting a genuine weakness in the perimeter defense model that could cause severe damage. The Snowden incident and the high-profile insider threat cases that emerged later (Chelsea Manning, Tesla, Capital One, and others) gave us the reason to change. But still, many of us haven't even begun the journey.

---

[82]Staff, 2019c. The State of SDP Survey: A Summary [WWW Document]. CSA. cloudsecurityalliance.org/blog/2019/07/02/the-state-of-sdp-survey-a-summary (accessed 12/17/22).

The reason is that for most of us, we have set ourselves a daunting task. We think that in order to achieve zero trust, we have to boil the ocean, throw everything out, and start over. Take a look at the NIST draft zero trust architecture document published in February 2020 to understand what I'm talking about (see Figure 3.6).[83]

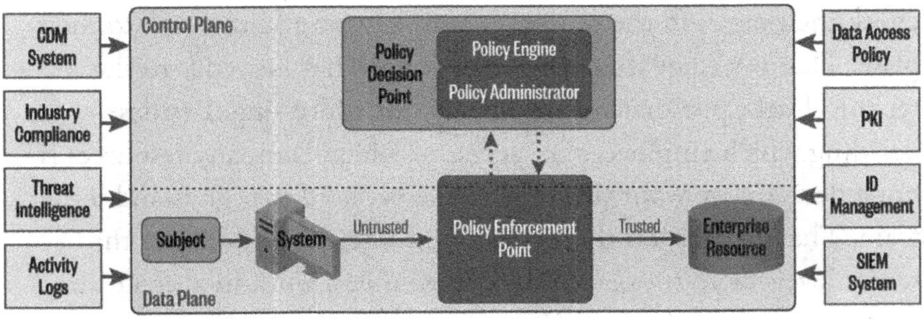

Figure 3.6 NIST logical components of zero trust architecture

Although the document is absolutely correct in how it organizes the zero trust ideas and the technical things you must have in place for it to work, NIST puts forward a proposed system of systems, an architecture of black boxes, that at first glance seems to be something none of us has, isn't available from the commercial sector, and is too big to build ourselves. But this just isn't true.

Here's the thing, though. Zero trust initiatives don't fail because the technology to implement it doesn't exist. Next-generation firewalls have been around since 2007 and were designed to do this very thing. Zero trust initiatives fail because network defenders don't allocate enough resources in terms of people and processes to manage them. At worst, some of us think that we can flip a switch and the system will manage itself. Let me count how many times that strategy has worked for me in my lifetime—that would be zero.

[83]Rose, S.W., Borchert, O., Mitchell, S. and Connelly, S. (2020). Zero Trust Architecture. [online] NIST. www.nist.gov/publications/zero-trust-architecture [Accessed 3 Oct. 2022].

At best, we use the two-guys-and-a-dog management approach. This team of crack IT management experts operate our routers, our security stack, our printers, and George in sales' persistent inability to connect a monitor to his laptop, and they also get coffee for the CEO in the morning. Now we want them to also manage the zero trust strategy inside our next-generation firewalls. They barely have time to check their email in the morning, and now we add this task to their plate. That is a train wreck in the making. That just adds to the technical debt pile that we are already not addressing. Besides, deciding which employees get access to which company resources is not a decision we want sitting with the vaunted two-guys-and-a-dog team. That's a decision that should be addressed in policy at the senior levels of your organization. Even if you work in a small- to medium-sized company, setting access policy is a business process decision, not an IT decision.

Whenever I'm involved in somebody's new idea about how a fantastic piece of tech is going to make things so much better for us, I tend to annoy the team by asking pesky people and process questions. I worked for a boss once who became enamored over a new data loss prevention (DLP) system that his favorite vendor was rolling out. It could automate so many things, things that we weren't currently doing manually. But, as I was listening to the sales rep tout the product's features (which were truly great I have to say), I kept doing the math in my head about how many people it would take to run the system and, maybe more important, who in the leadership chain was going to authorize all of the policies that this team was going to implement. There seemed to be a giant disconnect there. In one job I had, my predecessor had purchased all of the latest cybersecurity toys, and then he promptly left the organization to take a higher-paying job (good for him). We had everything, all of the bells and whistles that you could possibly want in a security stack. Well, he ran out of money buying the tools before he hired the people we needed to manage it all. My problem was that I had a rookie team in the security operations center trying to manage a fleet of Ferraris in the security stack. Those engines mostly sat idle while I tried to convince my boss to hire more expertise.

If zero trust is an essential building block for our first principle philosophy, surely it is important enough to build a team to manage it. And, as the sections in this chapter illustrate, zero trust is much bigger than just identity management. We need a team to create the processes for bringing new employees in and deciding which zero trust functional buckets they will belong to initially. The team will also decide how to change employee access when they move laterally within the organization to new jobs and new responsibilities. The team will further design the processes for when employees leave the organization by removing their access from the system. Finally, we'll need an entirely different team focused on automating these procedures so that the team managing it doesn't fat-finger the configuration changes and leave the digital windows and doors open for some bad guy to find. It takes people, process, and technology. You likely already have the right combination of people and technology to start creating these processes.

Conclusion

Many years after the fact, it's easy for network defenders to criticize the NSA for failing to install a zero trust network designed to reduce the impact of an Edward Snowden–type insider threat attack. The startling truth is that most of us didn't have that kind of zero trust network installed at the time either. The sadder reality is that most of us still don't have that kind of thing installed when we all know that we should, even if we think that the phrase *zero trust* has been overhyped by every single security vendor on the planet.

At first glance, the prospect of converting our old M&M networks (hard exterior; soft tasty center) into zero trust networks appears daunting and expensive. Instead of thinking of zero trust as a thing we have to do to finish, consider it a journey on the never-ending path of improvement; a strategy to pursue every day. There are probably a million things we can do on that zero trust journey. But there are things we can do right now with technology that we already own that will allow us to start closing those digital doors and windows. And even if we do leave one ajar by mistake, the data that the thief finds there will not significantly impact the organization. Kindervag has been refining his thesis since he wrote the foundational paper in 2010. He has some definite thoughts about how to tackle this strategy in most environments. His "Nine Rules" are a good place to start.

From my view, use tactics that will have the most impact to your organization first such as logical and micro segmentation, vulnerability management, SBOMS, and asset management in general. Begin now to improve your identity management program and, if you haven't already started, get single sign-on, two-factor authentication, and software-defined perimeter on the road map. While you're doing that, consider why zero trust projects fail in that it's relatively easy to buy new tech to accomplish some tactic but considerably harder to add head count to the team to manage that tech.

And remember that zero trust is a philosophy and a journey without end, not a product. It's a way of life, a strategy that directly supports our ultimate cybersecurity first principle: reduce the probability of material impact. It's not the only strategy to pursue in that endeavor, but it is something that should be part of every organization's DNA and their culture, not just the infosec team, but the entire organization.

Finally, the zero trust strategy is a general-purpose passive defensive strategy. It's entirely agnostic to the specific threats you face. But, if you want to concentrate on defeating specific known adversary behavior, you will need a more active defensive strategy. That is the subject of the Chapter 4, "Intrusion Kill Chain Prevention."

4 Intrusion Kill Chain Prevention

Kill chain analysis illustrates that the adversary must progress successfully through each stage of the chain before it can achieve its desired objective; just one mitigation disrupts the chain and the adversary.

—Hutchins, Cloppert, and Amin, Lockheed Martin Kill Chain Paper, 2010

The Diamond model integrates . . . and complements Kill Chain analysis by broadening the perspective which provides needed granularity and the expression of complex relationships amongst intrusion activity.

—Caltagirone, Pendergast, and Betz, Diamond Model Paper, 2011

When tracking the threat, "Groups are defined as named intrusion sets, threat groups, actor groups, or campaigns that typically represent targeted, persistent threat activity."

—Strom, Applebaum, Miller, Pennington, and Thomas, ATT&CK: Design and Philosophy, March 2020

Overview

In this chapter, I reveal precisely why intrusion kill chain prevention is a first principle strategy. Since its inception in 2010, it completely changed how infosec practitioners thought about defending their organizations in cyberspace. Instead of trying to block technical tools that hackers used, the strategy elevated the network defender's purpose to defeat the adversary behind the tools. The idea was disruptive. Three research efforts contributed to the thesis. The first published was the original Lockheed Martin Kill Chain Paper that described the strategy. The second was the DOD's Diamond model that operationalized Cyber Threat Intelligence (CTI) teams along the kill chain idea. The third was MITRE ATT&CK; the best open source collection of adversary playbook intelligence in the world.

I will discuss what it actually means when a CTI team attributes an attack sequence and just how many active campaigns are running on the Internet on any given day. I will then explain several tactics to consider when trying to deploy the intrusion kill chain prevention strategy.

- Security operations centers
- Orchestrating the security stack
- Cyber threat intelligence
- Purple team operations
- Intelligence sharing

The Beginnings of a New Idea

During the first Gulf War in 1991, Iraq's mobile SCUD missiles gave the U.S. Air Force and Navy pilots trouble. Iraqi soldiers were able to fire their missiles and move their platforms long before the U.S. planes could find their location and blow them up. After the war, around the year 2000, General John Jumper changed air combat doctrine to address that issue by formalizing the techniques necessary to compress the time it takes to find and kill the enemy on the battlefield. The Air Force's target acquisition model is called Find,

Fix, Track, Target, Engage, and Assess, also known as F2T2EA, because, you know, the military loves acronyms more than cyber folks. More simply, they call it the *kill chain*. Jumper's mandate to the Air Force was to compress the kill chain from hours or days to less than 10 minutes.[1] The Air Force's F2T2EA model is significant to our story because, 10 years later, Lockheed Martin researchers applied the same concept to cyber defense. That is the genesis of the intrusion kill chain.

The Lockheed Martin Kill Chain Paper

The year 2010 was big in cybersecurity with multiple groundbreaking milestones and revolutionary ideas. Google sent out shockwaves when it announced that it had been hacked by the Chinese government.[2] John Kindervag published his foundational "No More Chewy Centers" paper on zero trust.[3] The world also learned about the U.S./Israeli cyber campaign (Olympic Games, commonly referred to as Stuxnet) designed to slow down or cripple Iran's nuclear weapon production capability and demonstrated the difficulty of crafting attack sequences for hard cyber targets.[4] Finally, Lockheed Martin published its seminal paper, "Intelligence-Driven Computer Network Defense Informed by Analysis of Adversary Campaigns and Intrusion Kill Chains," written by Eric Hutchins, Michael Cloppert, and Rohan

---

[1]Hebert, Adam, 2008. Compressing the Kill Chain [WWW Document]. Air & Space Forces Magazine. www.airandspaceforces.com/article/0303killchain (accessed 12/17/22).

[2]Perlroth, N., 2021. This Is How They Tell Me the World Ends. Bloomsbury Publishing.

[3]Kindervag, J., 2010. No More Chewy Centers: Introducing The Zero Trust Model Of Information Security, Palo Alto Networks. Forrester.

[4]Zetter, K., 2015. Countdown to Zero Day: Stuxnet and the Launch of the World's First Digital Weapon. Crown.

Amin; this was the symbolic starting gun for the subject of this chapter: intrusion kill chain defense. What a tumultuous year.[5]

I can't emphasize enough the seismic shift in cyber defense thinking after the Lockheed Martin paper. Before the paper, the model that most network defenders followed was called *perimeter defense* or *defense in depth* (see Chapter 3). Back then, we were preoccupied with stopping offensive technical tools (such as malware, zero day exploits, and bad URL links). The common notion was that the adversary had to be lucky only one time to have success (like using a zero-day exploit), while the defender had to be precisely correct all the time (protect against all the possible zero-day exploits). That's why network defenders back then, and some even today, are always scrambling to keep every system fully patched. But the Lockheed Martin paper flipped that idea on its head. The authors demonstrated that adversaries had to string a series of successful actions together in a chain to be successful. All the defender had to do was break the sequence somewhere along that chain (the kill chain).

A key takeaway from the paper is that network defenders shouldn't focus only on passive cyber hygiene issues such as patching and blocking of known bad Internet things. The Lockheed Martin researchers proposed that of equal import is the more active deployment of prevention controls for all known cyber campaigns. In other words, perimeter defense is a more general-purpose defense. It's like locking the doors and windows to your house. The deployed defenses are not specific to any known criminal method of attack. They work against all criminals. But the kill chain paper proposes that network defenders should target known adversary behavior specifically. If you know that Butch Cassidy's hole-in-the-wall gang has been operating in the general vicinity of your neighborhood and

[5]Hutchins, E., Cloppert, M., Amin, R., 2010. Intelligence-Driven Computer Network Defense Informed by Analysis of Adversary Campaigns and Intrusion Kill Chains. Lockheed Martin Corporation.

you also know that they typically use doggy doors to break into houses, you might take measures to improve your doggy door security posture to precisely counter the hole-in-the-wall gang method.

According to the kill chain paper authors, "Network defense techniques which leverage knowledge about these adversaries can create an intelligence feedback loop, enabling defenders to establish a state of information superiority which decreases the adversary's likelihood of success with each subsequent intrusion attempt." See how they used the phrase, "decreases the adversary's likelihood of success?" That fits in nicely to our overall first principle strategy of reducing the probability of material impact due to a cyber event. From the paper, "Intelligence-driven computer network defense is a risk management strategy that. . .requires a new understanding of the intrusions themselves, not as singular events, but rather as phased progressions." It's a simple and elegant strategy: know the enemy.

The Kill Chain Model

Conceptually, the kill chain paper breaks an adversary campaign into several phases or links in a chain. See Figure 4.1.

- *Reconnaissance*: Research, identification, and selection of targets.
- *Weaponization*: Build tools to leverage those targets.
- *Delivery*: Transmission of the developed weapon(s) to the targeted environment.
- *Exploitation*: Pull the triggers on the weapon(s).
- *Installation*: Install tools to maintain persistence.

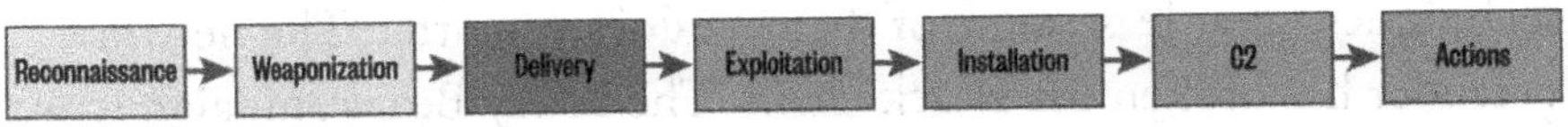

Figure 4.1 Phased progressions from the original 2010 paper

- *Command and control (C2)*: Establish connection to the outside world.
- *Actions on objectives*: Lateral movement inside the network and data exfiltration.

Think about each link in the chain as an opportunity to disrupt a known hacking campaign. For example, a well-known attack sequence that many network defenders have seen regularly in the wild throughout the 2010s has the colorful name of Fancy Bear. (I'm going to discuss adversary naming later in this chapter.)

If we want to develop a defensive plan to defeat a Fancy Bear campaign, we would design and deploy specific controls to counter how the Fancy Bear hackers recon victim weaknesses, for the malware they build and deploy (weaponization), for the techniques they use to deliver their malware to their victims, for the exploitation code they use to compromise victim zero, for the process they use to download and install additional tools to help them in their mission, for the interdiction of their communications channel, and finally, for how they move laterally within the victim's network looking for the data they have come to steal or destroy. (I'm going to discuss where to find these kinds of controls later in this chapter.)

Here's the genius of the Lockheed Martin kill chain idea. As of this writing, the MITRE ATT&CK Framework (see The MITRE ATT&CK® Framework section below) is tracking around 90 techniques used in a typical Fancy Bear campaign. Let's say that the hackers behind Fancy Bear developed a new zero-day exploit that they start using for the exploitation phase. Because the zero-day exploit is new, no defender has a countermeasure for it already deployed. But if they had prevention and detection controls deployed for the other 90 techniques, or at least some of them, it doesn't matter. The network defender has broken the attack chain. The Fancy Bear campaign won't work even with the new zero-day exploit because the rest of the sequence is broken.

As perimeter defense and defense in depth is passive (designed to defeat the generic hacker), the intrusion kill chain model is active and designed to defeat specific cyber adversaries. The kill chain paper's great insight is that regardless of the adversary's motivation (crime, espionage, warfare or low-level-cyber-conflict, hactivism, propagandists, or general mischief makers) and the tools they use to accomplish their objectives (malware, exploit code, phishing, etc.), all cyber adversaries have to string a series of actions together to complete their mission (see Figure 4.2). They called them *attack campaigns*. Today, attack campaigns compromise anywhere from 30 steps to more than 300 steps depending on how complicated and mature the attack campaign is.

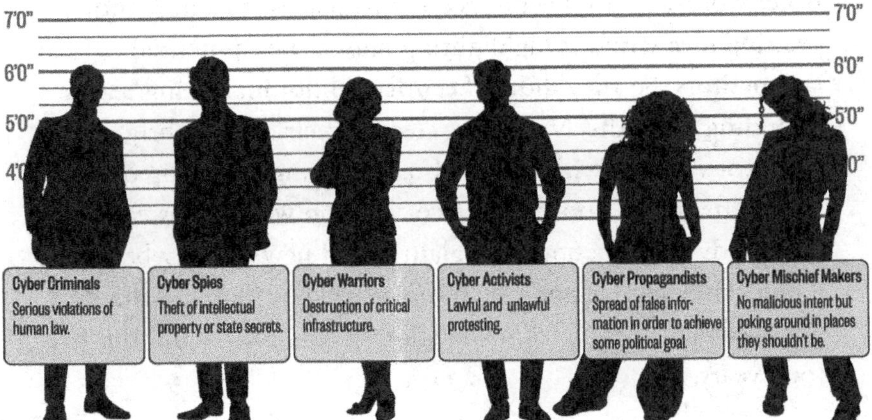

Figure 4.2 The unusual suspects: cyber motivations, modified and updated from a chart created by BAE Systems[6]

[6]Staff, n.d. The Unusual Suspects [WWW Document]. BAE Systems | Cyber Security & Intelligence. www.baesystems.com/en/cybersecurity/feature/the-unusual-suspects (accessed 12/17/22).

I was the Palo Alto Networks CSO from 2013 to 2019. I had just started getting excited about the intrusion kill chain idea when I began. As with many other CSOs and CISOs, I got invited to speak at various conferences around the world and I was ecstatic to describe how we were using Palo Alto Networks' products to implement our internal intrusion kill chain strategy. But, our lawyers quickly put a kibosh on that idea. It turns out that the Lockheed Martin leadership realized that they had a game-changing idea on their hands and wanted to ensure that they got the credit for it. In 2012, they applied to trademark the phrase "CYBER KILL CHAIN," which the U.S. patent office finally approved in 2019. In the interim, Lockheed Martin defended any use of the phrase in public without acknowledgment of the patent pending process. In other words, security vendors couldn't discuss this new and exciting idea without highlighting one of their potential competitors. So they didn't. Security vendor marketing teams, including Palo Alto Networks, created their own slightly different versions with subtle phrasing changes causing the idea to fragment into small pieces with no weight. Instead of everybody talking about this giant brand new idea, Cyber Kill Chain, the message got lost in the noise. The industry slowly got over their fear of acknowledging Lockheed Martin, but it took years.

Adversary Motivations: Cyber Warfare Morphing Into Low-Level Cyber Conflict

I want to take a small detour here—a slight tangential digression—to discuss the community's evolving thoughts about cyberwarfare. It's tangential in that the subject of cyberwarfare is not a discussion of what the intrusion kill chain strategy is. Cyberwarfare is more about how nation-states and other international actors use the kill chain to accomplish some political purpose. How nation-states use the kill chain—the tactics—have significantly changed since the early days (early 2000s).

Military cybersecurity professionals used to think that a war fought purely in cyberspace was possible, that nation-states would launch massive cyberattacks at each other without them also using their other physical assets such as fighters, bombers, aircraft carriers, artillery, tanks, and infantry. I was initially one of those people. That theory lost favor when everybody realized it was akin to saying we would fight wars with only artillery. Looking at it in that context, we realized how crazy that idea was. We came to understand that war fighters would use offensive cyber operations in support of a larger warfighting mission; in war, cyber operations would be used in conjunction with all the tools in the warfighting apparatus to accomplish some goal.

That said, some nation-states soon realized they could also accomplish some of their political goals on the international stage by conducting offensive cyber operations that were just short of war. In other words, they could achieve many things with a cyber operation by walking right up to the line where a victim nation-state would feel compelled to declare war in physical space with their military. But they wouldn't cross it. In that way, they could level the playing field for certain operations between wealthy nation-states and poorer ones.

The Chinese military championed the concept of asymmetric warfare in the 1990s,[7, 8] and the Russians have published similar military doctrine since the early 2010s.[9] Admittedly, where the

[7]Luke, C.B.K., 2012. Recognizing and Adapting To Unrestricted Warfare Practices by China. Air War College.

[8]Qiao, L., Xiangsui, W., Wang, X., 2002. Unrestricted Warfare: China's Master Plan to Destroy America. NewsMax Media, Inc.

[9]Greenberg, A., 2020b. Sandworm: A New Era of Cyberwar and the Hunt for the Kremlin's Most Dangerous Hackers. Anchor.

boundary is between acceptable cyber operations (campaigns that don't start an actual physical war) and unacceptable operations (ones that do start a physical war) is a bit fuzzy. To date, no cyber campaign has started an actual ground war. As a result, nation-states keep pushing the line, carefully doing the political calculus to see what is acceptable and what is not.

The most famous examples are probably the joint U.S./Israel Operation Olympic Games (Stuxnet) in 2010[4] and the Russian attacks against Ukraine in 2014 (notPetya, Sandworm).[9] The impact of those two infamous cyberattacks resulted in the destruction of physical infrastructure, a typical target of traditional military forces. But the victim nation-states didn't retaliate with traditional military assets. The cyberattacks didn't instigate the next physical war.

Other nation states such as India, Iran, North Korea, Pakistan, Vietnam, and others, use asymmetric cyber operations so often that David Sanger, a renowned journalist, started referring to this activity as *continuous-low-level-cyber-conflict.*[10] Although unwieldy to say, the phrase is a more accurate way to describe what is actually happening.

Continuous-low-level-cyber-conflict includes cyber campaigns across the intrusion kill chain to accomplish many goals: traditional espionage (steal government secrets), economic espionage (steal intellectual property), destruction of critical infrastructure, influence operations, etc. We haven't had "cyber warfare" as we originally conceived it in the early 2000s, but every year, the public becomes aware of international actors running continuous-low-level-cyber-conflict cyber campaigns to accomplish some political goal.

---

[10]Sanger, D.E., 2019b. The Perfect Weapon: War, Sabotage, and Fear in the Cyber Age. Crown.

The Lockheed Martin Cyber Kill Chain Is Great, but. . .

As I have said, the Lockheed Martin kill chain paper is a disruptive idea that challenged the industry about how we thought about defending the enterprise. That's the good news. The bad news is that although it's brilliant as a conceptual model, it's severely lacking in one major aspect: operations. There isn't a lot of detail in the original white paper about how to operationalize the concept. Things like how to collect adversary playbook intelligence, analyze the data, make prudent decisions about how to prevent playbook actions, and actually deploy the mitigation plan are left to the reader. But that's a nit-pick. The paper wasn't designed for that. The authors disrupted the industry by upending commonly understood best practices and proposed a strategy that was better suited to preventing material impact to our organizations. The operational void would be filled by other big thinkers.

Our foundational first principle is to reduce the probability of a material impact to our organization due to a cyber event. We can play whack-a-mole by blocking technical tools all day long and will probably have some effect. But if we decide to utterly defeat the humans that are behind those tools, our impact can be so much larger. We shouldn't just be blocking a random offensive tool with no relation to the hackers behind it. We should be blocking every single tool the hackers use in their campaign at every phase of the intrusion kill chain. With intrusion kill chain prevention, we design defensive campaigns to defeat the ultimate purpose of the Fancy Bear hackers, not just the individual tools they use.

Kill Chain Models

An adversary playbook assembles all known intelligence on a hacker group's attack sequence: tactics, techniques, indicators of compromise, attack time frame, and context about motivation as well as attribution.

In a paper that Ryan Olson, a longtime colleague, and I published in 2020, "Implementing Intrusion Kill Chain Strategies by Creating Defensive Campaign Adversary Playbooks," we provided a standard framework designed to ease the burden of collecting intelligence and sharing it with other network defenders.[11] It facilitates the receiver writing code to absorb that intelligence systematically and provides the means to automatically deploy new and updated security controls to their already deployed defensive posture within their DevSecOps infrastructure.

When you create adversary playbooks, three exemplars have emerged as accepted best practice to model the intelligence.

- Lockheed Martin's intrusion kill chain paradigm[5]
- MITRE's ATT&CK framework[12]
- The Department of Defense Diamond model[13]

But, when the community talks about adversary playbooks, you get the sense that all these models are different approaches to the same thing. That just isn't true. One is a strategy document (Lockheed Martin), one is an operational construct for defensive action (MITRE), and one is a methodology for cyber threat intelligence teams (Diamond). For adversary playbooks, you don't choose one model over the other. All of these models work in conjunction with each other. If the metaphor for preventing the success of cyber adversaries is an elephant, each of these models represent different parts of the elephant. Let's look at each one in turn.

---

[11]Howard, R., Olson, R., 2020. Implementing Intrusion Kill Chain Strategies by Creating Defensive Campaign Adversary Playbooks. The Cyber Defense Review 4.

[12]Strom, B., Applebaum, A., Miller, D., Nickels, K., Pennington, A., 2020a. MITRE ATT&CK: Design and Philosophy.

[13]Caltagirone, S., Pendergast, A., Betz, C., 2011. The Diamond Model of Intrusion Analysis, Active Response.

The MITRE ATT&CK Framework

MITRE released its first version of the ATT&CK framework in 2013, three years after the original Lockheed Martin paper. The acronym stands for Adversarial Tactics, Techniques, and Common Knowledge. At first glance, the casual reader would assume that the framework is a slight improvement on the original Lockheed Martin model. The framework extends the original phases and corrects for some of the limitations. It eliminates the recon phase and expands the actions on the objective stage with more clarity and detail. That's all true.

But, the framework's significant innovation is an extension of the list of information requirements intelligence analysts collect for adversary playbooks. They added tactics, techniques, and procedures (TTPs). Before the framework, we would all collect indicators of compromise, like bad IP addresses or URLs, without connecting them to known adversary behavior. They would just be lists of bad things. These lists are not useless per se, but they are ephemeral and hackers can easily change them at the drop of a hat. By the time infosec teams deployed countermeasures, the bad guys had likely already changed their behavior.

MITRE's extension to the Kill Chain model includes the grouping of tactics (the "why"), the techniques used (the "how"), and the specific implementation procedures the adversary group used to deploy the tactic (the "what"). That intelligence is not as ephemeral, is tied to known adversary group behavior, and is conducive to designing impactful countermeasures. Where the Lockheed Martin Kill Chain model is conceptual, the MITRE ATT&CK framework is operational. The network defenders can use the provided TTPs to detect and prevent actual cyber campaigns that have been observed in the wild.

MITRE shares framework intelligence with the public that its own teams collect. They also synthesize intelligence received from members of the Defense Industrial Base (DIB). According to the U.S. Cybersecurity and Infrastructure Security Agency (CISA), the DIB is a worldwide industrial complex of more than 100,000 companies and their subcontractors that provide goods and services to the U.S. military. All are prime targets for nation-state cyber operations activity. MITRE's intelligence teams sift through the intelligence collected by the DIB companies and eventually publish it in the ATT&CK framework wiki as open source intelligence for anybody to use.

Although the wiki tracks several crime groups, that's not the focus. It primarily covers how advanced persistent threat (APT) groups run their own playbooks. In other words, they are tracking nation-states. Most important, though, the framework standardizes the taxonomy vocabulary that network defenders use to describe both offensive and defensive actions. Before the framework, each vendor and government organization had their own language. Any intelligence product coming out of those organizations couldn't be shared with anybody else without a lot of manual conversion grunt work to make sense of it all. We were all looking at the same activity and couldn't talk about it collectively in any way that made sense. The MITRE ATT&CK framework fixed that. The bottom line is that the MITRE ATT&CK framework has become the industry's *de facto* standard for representing adversary playbook intelligence. In other words, it has helped us to operationalize the cyber threat intelligence process.

That said, there is still a lot of work that needs to be done. Users of the wiki still need to automate the process of collecting the ATT&CK intelligence and using it to upgrade their internal defenses. They could also streamline the intelligence to make it easier for their red teams and penetration teams to use. Lastly, the intelligence collected and distributed by MITRE is not in real time. They update the wiki only every few months. That said, since adversary groups don't make wholesale changes to their attack playbooks that often, that's not a major concern at the moment.

Creating attack campaigns that generally work against multiple operating systems and routinely slip by vendor tools in the security stack is not easy or cheap. Typically, adversaries don't throw out entire attack sequences when they need to make a change. If one element in their attack sequence doesn't work anymore or needs an upgrade, they change that element, not the sequence. It's just more economical. And, quite frankly, they haven't had to. Most network defenders are trying to defeat individual tools with no relation to the step-by-step progression adversaries have to take to be successful. The beauty of the kill chain philosophy is that if we are deploying defenses designed to defeat the adversary and not individual unrelated tools, then we have multiple prevention and detection controls deployed across the kill chain looking for known specific adversary activity. If the adversaries change something in the sequence that avoids one of those controls, they still have to get by all the others. So, the fact that MITRE doesn't update the wiki in real time isn't ideal, but it's not a showstopper. But it would be exceptional if all the network defenders in the world could have an open source collection of adversary playbook intelligence that's updated regularly and could be automatically consumed, processed, and tailored for detection and prevention controls for the security stack in place, and automatically deployed in real time (see Chapter 7).

Lastly, it would be better if MITRE covered the non-nation-state hacking campaigns too: criminals, activists, and mischief makers. Let's call these the CAMM campaigns. Except for a small handful, the MITRE ATT&CK wiki doesn't really collect on these. And, as of this writing, there is no equivalent of the MITRE ATT&CK wiki for CAMMs. You can buy it through commercial cyber intelligence companies, but there's no open-source equivalent.

Still, we've come a long way since 2010. The Lockheed Martin research team gave us a new strategy, and the MITRE team helped us to operationalize it. The remaining task is how to collect that adversary playbook intelligence with some rigor. In other words, can we formalize the process so that all cyber threat intelligence teams can use the same basic procedures and can easily share and compare their notes with peers and colleagues? That's where the Diamond model comes in.

The Department of Defense's Diamond Model

About the same time that the Lockheed Martin research team was working on its intrusion Kill Chain model (2006), three researchers working for the U.S. Department of Defense started coming to similar conclusions but in a slightly different context. They were trying to establish a formal mathematical method for cyber threat intelligence work that they could apply to "game, graph, and classification/clustering theory to improve analysis and decision-making."

Like the Lockheed Martin researchers, the Diamond model's authors were also first principle thinkers. They asked the question, "What is the basic atomic element of any intrusion activity?" By the time they published their disruptive paper, "The Diamond Model of Intrusion Analysis,"[14] in 2011, Sergio Caltagirone, Andrew Pendergast, and Christopher Betz had their answer, something they called an *event* that consists of four core elements arranged around the vertices of a diamond shape. See Figure 4.3.

In 2019, Pendergast, now working for a commercial intelligence company (ThreatConnect), showed the diagram with an additional vertical line connecting the top and bottom vertices.[15]

From the paper, "The core features are linked via edges to represent the fundamental relationships between the features, which can be exploited analytically to further discover and develop

[14]Baker, W., Pendergrast, A., 2020. Diamond Presentation v2 0: Diamond Model for Intrusion Analysis – Applied to Star Wars' Battles. YouTube.
[15]Baker, W., Pendergrast, A., 2020. Diamond Presentation v2 0: Diamond Model for Intrusion Analysis – Applied to Star Wars' Battles. YouTube.

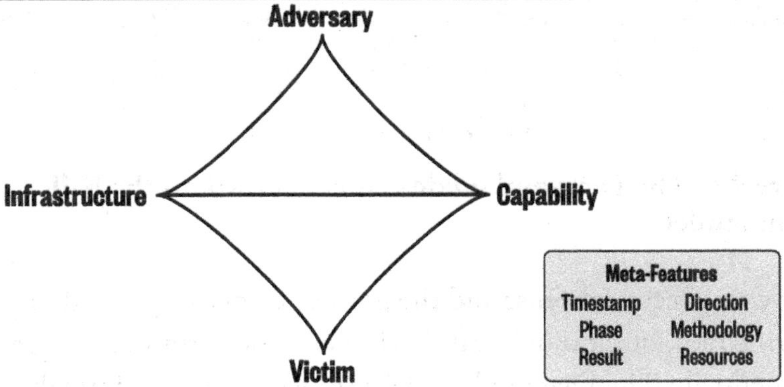

Figure 4.3 The original Diamond model from the 2011 paper

knowledge of malicious activity." In other words, adversaries (top vertex) develop attack capability (right vertex) and apply it to exploit infrastructure (left vertex). Adversaries (top vertex) also build and maintain their own infrastructure (left vertex). Victims (bottom vertex) run and maintain infrastructure (left vertex) and are exploited by the capability (right vertex). Finally, adversaries (top vertex) exploit victims (bottom vertex).

The idea is that as intelligence teams describe cyber incidents, they are filling in the blanks of these relationship pairs. According to the paper, "This allows the full scope of knowledge to be represented as opposed to only the observable indicators of the activity."[16]

The authors were riffing off something called *attack trees* originally proposed by Bruce Schneier, a Cybersecurity Canon Lifetime Achievement winner by the way and my first boss in the civilian world when I retired from the U.S. Army. Schneier's idea was that attack graphs "attempt to generate all possible attack paths and vulnerabilities for a given set of protected resources to determine the

[16]Baker, W., Pendergrast, A., 2020. Diamond Presentation v2 0: Diamond Model for Intrusion Analysis – Applied to Star Wars' Battles. YouTube.

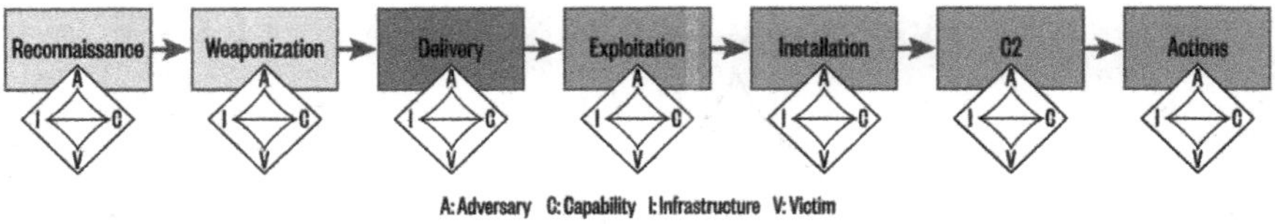

Figure 4.4 The Diamond model superimposed on the Kill Chain model

most cost effective defense and the greatest degree of protection."[17] It's a terrific idea, but it didn't scale back then. The permutations grew exponentially. The Diamond model author's attempt to formalize the language around cyber incidents was a first step to improve that situation. In their model, they build "activity threads" that combine intelligence and traditional attack graphs into activity-attack graphs by merging "traditional vulnerability analysis with knowledge of adversary activity."[18] This is the point where it becomes apparent that the Diamond model is not an alternative to the Lockheed Martin Kill Chain model and the MITRE ATT&CK framework; it is an enhancement. The Diamond model's atomic element, the event, with its four core features, is present at each phase of the intrusion kill chain. See Figure 4.4.

From the Diamond model paper, "The 'Kill Chain' provides a highly effective and influential model of adversary operations, which directly informs mitigation decisions. Our model integrates their phased approach and complements Kill Chain analysis by broadening the perspective, which provides needed granularity and the expression of complex relationships amongst intrusion activity."[19]

[17]Baker, W., Pendergrast, A., 2020. Diamond Presentation v2 0: Diamond Model for Intrusion Analysis – Applied to Star Wars' Battles. YouTube.
[18]Baker, W., Pendergrast, A., 2020. Diamond Presentation v2 0: Diamond Model for Intrusion Analysis – Applied to Star Wars' Battles. YouTube.
[19]Baker, W., Pendergrast, A., 2020. Diamond Presentation v2 0: Diamond Model for Intrusion Analysis – Applied to Star Wars' Battles. YouTube.

In practice, your own intel team might be analyzing multiple incidents that may or may not be related to each other. For each, using the Lockheed Martin strategy, you are monitoring adversary activity across all kill chain phases. You collect that intelligence by filling in the blanks of the four feature pairs (the event) from the Diamond model, and you standardize the language by using the MITRE Framework's vocabulary of tactics, techniques, and procedures. As the story develops, your knowledge of the adversary's kill chain becomes more complete with data for all the incidents.

At a certain point, you might note that the Diamond model events for the delivery phase and the Command and Control phase in incident 1 are remarkably similar to the events captured in incident 2. These "activity threads" connect the two incidents, may indicate that the attacks have originated from the same adversary, and imply a much broader campaign against your network. According to the paper, "The Diamond model's Events can then be correlated across activity threads to identify adversary campaigns, and coalesced into activity groups to identify similar events and threats, which share common features." This process is how we get all of those colorful names that splash across as headlines in the cybersecurity news space.

- "Chinese APT10 hackers use Zerologon exploits against Japanese orgs"
- "Ferocious Kitten: 6 years of covert surveillance in Iran"
- "Lazarus Group May Have Been Behind 2019 Attacks on European Targets"

When intelligence teams have high confidence that they are seeing similar "activity threads" across multiple incidents targeting the same victim or described in other "activity threads" for other victims, they assign the activity group a colorful name as a kind of shorthand to readers of the news and readers of intelligence reports, a label that says that all of this information is related.

Some Thoughts About Attribution

There are many sources of these names. Most security vendors do the bulk of name attribution by publishing blogs describing what they have discovered with their own security products and services. One reason for the colorful names is to get attention in the marketplace. Some vendors have become famous for their naming schemes.

- Mandiant uses numbers as in APT1.
- Crowdstrike uses animal names like Fancy Bear.
- Microsoft uses elements like Hafnium.

There are many other schemes. But government computer emergency response teams (CERTs) and law enforcement agencies from around the world publish intelligence reports too. While interesting, most are not that operationally useful in a real-time kind of way. Analysts write them in blogs of text guaranteeing that the consumer of the report has to spend time picking out the most important bits. While many vendor and government analysts have made some effort to follow the standardized vocabulary made possible by the MITRE ATT&CK framework, they have not fully embraced the intrusion kill chain concept in total and have mostly ignored the Diamond model.

One possible reason for this reluctance to adopt these models is that not all organizations need the same kind of intelligence reports. I'm going to cover cyber threat intelligence in detail below (Cyber Threat Intelligence – A Tactic for All First Principles Strategies) but for now, understand that the kinds of intelligence reports needed change depending on the nature of the organization. Law enforcement, government spy agencies, the military, and commercial and academic organizations require different kinds of intelligence to be useful in cyberspace. Law enforcement is looking to arrest criminals, spy agencies are pursuing national political objectives, the military is looking for on-the-ground targets, and commercial and academic organizations are looking to prevent material impact due to a cyber event.

In the MITRE ATT&CK wiki, you can find intelligence on famous adversary campaign names that you've probably read about in the news like APT1, the Lazarus Group, and Sandworm. There are many more that you likely haven't heard that much about with cool code names like Ferocious Kitten, Nomadic Octopus, and Wizard Spider. The thing about these code names is that they don't attribute adversary groups as in, here are a bunch of real people (cyber bad guys) that are behind the activity we are calling Nomadic Octopus. We use group names to identify unique adversary attack patterns across the intrusion kill chain that have been seen repeatedly in the wild.

What I mean by that is when the MITRE ATT&CK wiki publishes intelligence about Ferocious Kitten, it doesn't normally include information about Kevin (day job: Walmart greeter) as the hacker behind the attacks. The wiki just outlines a set of attack techniques and specific procedures observed in the wild that intelligence analysts have grouped together as belonging to the same adversary playbook.

Sometimes, intelligence analysts are pretty sure that these pattern names, like APT1, originate from a specific government or CAMM group. In the APT1 case, the security vendor Mandiant actually hacked back to one of the bad guy's computers, compromised his camera, and watched his team operate in the room in real time.[20] You can view some

[20]Mandiant, 2021. APT1: Exposing One of China's CyberEspionage Units. YouTube.

of the videos on YouTube. After that operation, Mandiant intelligence analysts had high confidence that the hackers behind APT1 are a Chinese military hacking group belonging to the 2nd Bureau of the People's Liberation Army (PLA) known as Unit 61398. But that kind of attribution is an exception to the norm in the commercial space. For the rest of the groups like Nomadic Octopus, intelligence analysts may have some suspicions that the group hails from Russia, but they rarely have irrefutable proof as concrete as the APT1 evidence.

The point is for most of us, it doesn't matter which government is behind the attacks. If you know that North Korea is attacking you, who cares? Unless you're a nation-state spy organization tracking useful human intelligence sources or a law enforcement agency seeking to indict people, that knowledge doesn't help a typical network defender at all. What is important is knowing whether your team is observing attack patterns consistent with the Lazarus Group in your networks and whether they have deployed prevention controls to counter them at each stage of the intrusion kill chain.

What makes this code name situation even more confusing is that the industry has no standard for naming attack patterns. Every vendor and every government intelligence agency has their own system. In some cases, we end up with a smorgasbord of names for the same attack patterns. For example, MITRE lists APT29 as one of the groups it tracks. With a simple Google search, I found 14 aliases that other organizations use to track the same activity like Cozy Bear, the Dukes, and Office Monkeys.

Further, in news and intelligence reports, you might read that Cozy Bear is associated with the Russian foreign intelligence service SRV (formerly the KGB). But you have no idea if that attribution is correct. And how could you? You're tracking network traffic, not people in the real world. Government spy agencies can attribute activity at this level, but they're not likely to tell you what they know except for some niche special cases. For the most part, they're trying to protect their sources and methods. The chances that your favorite security vendor's intelligence team has any inside information to confirm the assertion is low. They might have some suspicions (like language used in the code, IP address geographical location, time of day, etc.), but if I'm the President of the United States, I'm not launching the nukes on that flimsy evidence.

What is likely when you read the attribution is that some other intelligence team in the past attributed Cozy Bear to the SRV and this new report you're reading is just passing the information along without telling you the source. The bottom line is that for public intelligence reports, the fidelity of most attributions to some nation-state is not supported by strong evidence.

On the other hand, the fidelity for the listed MITRE ATT&CK TTPs associated with Cozy Bear is high. And that causes confusion. Public threat intelligence teams, especially from security vendors that have products deployed around the world collecting security telemetry 24/7, know exactly if they're seeing the same Cozy Bear attack sequence in one of their customer's networks. Because of their accuracy about the TTPs, when they also mention that Cozy Bear has been associated with the Russian SRV, readers conflate the two assertions with the same precision.

Here's the thing: don't get lost in naming and attribution. Besides being fun to say in board rooms as in "we have intelligence that the attack sequence associated with the threat group Office Monkeys has been attacking our competitors with BananaPeel malware," the name is not important. When I'm talking about TTP attribution, I try to avoid the entire confusion by saying things like "The adversary playbook associated with the Cozy Bear attack sequence." I try not to say "The hacker group called Cozy Bear." It's a subtle distinction but well worth it to avoid confusion.

How Many Active Adversary Playbooks Are There?

When I speak at conferences and discuss adversary playbooks and intrusion kill chain prevention, I normally like to pause and poll the audience. "How many active adversary playbooks are running on the Internet at any given time? In other words, how many campaigns are hackers running at this very moment?" Most have no idea, so I try to bracket them. "How many think that it's over a million?" Usually I get about half the audience to raise their hands here. "How many think it's over a thousand?" More hands go up. "How many think it's less than a thousand?" Many people drop their hands here. "How many think it's less than 500?" Usually, only one or two brave souls keep their hands raised. "What if I told you that the number is likely between 231 and 281?" This is normally met with stunned silence.

At the time of this writing, the MITRE ATT&CK wiki tracks about 125 nation-state campaigns across the intrusion kill chain. In other words, MITRE analysts have intelligence on the TTPs of 125 adversary playbooks. Let's assume that some adversary playbooks have not been discovered yet, say 25 percent. That adds about 31 more campaigns for a total of 156. And what about the CAMM campaigns that MITRE doesn't cover? If you just count CAMM campaign activity that has appeared in the news between 2021 and 2022, there are roughly 80 groups that have ongoing operations. For the sake of argument, let's assume that 25 percent of CAMMs haven't appeared in the news these past two years either. That bumps that number up to about 100.

That means that the total number of adversary campaigns (nation-state + CAMMs) operating on the Internet on any given day is roughly 256. Since we're doing some back-of-the-envelope calculations here (see Chapter 6), we know that's not a precise number, just an educated guess. If we build in a 10 percent fudge factor to give us a range, I'd bet $100 that the number of active campaigns on the Internet on any given day is between 231 and 281.

That number seems low, doesn't it? When you read the news, it's easy to get the feeling that there are millions of cyber adversaries operating in the world. Every day it seems like there is some new doomsday attack. They appear so often that our sense is that the number of campaigns must be much larger. It's daunting and seems impossible to keep track of everything. But that just isn't true. It's only 250ish. You could keep track of the entire problem set in a spreadsheet if you wanted. I'm not saying that collecting intelligence on all known adversaries across the intrusion kill chain, processing that intelligence in order to design detection and prevention controls for the tools in your security stack, and then automatically deploying those controls in a DevSecOps kind of way is easy. It's not (see Chapter 7). But the scope of the problem is much smaller than we have made it out to be.

The Adversary Intelligence Trifecta: Kill Chain, ATT&CK, and Diamond

To reduce the probability of material impact to our organization due to a cyber attack, our first principle cybersecurity strategies include risk forecasting, zero trust, resilience, automation, and intrusion kill chain prevention. Out of the four, the strategy that I personally enjoy the most is intrusion kill chain prevention. The others are great and necessary, but they're passive. They're like eating your vegetables or getting the oil changed in your car. You have to do them, but they're not sexy. Intrusion kill chain prevention, though, that's exciting. That's me and the adversary, in the ring, duking it out, every day. And it has taken the network defender community more than a decade to figure out how to do it in terms of strategy, operations, and cyber threat intelligence best practices.

Big thinkers from Lockheed Martin (kill chain), the Department of Defense (Diamond model), and MITRE (ATT&CK Framework) gave us the blueprints of how to be good at this more than a decade ago. It's taken that long for the rest of us to get our heads around the key concepts. The bottom line is that we build adversary playbooks so that we can automatically collect threat intelligence on what adversaries are actually doing across all the Lockheed Martin kill chain phases. We operationalize that process by standardizing on the MITRE ATT&CK framework's established vocabulary for adversary tactics, techniques, and procedures. We instruct our cyber threat analysts teams to fill in the blanks of event pairs, identify activity threads across multiple incidents, and establish activity groups for common behavior in the Diamond model. Finally, we automate the deployment of our mitigation plan across our entire security stack. We do all of that with the adversary intelligence trifecta: kill chain, ATT&CK, and Diamond.

Security Operations Centers: A Tactic for Intrusion Kill Chain Prevention

The idea of operations centers has been around seemingly forever. Friedrich Klemm in his "A History of Western Technology" suggests that the concept goes as far back as 5,000 B.C.[21] Klemm said that any time an organization grows big enough, either in terms of people or in function, where one small team can't do everything, leaders have built these centers to manage the workflow and status of the various groups and to coordinate actions among them. If you fast-forward to the early days of the technological revolution (early 1900s), we started seeing organizations that began looking like a modern-day SOC but weren't quite there yet.

When telephone networks started appearing in the early 1920s, phone companies like AT&T built traffic control bureaus to handle

[21]Klemm, F., 1964. A History of Western Technology. MIT Press.

long-distance traffic issues. By the early 1960s, AT&T handled most telephone switching through mechanical devices and built a network control center (NOC) to manage it. AT&T historians consider this to be the first NOC ever built.[22] By 1977, Bell Systems had built the first national NOC in Bedminster, New Jersey, which looked a lot like modern NOCs today. There wasn't much security yet, but if there was any, NOC operators were doing it.

Meanwhile, in the U.S. intelligence community, the 1960s were fraught with international incidents like the following:

- *1962*: Cuban Missile Crisis
- *1967*: Arab–Israeli Six-Day War
- *1968*: The U.S.S. Pueblo capture
- *1968*: the Prague Spring Crisis in Czechoslovakia
- *1969*, The EC-121 shootdown crisis

The National Security Agency (NSA) decided that they needed an operations center to manage their efforts across a wide swath of international activity. Based on a Freedom of Information Act request, the NSA released a document in 2007 that described the formation of the first National SIGINT Operations Center (NSOC) in 1973.[23] According to Charles Berlin, a former NSOC director, NSA kept adding more responsibility to it over time. He said that its secret sauce was when the NSA decided to pair offense (SIGINT) and defense (COMSEC) in the same place. Eventually, they replaced the word "SIGINT" in the title with "Security." In other words, it

---

[22]Staff, 2012. A tour of AT&T's Network Operations Center (1979) - AT&T Archives. AT&T Tech Channel.

[23]Staff, 2007. The National Sigint Operations Center [WWW Document]. Wayback Machine. web.archive.org/web/20100527224956/www.nsa.gov/public_info/_files/cryptologic_spectrum/nsoc.pdf

became the National Security Operations Center. Berlin said that when cyber came along years later, the total mission became too big to keep in the NSOC, and the NSA created the National Cyber Threat Operations Center (NCTOC) to deal with it.[24] But with the addition of the COMSEC mission, these operations centers started to lean toward defensive security. Today, NSA has many operations centers all focused on different parts of NSA's mission, but NSOC is still the main center at the heart of the agency's operations.

On the general-purpose government side, in the aftermath of the Morris worm[25]—the first destructive Internet worm—the Defense Advanced Research Projects Agency (DARPA), a science and technology organization of the U.S. Department of Defense, sponsored Carnegie Mellon University to establish the first CERT/coordination center (CERT/CC) in 1988.[26] By 1990, the Forum of Incident Response and Security Teams (FIRST) had become a nonprofit "to bring together incident response and security teams from every country across the world to ensure a safe Internet for all." As of 2022, there are 657 teams in 101 different countries that belong to FIRST.[27]

According to Rich Pethia, the first CERT/CC director, one of his missions was to help the military services build their own CERTS,

---

[24]Howard, R., Berlin, C., 2020b. National SIGINT Operations Center (NSOC).
[25]Staff, 2018. The Morris Worm [WWW Document]. Federal Bureau of Investigation. www.fbi.gov/news/stories/morris-worm-30-years-since-first-major-attack-on-internet-110218 (accessed 12/17/22).
[26]Staff, 1996. Testimony of Richard Pethia, Manager, Trustworthy Systems Program and CERT Coordination Center Software Engineering Institute, Carnegie Mellon University, Before the Permanent Subcommittee on Investigations U.S. Senate Committee on Governmental Affairs [WWW Document]. Federation of American Scientists (FAS. irp.fas.org/congress/1996_hr/s960605m.htm (accessed 12/17/22).
[27]About FIRST [WWW Document], n.d. . FIRST — Forum of Incident Response and Security Teams. www.first.org/about (accessed 11/1/22).

which they did.[28] The Air Force established the Air Force Computer Emergency Response Team (AFCERT) in 1993.[29] The other services followed suit soon thereafter. The work done in the military CERTS contributed to the eventual stand-up of the Joint Task Force – Computer Network Defense (JTF-CND) in 1998.[30] With the creation of these military CERTS, the requirement for a SOC—coordination of defensive actions and intelligence within an organization—began establishing itself as a general-purpose best practice for network defenders working for sizable organizations in military, governments, commercial, and academic institutions.

On the commercial side, it's unclear of the exact date, but we started to see the first managed security service providers (MSSPs) in the late 1990s and early 2000s. MSSPs are essentially contracted SOCs. President Clinton established the ISAC system, the information sharing and analysis center framework, when he signed Presidential Decision Directive-63 (PDD-63) on May 22, 1998, in an effort to better protect the country's critical infrastructure.[31] In February 2015, President Obama established the Information Sharing and Analysis Organization (ISAO) framework clearing the legal

---

[28]Howard, R., Pethia, R., 2020b. CERT/CC helping the military build their own CERTS.

[29]Bejtlich, R., 2014. A Brief History of Network Security Monitoring. Blogger. taosecurity.blogspot.com/2014/09/a-brief-history-of-network-security.html (accessed 12/17/22).

[30]Staff, 2019. Joint Task Force—Computer Network Defense: 20 Years Later [WWW Document]. National Security Archive. nsarchive.gwu.edu/briefing-book/cyber-vault/2019-06-29/joint-task-force-computer-network-defense-20-years-later (accessed 12/17/22).

[31]Clinton, Bill, 1998. PRESIDENTIAL DECISION DIRECTIVE/NSC-63 [WWW Document]. White House. irp.fas.org/offdocs/pdd/pdd-63.htm (accessed 12/17/22).

hurdles for all like-minded organizations, not just critical infrastructure groups, to share threat intelligence with each other.[32]

CERTs, ISACs, ISAOs, and MSSPs provide SOC-type services for those that can't do it themselves or provide supplemental help for those that can. At some point between 2002 and 2012, the idea that network defenders in the commercial space should build and operate their own in-house SOCs started to gain traction.

Current State of Security Operations Centers Today, many medium-to-large commercial organizations either have their own internal SOCs or contract the function (or at least a part of the function) to a third-party MSSP. Sometimes the SOC is adjacent to the NOC, and other times the SOC functions are just a subsection of the NOC.

Small organizations usually accept more risk and don't have a centralized point to coordinate the activities of multiple groups. IT and security are often done by the same small team. The latest development in the commercial space is SOC services delivered as SaaS applications, what some call "SOC in a box."

However, the functionality of any specific SOC compared to another varies wildly. Based on the history and evolution of the operations concepts, you would think that the SOCs would be the one point in the organization that coordinates all security issues, but that just isn't the case. The functions range from simply monitoring certain pieces of the network with no ability to make changes to the security policy on one end of the spectrum to having complete control of the security stack across all deployments of data.

[32]Obama, Barack, 2013. Executive Order — Improving Critical Infrastructure Cybersecurity [WWW Document]. whitehouse.gov. obamawhitehouse .archives.gov/the-press-office/2013/02/12/executive-order-improving-critical-infrastructure-cybersecurity (accessed 12/17/22).

As an aside, SOCs also manage the organization's incident response. I will talk about that function in Chapter 5.

SOCs: An Essential First Principle Intrusion Kill Chain Prevention Tactic Earlier in this chapter, I made the case that intrusion kill chain prevention is an essential follow-on strategy from our absolute cybersecurity first principle. And just like identity and access management (IAM) is an essential first principle tactic for our zero trust strategy (because you can't do zero trust without IAM), deploying a SOC, or something that functions as a SOC, is an essential tactic for the intrusion kill chain prevention strategy. You can't do intrusion kill chain prevention without one. Somebody in the organization has to do the following:

- Keep track of adversary playbook intelligence (this chapter).
- Orchestrate and monitor the internally deployed tools in the security stack (this chapter).
- Manage the incident response team (see Chapter 5).
- Design, manage, and distribute key learning points from purple team exercises (this chapter).
- Manage the intelligence sharing program (this chapter).
- Monitor the vulnerability management program (see Chapter 3).
- Plug into the DevOps process (see Chapter 7).

Those are tactics that directly or indirectly support the intrusion kill chain strategy. SOCs also support other first principle strategies.

- Zero trust: Monitor the software bill of materials program (see Chapter 3).
- Zero trust: Monitor the identity and access management program (see Chapter 3).

- Resilience: Monitor and help design the backup and restore exercises (see Chapter 5).
- Automation: Design, manage, and distribute key learning points from chaos engineering exercises (see Chapter 7).
- Resilience: Monitor the compliance program (see Chapter 7).
- Risk forecasting: Calculate cyber risk for the organization (see Chapter 6).

Of course, not every SOC performs all of these tasks, and some SOCs get additional responsibilities not captured here. But remember, the SOC doesn't typically own the responsibility for all of these tactics within the organization as well as the business units that will be most impacted by the decisions made inside the SOC. It's likely that no single team inside the organization does. That's the very characteristic that leadership has used to justify the building of operations centers for centuries, but especially in the modern era. When a task gets so big in scope that it requires multiple teams to complete it, an operations center is needed to coordinate those efforts. The point is that when your organization grows large enough that Kevin (the IT guy who fixes laptops, mobile phones, and printers in the office) can't handle the volume of work anymore, security teams build SOCs to manage the workflow and status of the internal security function, just like Friedrich Klemm said.

For the pursuit of cybersecurity first principles to be effective, network defenders must have a centralized point (physical or virtual) where they bring in relevant information from all corners of the cybersecurity first principle space. Analysts review the information and make recommendations to leadership. Leadership makes decisions, and then the SOC coordinates the deployment of those actions out to the individual first principle teams to execute or, even better, uses automation to deploy those decisions without having to put people in the loop.

Aspirations Let me be clear. There might be a handful of organizations in the world that design and operate their SOCs to accommodate all of these first principle tactics. Most come nowhere near it. They monitor. They collect data. Their SOC analysts grind their way through billions of log entries trying to find the one item that may mean they've been compromised. Most don't try to defeat adversary campaigns across the intrusion kill chain. Instead, they focus on blocking access to technical vulnerabilities that an adversary might use to be successful. Most SOC analysts aren't involved in the resilience plan at all. Many can't even spell DevSecOps let alone contribute to the infrastructure-as-code philosophy. The SOC may have some control over the zero trust deployment and policy, but not the entire plan. Most SOC analysts have no idea how to calculate the risk probability of a material cyber event in some future time frame, not because they can't but because no leader has trained or tasked them to do it. The one tactic that many do have control of is the intelligence tactic. But even that effort isn't completely focused on defeating the adversary across the intrusion kill chain, and leadership most likely doesn't use the intel team to calculate the cyber risk probability of the organization.

That is the reason to rethink your security program through a first principle lens. It isn't enough to have an organization called the SOC. The SOC you build must absolutely support our first principle strategies, or why bother? And I realize that this is hard to do. This refocusing of the SOC along first principles goes against 20 years of established infosec practice. Even if you agree with me that a change is required, the chances aren't good that you can convince senior management to centralize security decisions in one place and to break across many swim lanes of established bureaucracy over decades of not doing that. But it has to be done, and it can be done.

In Chapter 2, I discussed one of the reasons that the Elon Musks of the world have succeeded. Musk, in particular, had the strength of his convictions that incrementally improving something without considering the ultimate purpose of what he was trying to do was a recipe for failure. By using first principles, he was able to build a Mars rocket, a luxury electric car, and affordable solar power when most thought it was impossible to build even one of those things. I'm not saying that first principle thinking is the only thing that made Musk successful. I'm just saying that it was an essential part, and that, without it, none of it would have happened.

The concept of a modern-day SOC has a winding, interesting, evolutionary, and incremental improvement backstory that started in the early 1900s and continues today—but we are not done. We have a long way to go to create a SOC in the future that can easily support every tactic in our collection of first principle strategies.

Orchestrating the Security Stack: An Intrusion Kill Chain Prevention Tactic

I mentioned that I was the Commander of the Army Computer Emergency Response Team (ACERT) in the early 2000s. The modern Internet was just really taking off then. Wikipedia had just launched a couple of years before. Apple launched iTunes that year, but we were still four years away from seeing our first iPhone. Meanwhile, in the military, we were still trying to figure out what cyber operations meant, and every organization that could spell *cyber* correctly, three times out of five, thought that they should own it.

One of my ACERT responsibilities was to coordinate offensive and defensive cyber operations for all of the Army cyber stakeholders (intelligence, networking, law enforcement, legal, information operations, and many others) with our sisters and brothers in the joint world (Air Force, Navy, and the Marines). These were the "Title 10" forces, as they say, and my job was to make sure that whatever they were doing didn't step all over what the "Title 50" cyber forces at the NSA and the Central Intelligence Agency (CIA) were doing.

Title 10 and Title 50 refer to the chapters in the U.S. Code that provide, among other things, the laws governing the Armed Forces and their use (Title 10) and things like spying, covert operations, and espionage (Title 50). Many people probably don't know that spying and espionage (Title 50) are things primarily reserved to the American spy organizations. Title 10 forces mainly fight the nation's wars. There are some exceptions to this, but on the whole this is the general division of labor. In theory, this means the Army doesn't do espionage missions unless it's working directly for the NSA, and the intelligence community doesn't fight wars unless they are directly supporting the military.

I mention all of this because, during this time (early 2003), the United States and some of its allies were about ready to launch the invasion of Iraq. In preparation for that event, the Army's cyber stakeholders realized that we were caught flat-footed. Previously, we had divided operational control of the Army's cyber assets into various regional CERTS (RCERTS): North America, South America, Europe, Pacific, and South Korea. But we had no presence in South West Asia (SWA). And we needed one. So we built one lickety-split, recalled a bunch of reservists to man it, and shipped them all out to the sandbox in time to support the invasion.

Immediately, the RCERT team noticed several continuous, low, and slow probes of the RCERT SWA electronic perimeter coming from multiple locations and countries in the Middle East. That couldn't be good. We began to worry that whomever those bad guys were might be gearing up to degrade or dismantle this fledgling network designed to support the tanks and the infantry when they crossed the line of departure on H-Hour. We needed a plan to counter that contingency.

We basically went into stealth mode.

We orchestrated a plan across all Title 10 interested parties where, at the push of a button, we switched the entire RCERT SWA infrastructure to new domains and IP addresses. Essentially, when H-Hour arrived, the RCERT SWA infrastructure went dark from the perspective of any outside entity trying to keep tabs on us. Internally, we were fully functional, but to the outside world, RCERT SWA disappeared off the board just like a Klingon Bird of Prey using its cloaking device. It didn't last long, maybe a day, and we knew that going in. Our goal was to cause confusion and disorientation to whomever might want to cause the Army harm at the beginning of the war.

I love that story because it highlights a capability that all network defender organizations need and most don't have: orchestrating the security stack, in other words, deploying the policy and strategy to the operational equipment on the ground in real time.

Why Do We Need Orchestration? In the early Internet days (the late 1990s), orchestration wasn't a problem. We had only three tools in the security stack: firewalls, intrusion detection systems, and antivirus systems. When we wanted to make a change to the policy, we manually logged into each tool and made the change. Fast-forward to

2021, and our environments have morphed into enormously complex systems of systems deployed across multiple data islands (hybrid cloud, SaaS, internal data centers with legacy systems, and mobile devices). Orchestrating the security stack for our first principle strategies (zero trust, intrusion kill chain prevention, resilience, and automation, and risk forecasting) across all those data islands in some consistent manner with velocity is exponentially hard to do compared to the early days. Truth be told, most of us don't do it very well at all.

There are a number of approaches security practitioners can take to ease this burden. One is DevOps or DevSecOps.

DevOps and DevSecOps In 2003, when Google was still nothing but a search engine, it decided to give the task of network management to the developers.[33] What do developers do when they get a task like that? They automate it. Instead of technicians manually logging into network devices to update configurations, Google's site reliability engineers automated those low-level tasks, or *toil*, as they call it. In the same year, Amazon rolled out its infrastructure-as-code program internally: a set of common infrastructure services anyone in the company could access without reinventing the wheel every time. Amazon business leaders soon realized that they could build the operating system for the Internet from these services. This eventually led to AWS in 2006.[34]

Today, we call what Google and Amazon were doing back then as DevOps or infrastructure as code, but the industry didn't come up with that name until 2010. Today, 20 years from inception, Google

---

[33]Beyer, B., Jones, C., Petoff, J., Murphy, N.R., 2016. Site Reliability Engineering: How Google Runs Production Systems. O'Reilly Media.
[34]Javatpoint, n.d. History of AWS [WWW Document]. www.javatpoint.com/history-of-aws (accessed 11/1/22).

and Amazon are among a handful of Internet giants (like Netflix, Microsoft, and others) that dominate electronic commerce.

Innovative startup companies, the ones that came up with the DevOps name in 2010, realized that the way they could distinguish themselves in the marketplace was to deliver their services from a SaaS model using infrastructure as code. Two Cybersecurity Canon Hall of Fame books talk about this history and how to think about this philosophy: *Site Reliability Engineering* from the team at Google[28] and *The Phoenix Project* by Gene Kim.[35] With this approach, as part of the app development process, practitioners build into the system the way to manage the security stack at scale and velocity. Read the Netflix Chaos Monkey case study (Chapter 7) if you want to get a lesson on how to think about a hard-core resiliency strategy that is powered by DevSecOps, essentially cybersecurity as code.

Orchestration Platforms A second approach is to deploy a commercial tool that does the bulk of the work for you. Security pundits, like Jon Oltsik (the principal analyst at Enterprise Strategy Group), started talking about this concept as early as 2015.[36, 37] They were describing the need for the security industry to develop services that automated the collection of security tool telemetry, made policy decisions based on that telemetry, and deployed new and updated policies back to the security stack. This concept is rooted in the feedback loop, or control loop, of systems engineering. It's a good idea.

---

[35]Kim, G., Behr, K., Spafford, G., 2013. The Phoenix Project: A Novel about IT, DevOps, and Helping Your Business Win. It Revolution Press.
[36]Howard, R., 2021i. XDR Explainer Interview with Jon Oltsik. The CyberWire.
[37]Oltsik, J., 2018. The evolution of security operations, automation and orchestration [WWW Document]. CSO Online. www.csoonline.com/article/3270957/the-evolution-of-security-operations-automation-and-orchestration.html (accessed 12/17/22).

One big problem is that most medium- to large-sized organizations have too many tools. According to a survey of 1,200 security VPs presented in the Panaseer 2022 Security Leaders Peer Report, the average number of security tools that we all manage is 76.[38] This is significantly higher than the three we were managing two decades earlier.

All-in-one orchestration platforms started appearing in the market around 2017 from the big firewall vendors such as Checkpoint, Cisco, Fortinet, Juniper, and Palo Alto Networks. These platforms still did traditional firewall-type things, but they also started adding subscription service add-ons to help with zero trust, intrusion kill chain prevention, and resiliency. Instead of the practitioner managing the integration of 76 stand-alone security tools, they deployed one orchestration platform in various form factors to each data island. The platform performed many of the same tasks as the individual tools, but it was all controlled under one coherent platform policy. Where it was possible, each subscription service integrated with the others automatically. The downside was that this collection of services probably didn't represent the best of breed for any particular security tool category. The upside was that they were likely good enough, had the added benefit of being fully integrated with other subscription services where possible, and were automatically updated with the latest prevention controls discovered by the vendor. Since these firewall vendors had multiple customers scattered around the world, they saw a lot of bad guy telemetry in real time. If they developed new prevention controls because of something they saw in customer A's network, all of their customers benefited from that process.

---

[38]Finnane, T., 2021. Panaseer 2022 Security Leaders Peer Report [WWW Document]. Panaseer. panaseer.com/reports-papers/report/2022-security-leaders-peer-report (accessed 11/4/22).

SOAR But the idea that you could trust one single vendor to do the bulk of the security work was a tough sell. Most security practitioners wanted to hedge their bets with multiple vendors. The platforms were expensive too. Small- and medium-sized organizations couldn't afford them. These same small- and medium-sized companies were likely not doing DevOps either despite the disruptive success of startup companies in the early 20-teens. That brings us to a third hybrid approach: security orchestration automation and response (SOAR).

Gartner coined the term in 2017 about a new kind of SOC tool that, in general terms, knew how to communicate with every device in the security stack and provided basic automation capability to handle repetitive data patterns.[39] For example, if newbie SOC analysts swipe left on the same intrusion detection system alert a thousand times during their shift, the SOAR tool facilitates the automation of that swipe. The automation piece made SOAR tools unique compared to security information and event management (SIEM) tools that just collected the telemetry for the most part. But I expect at some point that these two capabilities will start to merge. SOAR companies already have SIEM functionality, and SIEM tools already have SOAR functions. It's only a matter of time before there will be no distinction between them.

SOAR tools excel at reducing the noise inside the SOC. At my last CSO gig, we went from 1 billion alerts coming into the SOC every quarter that humans had to process to just under 500 every quarter. That's amazing. If SOC analysts just did that, their life would be so much easier. But there is this untapped capability with SOAR/SIEM platforms. We don't have to be in the one-way receive mode. They already know how to talk to all of the devices in the security stack. What if we used these tools as our DevOps bridge? We could

---

[39]Engelbrecht, S., 2018. The Evolution of SOAR Platforms [WWW Document]. SecurityWeek.Com. www.securityweek.com/evolution-soar-platforms (accessed 12/17/22).

build zero trust, intrusion kill chain prevention, resiliency, and risk forecasting frameworks within the SOAR tools that might be able to give us push button capability to update our security stack. But I haven't seen anybody doing that in the real world.

SASE and SSE One last option is to use a secure access service edge (SASE) vendor or its near cousin security service edge (SSE). SASE and SSE flip the old perimeter defense model on its head by using a cloud provider as the first hop destination for any network traffic leaving the local site. See Figure 4.5.

Local sites could be headquarters buildings, sales offices, data centers, cloud workloads, and remote employees working from home or at the local Starbucks. Gartner coined the term SASE in 2019 and defined three elements that would distinguish a SASE vendor from, say, a standard managed security service provider (MSSP).

- *Security stack*: In a shared responsibility model, the SASE vendor keeps the blinky lights working on whatever security stack tools they provide. The customer sets the policy. The range of options for the security stack is wide. Buyer beware. If you're doing this, make sure that the SASE vendor's security stack can handle all of the first principle strategies discussed in this book.
- *SDWAN*: The SASE vendor plugs into your SDWAN meta layer to ensure that all traffic goes through the security stack and routing is as efficient as it can be. That's the good news. The bad news is that you have to have an SDWAN meta layer. I'm not saying that SDWAN is bad. I'm just saying that it's another element in your security stack that adds complexity.
- *Peering*: The only way this SASE model works is if it doesn't slow down normal Internet traffic. If your SASE vendor has only a handful of cloud locations around the world, that could impose

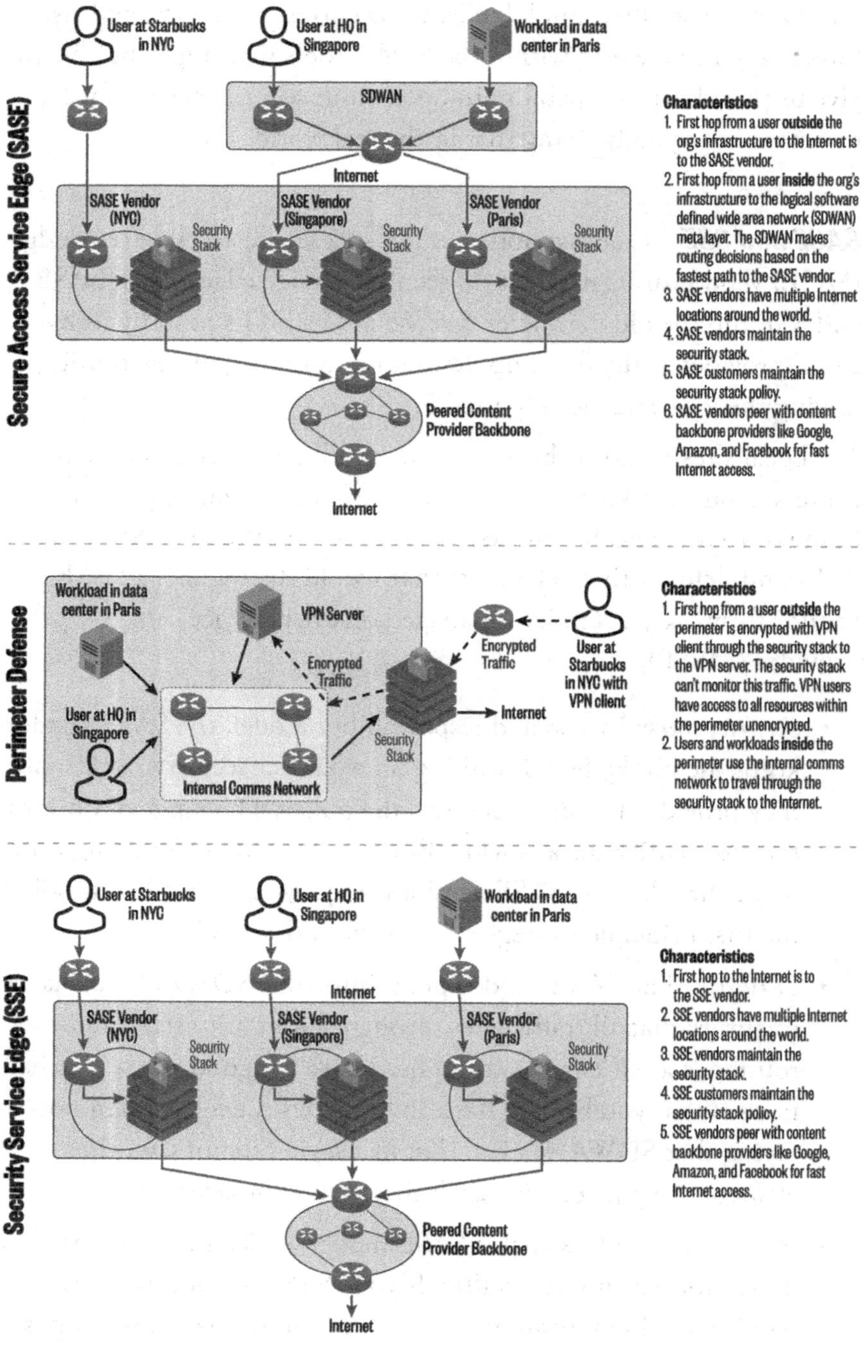

Secure Access Service Edge (SASE)
User at Starbucks in NYC
User at HQ in Singapore
Workload in data center in Paris
SDWAN
Internet
SASE Vendor (NYC)
SASE Vendor (Singapore)
SASE Vendor (Paris)
Security Stack
Security Stack
Security Stack
Peered Content Provider Backbone
Internet
Characteristics
1. First hop from a user outside the org's infrastructure to the Internet is to the SASE vendor.
2. First hop from a user inside the org's infrastructure to the logical software defined wide area network (SDWAN) meta layer. The SDWAN makes routing decisions based on the fastest path to the SASE vendor.
3. SASE vendors have multiple Internet locations around the world.
4. SASE vendors maintain the security stack.
5. SASE customers maintain the security stack policy.
6. SASE vendors peer with content backbone providers like Google, Amazon, and Facebook for fast Internet access.
Perimeter Defense
Workload in data center in Paris
VPN Server
Encrypted Traffic
Encrypted Traffic
User at Starbucks in NYC with VPN client
User at HQ in Singapore
Internet
Security Stack
Internal Comms Network
Characteristics
1. First hop from a user outside the perimeter is encrypted with VPN client through the security stack to the VPN server. The security stack can't monitor this traffic. VPN users have access to all resources within the perimeter unencrypted.
2. Users and workloads inside the perimeter use the internal comms network to travel through the security stack to the Internet.
Security Service Edge (SSE)
User at Starbucks in NYC
User at HQ in Singapore
Workload in data center in Paris
Internet
SASE Vendor (NYC)
SASE Vendor (Singapore)
SASE Vendor (Paris)
Security Stack
Security Stack
Security Stack
Peered Content Provider Backbone
Internet
Characteristics
1. First hop to the Internet is to the SSE vendor.
2. SSE vendors have multiple Internet locations around the world.
3. SSE vendors maintain the security stack.
4. SSE customers maintain the security stack policy.
5. SSE vendors peer with content backbone providers like Google, Amazon, and Facebook for fast Internet access.

Figure 4.5 Comparison: SASE, perimeter defense, SSE

> a serious bandwidth limitation if all of your traffic has to go through those nodes. The fix for that is for your SASE vendor to establish peering connections in their data centers with some of the big content provider networks like Google, Amazon, and Netflix. For example, your employees in Singapore could ride the vast fiber network of Google to get to the SASE vendor's security stack. When you are talking to SASE vendors, make them describe their peering connection road map.

By 2022, IT practitioners realized that maybe the SDWAN component of the SASE architecture model wasn't essential. It was a good idea, and if you have an SDWAN component, then by all means use it. But for everybody else, Gartner offered SSE as an alternative; it's essentially SASE without the SDWAN meta layer.[40]

SASE/SSE is a modified version of using a single vendor's orchestration platform. The good news is that this model is even less complex than deploying and maintaining the orchestration platform yourself on all of your data islands. The SASE/SSE vendor maintains everything. All the customer has to do is manage the policy. The bad news is that it's not clear how expensive these SASE/SSE services will be in the future. As of this writing, we are in the first innings of this ball game. But security vendors will likely reach some economies of scale as their customer base grows, and that may lead to prices falling.

Of the four options, using a SASE/SSE vendor is probably the easiest in terms of complexity, followed closely by deploying a single orchestration platform. Today, both tend to be more expensive. If the SASE vendors can keep the costs down, the SASE/SSE architecture is the future especially for small and medium-sized organizations. Adopting a DevSecOps mentality is probably the right way to go if your organization is trying to be the next Internet giant in the wake of the Googles, the Netflixes, and the Amazons. But if you are just

---

[40]Staff, 2022d. Security Service Edge [WWW Document]. Gartner. www.gartner.com/reviews/market/security-service-edge (accessed 11/5/22).

starting that now, you are years away from having something useful. I expect that most organizations are in the middle somewhere with the SOAR/SIEM model, but they most likely are using it only as a SOC noise reducer and not as an orchestration platform.

The Importance of Orchestration to Intrusion Kill Chain Prevention The essence of the intrusion kill chain prevention strategy isn't complicated. Deploy detection and prevention controls for all known adversary playbooks on all data islands across the entire kill chain. Easy. But as you parse that sentence, each noun (controls, playbooks, data islands, kill chain) exponentially increases the complexity of the task. SOC personnel trying to do this manually have been completely overwhelmed by it. To keep up with the changing adversary landscape, network defenders need to find ways to reduce the complexity of their environments and to automate the process as much as possible. That's what security orchestration buys you, and there are a number of architectures to think about. We covered some of them in this section.

- DevOps and DevSecOps
- Orchestration platforms
- SOAR
- SASE and SSE

To be successful at pursuing the intrusion kill chain strategy, network defenders have to become masters of orchestration.

Cyber Threat Intelligence: A Tactic for All First Principles Strategies but Primarily for Intrusion Kill Chain Prevention

Cyber threat intelligence (CTI) isn't a new concept. It has been practiced in some form as early as the 2000s by various military organizations in the United States and elsewhere. The idea of it being a best practice for the commercial sector didn't really gain traction until roughly 2015, sometime after the publication of the famous intrusion kill chain paper by Lockheed Martin in 2010, the publication of Mandiant's APT1 report in 2013, and the first release of the MITRE ATT&CK framework in 2013. Some commercial organizations were doing it early, but the bulk of the network defender community weren't. By 2015, most of the established security vendors had their own intelligence team publishing public reports for marketing purposes. Mature infosec teams not working for a security vendor realized they needed some kind of intelligence team to take advantage of all of this great open source intelligence.

What Is CTI? CTI operations are really nothing more than regular intelligence operations applied to the cyber landscape. And intelligence operations have been around since the world was young. According to Professor Vejas Gabriel Liulevicius of the University of Tennessee, "Our earliest evidence of intelligence work comes from the clay tablets of Mesopotamia, and we know from the Bible that spies were used not only by political rivals but also by religious ones in ancient Israel."[41]

The subject of intelligence—what it is, how to do it, how to measure its effectiveness—is vast. Until the early 2000s, the study of it had mostly fallen to government employees and academics. In the last 20 years, the commercial security sector has started to pick it up because it has a direct impact on how to protect their organizations in cyberspace or improve their own security products. When interested parties search for a definition, though, they are likely to find a wide array of descriptions.

[41]Liulevicius, V.G., 2011. Espionage and Covert Operations: A Global History. The Great Courses.

For example, A.C. Wasemiller, writing for the Central Intelligence Agency in 1996, said that intelligence operations produce "reliable information about all those enemies of a country who attack it by stealth."[42] He also said that those intelligence products help the government prepare "passive or static defenses against all hostile and concealed acts." Finally, he said that they identify specific adversary operations so that they may be countered through penetration and manipulation "so that their thrust is turned back against the aggressor."

> I love the way that Wasemiller thinks. Notice here that his passive defense corresponds to our zero trust prevention strategy and that he is also trying to defeat the adversary just like what we are trying to do with the intrusion kill chain strategy. If I ever see Wasemiller in a bar somewhere, I owe him a beer.

On the academic side, Christopher Gabel, writing for the Scholastic blog, defines intelligence operations this way:

> *"An intelligence operation is the process by which governments, military groups, businesses, and other organizations systematically collect and evaluate information for the purpose of discovering the capabilities and intentions of their rivals. With such information, or intelligence, an organization can both protect itself from its adversaries and exploit its adversaries' weaknesses."*[43]

I have been a cyber intelligence guy for more than 20 years both in the military and in the commercial sector. I like to describe it this

---

[42]Wasemiller, A.C., 1996. The Anatomy of Counterintelligence. Center for the Study of Intelligence 13.

[43]Gabel, C., 2020. Intelligence Operations. Scholastic.

way: "The process of turning raw information into intelligence products that leaders use to make decisions."

All of these descriptions are correct to a point. If I had to choose one that most closely hits the mark, I would choose the academic's definition. But I believe the vast array of opinions about what CTI is has slowed the adoption of the practice in the network defender community. What is absolutely true is that CTI operations in one organization will likely not look like CTI operations in another.

The Intelligence Process: The Life Cycle Any discussion of the intelligence process, cyber or otherwise, must start with an explanation of the intelligence life cycle. See Figure 4.6.[44]

According to Mark Phythian in his book *Understanding the Intelligence Cycle*, the origins of the intelligence life cycle are unclear.[45] Most scholars generally agree that it came out of WWII as allied intelligence officers tried to explain what they did during the war. Phythian says, "After 1945, this experience began to appear in US training manuals, such as 'Intelligence is for Commanders' by LTC Phillip Davidson and LTC Robert Glass."[46] Although Phythian's book is a criticism of the cycle in that the process for most government intelligence organizations is much more complicated than a five-step process that repeats, this simplified intelligence life cycle is a good summary of the big moving parts.

- *Plan*: Get guidance from the boss by creating critical information requirements (CIRs). They are called Commander's *critical information requirements* (CCIRs) in the military.

---

[44]Army, T.U.S., 2007. Army Field Manual FM 2-0 (Intelligence). Digireads.Com.
[45]Phythian, M., 2013. Understanding the Intelligence Cycle. Routledge.
[46]Glass, R.R., Davidson, P.B., 1948. Intelligence is for Commanders. Military Service Publishing.

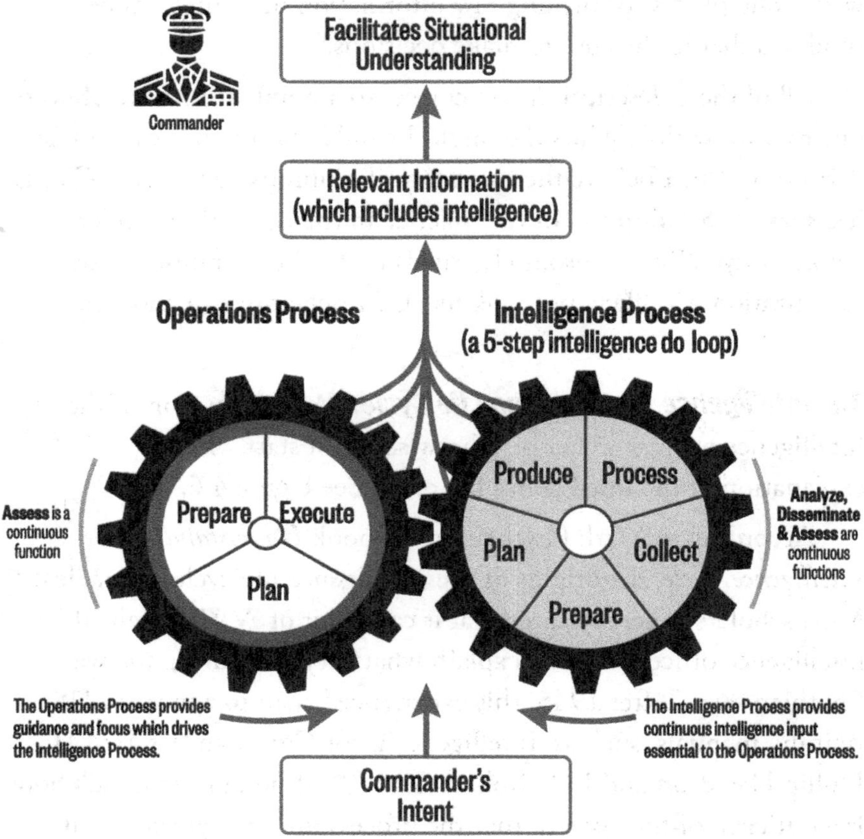

Figure 4.6 2004 version of the U.S. Army's intelligence process[44]

- *Prepare*: Break that guidance down into smaller more manageable questions called *priority intelligence requirements* (PIRs) and *intelligence requirements* (IRs).
- *Collect*: Gather raw data that will help answer those PIRs. Decide if the data you have on hand will answer all the PIRs and ultimately the CIRs. If not, go get the data you need.
- *Process*: Transform that raw data into intelligence products that answer the PIRs.

- *Produce*: Build one or more intelligence products that use PIR answers to address the boss' CIRs. Deliver those intelligence products to key leaders at the right time and enable them to make better-informed decisions.
- *Plan*: Collect feedback from the key leaders for improvement suggestions.
- *Rinse and repeat*: Or as I like to call it, the intelligence do-loop.

Intelligence Life Cycle: The Plan and CIRs Start with the organization's leadership. In the military, this is the commander. In business, it's the CEO, board, and other senior business leaders. When combat units begin preparing for the next operation, whether it is defensive or offensive, commanding officers tell their intelligence teams the questions they need answered to be successful. Which direction will the enemy come from? How big will the enemy force be? What kinds of weapons will they bring to the fight?

> When Lee Marvin briefed his commandos on the plan to attack the German chalet in the 1967 movie *The Dirty Dozen*, where do you think he got the layout of the building? When General Dodonna told his fighter pilots about how to blow up the Death Star in the 1977 movie *Star Wars*, how do you think Princess Leia got the engineering plans for the Death Star's weakness? Senior leaders told the intelligence team to go get them.

In the commercial space, it's the same process, just a different set of questions. By design, CIRs don't change that often. In the commercial sector, they might need to be revisited about once a year.

They are high level and probably complex. They are likely open-ended. As an example, here is a generic list that might apply to any organization:

- *Intrusion kill chains (this chapter)*: What are the most likely attack campaigns hackers will use to cause material harm to our organization?
- *Zero trust (see Chapter 3)*: What are the material systems and information within our organization and who needs to access them?
- *Resilience (see Chapter 5)*: In the event of a material cyber event, which systems and data sets must be available to continue delivering service to our customers?
- *Risk Forecasting (see Chapter 6)*: What is the probability of a material cyber event in the next three years?
- *Automation (see Chapter 7)*: What are the priority DevSecOps projects that will have the greatest impact on reducing the probability of material impact due to a cyber event?

All of these are valid CIRs for the intelligence team. Since we're talking about cybersecurity first principles, I want to focus the intelligence function on tasks that will directly reduce the risk of material impact due to a cyber event. CTI could absolutely be used to support all of our first principle strategies, and more mature organizations will do just that, but what most organizations use CTI for first is to support the intrusion kill chain prevention strategy.

Note that this discussion assumes you have unlimited resources to pursue this endeavor. Nobody has this, I know. Later, I offer ideas about how you might do this on a shoestring budget.

I've said that the CIRs apply to what the CEO wants to know about in the cybersecurity landscape. But it doesn't have to be the CEO.

The leader we are crafting the CIRs for can be anybody on the executive staff, general managers of the various business units, product managers, or whoever the leader is who owns the intelligence team.

Intelligence Life Cycle: Preparation and PIRs The intelligence team takes the CIRs and breaks them down into smaller, more answerable bits. This is classic problem solving; you keep breaking the problem down into tinier chunks until you get a piece that you can solve and work your way back up from there. It's the same with PIRs. Typical CIRs can generate as few as one to well over 20 PIRs depending on the complexity. For example, see Figure 4.7.

PIRs are dynamic. Where the CIRs might change once a year, PIRs might change daily, weekly, monthly, or whenever. And, if you answer one, you might find that it didn't help you answer the larger CIR at all. For example, take this PIR:

"How many cyber adversary campaigns are running on any given day?"

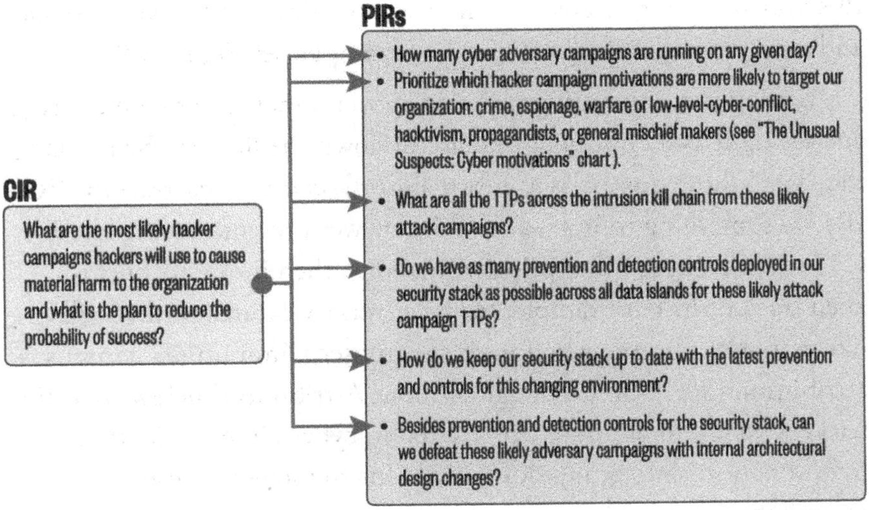

Figure 4.7 Example: CIR into many PIRS

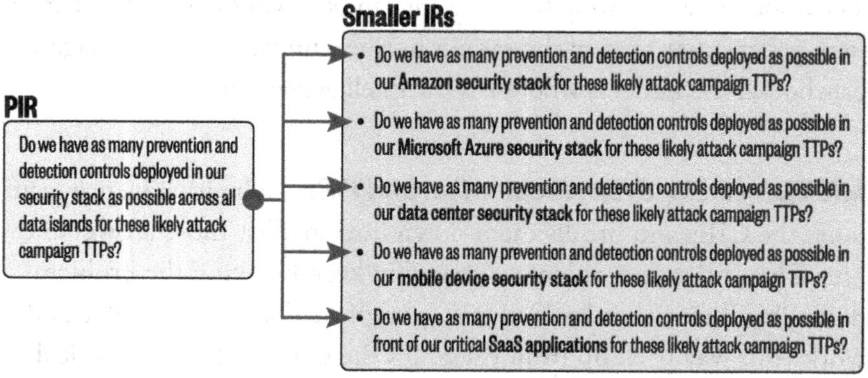

Figure 4.8 Example: one PIR into smaller IRs

That doesn't really help you answer the overall CIR. It's interesting and might help you down the line, but it's not directly applicable. So, you modify it and try again: How many of the most likely cyber adversary campaigns are running on any given day?"

As you answer one PIR, five more might pop up to replace it as you learn more detail about the problem set or you realize that the PIR you are trying to answer can be broken down into several smaller and more manageable questions. For example, see Figure 4.8.

Sometimes, interesting questions pop up that are not a priority to answer right away but might be useful down the line. In the military, they label those questions as just plain *information requirements* (IRs). IRs are something to note, and if the answer presents itself while the CTI team is doing other priority missions, then it doesn't hurt to keep track of it. For example, for an adversary campaign that will likely attack your organization, is the infosec community's consensus attribution (See "Some Thoughts About Attribution" below) that the hackers behind it are purely interested in cybercrime, or are they a hybrid nation-state group doing work for the state but also moonlighting as a cybercrime group bringing in additional revenue to fund their operation? This is not important to know in terms of intrusion kill chain prevention strategy, but it might prove useful later if we happen to know the answer.

Intelligence Life Cycle: Collection Once you establish the PIRs, the intelligence team looks at the raw information at its disposal and decides if it can answer them. If they can, that's great. If not, then they need to seek new sources of information that will. This is called *collection management*, and it is a never-ending process of evaluating the PIRs against the raw intelligence coming into the organization. There are many places you can get this kind of raw intelligence.

- Internal network and security stack telemetry
- Open source intelligence (OSINT) such as security blogs, news outlets, and government alerts from CERTs and law enforcement
- Subscription or commercial intelligence feeds
- Intelligence sharing organizations (like the FS-ISAC and the Cyber Threat Alliance)
- One-on-one sharing arrangements with partner organizations
- Many others

This is an important job. The fuel that feeds the CTI team is raw information. If your sources are inconsistent, just plain bad, or even hard to use, the quality of the CTI's work will suffer. As your CTI group becomes more mature, this could consume one or more people full time. The job entails not only managing all of the intelligence sources but also automating the collection processes involved and building other intelligence products to make that incoming intelligence useful to the team.

Intelligence Life Cycle: Process and Intelligence Products This is where the intelligence analysts come in. Their job is to consume the raw information, synthesize it to answer the PIRs, and create one more deliverables (intelligence products) that leadership can use to make a decision. The conversion of raw information into something useful—actionable intelligence—is the characteristic that distinguishes a news reporter from an intelligence analyst. Both are valuable services. In fact, an intelligence analyst performs many of the same functions as a news reporter but has the added responsibility of advising the leadership about what specifically to do with the information. That advice comes in the form of intelligence products.

They don't have to be complicated. The product can be a well-crafted but brief email message informing the CEO that the CTI team's first assessment of the newly acquired company shows some gaps in their intrusion kill chain prevention coverage. The CEO may want to accelerate the timetable to bring them under our internal security stack protection. An email may be simple, but if the CTI team is using it to help the CEO make a decision, then it's an intelligence product.

On the other side of the spectrum, an intelligence product can be a well-defined automatic dashboard where CEOs can keep track of the progress of prevention and detection controls across the kill chain for their companies and make decisions about resource allocation depending on how well or how poorly the organization is doing. It all depends on what they need.

Interestingly enough, the government intelligence community and the commercial sector both use the same terminology to describe the service they deliver to their customers. They each call them products. I have no evidence of this, but I believe that the common usage is purely coincidental. Regardless, both groups should treat them the same way. In the best-case scenario, each commercial product and intelligence product should have a product manager assigned whose job it is to capture the current state of the product, design the road map for future changes, and plan for end of life.

The point is that the design of the intelligence product is at least as important as the intelligence itself. The CTI team could have done outstanding work throughout the intelligence life cycle, but if they didn't present the intelligence to the respective bosses in a way that they could understand easily and make decisions, then the entire process fails.

> When I was a second lieutenant stationed at Fort Polk, Louisiana, we had a commanding general go around and ask everybody if they had made coffee this morning. He was a teacher by education, and he had this theory. If you were going to school to learn how to make coffee, there were 10 steps in the process, and on your first test you performed the first nine steps flawlessly but failed to plug the coffee pot in, what grade would you get? Is that an A- for getting 90 percent on the test? Or is it an F because you failed to make the coffee? He said that was an F because no coffee was made. When it came to Army training, his point was to boil everything down to the essential tasks and don't worry about all of the extraneous stuff. But, perform the essential tasks without error. Come to think of it, that idea is similar to our absolute first principle: reduce the probability of a material cyber event, not all the small things that have no impact on the organization.

Intelligence Life Cycle: Production and Distribution This seems like an obvious step, but how you distribute these intelligence products will determine how useful they will be to leadership. Do you push the products via email or Slack or some other mechanism? Do you have the customer pull them from a website, SaaS drive, something else? Or is this intelligence suitable for the DevSecOps infrastructure-as-code engine (see Chapter 7) that can eliminate the human-in-the-loop decision process? And how timely is the intelligence once you deliver it? As with intelligence product design, this seems almost trivial, but it's not. Of course, you have to send the intelligence product to somebody who will read it and do something with the information. However, if your weekly intelligence summary product has the information within that could save the company millions of dollars and it gets lost in the CEO's spam filter or is not read because it's buried in an avalanche of other items the CEO doesn't have time to read or if the product arrives after the event has occurred, then the life-cycle process has failed. How you avoid that is dependent on the organizational structure, the distribution tools you have at your disposal, the culture, and the personalities of the leadership team. There is no one solution that fits everything, but the delivery mechanism for each intelligence product needs to be well thought out and adjusted over time. That means that the intelligence life cycle needs a feedback loop, which it has.

Intelligence Life Cycle: Plan and Feedback It goes without saying that if the intelligence products you create aren't useful, then maybe you shouldn't make them. Getting feedback on their usefulness and how you can make them better is essential to the entire intelligence process. Just like the product managers for commercial tools and services and just like senior security executives, a key component to the intelligence product manager's job is polling customers for the features they like, the ones they don't like, and the features they want in the future.

In my career, I've been a CISO officially three times, and if you count the work I did as the ACERT Commander (the U.S. Army's CISO), make that four. If I had any success at all in those roles, it was due in part because I was checking in on a regular basis with the organization's business leaders (customers) to get their feedback on the programs I was working on.

Be ruthless here. If the intelligence product that you lovingly put together each week through the toil and sweat of your CTI team, that you think is the best thing since sliced bread but has nobody consuming it, then you have a problem on your hands. Either none of your business leaders think it's useful, they don't understand it, or it's delivered in a way that's too hard to find. You either need to make the decision to end-of-life the intelligence product or decide to massively re-design it.

Like me, Steve Winterfeld (one of my editors on this book) was a new network defender in the early cyber days for the U.S. Army (early 2000s). Back then, we weren't sure what was important to track and what wasn't. We both briefed our respective commanders on a regular basis about lists of technical things: like top 10 Army software vulnerabilities, top 10 IP addresses coming from China, top 10 viruses seen on Army networks, etc. After a while, we noticed that our commanders stopped paying attention to what we were saying. It wasn't until much later that we realized that the reason they were checked out was because they couldn't make a decision with that information. We were presenting them with news, not intelligence. We needed to jettison that intelligence brief for something more useful. Much later, after we started to track nation-state activity within our networks, we could provide intelligence that the commander could use to plan and utilize to make decisions.

This goes for commercial intelligence services too. I ran one called iDefense (a VeriSign business unit) in the late 2000s. Many of the intelligence products we sold were much like those top 10 lists I presented in the Army; meaning they were background news reports on what various hacker groups were doing around the world. Back then, there wasn't a glut of reporting on those kinds of things in the open press, so some organizations valued them. Today, there's so much open source information in that vein that it's tough to consume it all. But, in hindsight, they weren't strictly intelligence reports. I have to admit, leaders couldn't make decisions with them.

The Intelligence Process on a Shoestring Budget The generic life-cycle process described earlier for the intrusion kill chain strategy assumes unlimited resources. Most of us don't have that, especially if we run a small- to medium-sized business. What is a network defender to do in that circumstance?

Regardless of the size of your organization, seek security vendors who are already doing this for you. I would focus on the mainstream security platforms and endpoint products. These vendors invest heavily in their intelligence teams, both to improve their product sets and to demonstrate to the world how smart they are about the security landscape. Pursue those that have already bought into the intrusion kill chain strategy. They should be tracking adversary campaigns and building prevention controls for their products to defeat them. Influence them with your checkbook. Don't buy them unless they directly support your first principles infosec program and specifically your intrusion kill chain strategy. Point them to the MITRE ATT&CK Evaluation website, a place where vendors prove that their product set can defeat specific known adversary campaigns.

Better yet, seek vendors who belong to the Cyber Threat Alliance (a security vendor information security analysis organization [ISAO]). As of this writing, it is a group of some 34 vendors who have agreed to share adversary playbook intelligence with each other so that their customers don't have to do the work themselves. They have all agreed that they wouldn't compete on the quality of intelligence collected, processed, and shared. Instead, they'd compete on how well their product sets used that intelligence to prevent the success of adversary campaigns. The thing that makes them different from other sharing organizations is that all members have to share or they can't be in the club, and there is a minimum daily quota. If you buy and install one of these vendors' products, not only do you get the adversary campaign tracking from their intelligence team, you get the work of all 34 vendors combined. The CTA's collection of adversary campaign intelligence is likely the most comprehensive and useful in the industry and can compete head to head with what the U.S. government collects with its intelligence agencies. They have standardized on the STIX™ language[47] and the MITRE ATT&CK framework to build their sharing platform.

According to the Organization for the Advancement of Structured Information Standards (OASIS), a nonprofit that promotes the development of open standards on the Internet, STIX stands for Structured Threat Information Expression and is an "open source language and serialization format used to exchange cyber threat intelligence (CTI)."[48] The concept emerged from the Idea Exchange Working Group (IDXWG) email list established by members of the US-CERT and CERT.org in 2010 to discuss automated data exchange for cyber incidents.[49] In 2022, STIX has become the de facto standard format for storing CTI information.

---

[47]Staff, 2022. What is STIX (Structured Threat Information eXpression)? [WWW Document]. Information Security Asia. informationsecurityasia.com/what-is-stix (accessed 11/2/22).
[48]Introduction to STIX [WWW Document], n.d. Oasis. oasis-open.github.io/cti-documentation/stix/intro (accessed 11/2/22).
[49]Staff, n.d. The CERT Division [WWW Document]. Software Engineering Institute. www.sei.cmu.edu/about/divisions/cert/index.cfm#history (accessed 11/2/22).

If your organization is small and doesn't have the resources to build an intelligence team that can track all known adversary campaigns, buy and install security products from vendors that do. Use your checkbook to encourage your security vendors to participate in programs like the MITRE ATT&CK Evaluation program and the Cyber Threat Alliance.[50] It costs you nothing to do so, but it makes the entire community safer. The best part is that you get to leverage those high-end intelligence teams to support your intrusion kill chain strategy.

Cyber Threat Intelligence Operations As a Journey

In the early days of the Internet, building a fully functional intelligence team felt like a luxury to most network defenders. In light of a first principle analysis of our infosec program, though, we have learned that we can't pursue our key strategies of zero trust, intrusion kill chains, resilience, automation, and risk assessment without it—but it's a big ask. For many, they don't have the resources to do it. But remember, strategies are a direction. You don't have to build the equivalent of the NSA today to get the benefit of this work. It is something we should all be building toward. In the meantime, seek vendors who are doing the work for you. Encourage them with your checkbook to support your first principle programs. Take advantage of the good work that the MITRE ATT&CK Evaluation program and the Cyber Threat Alliance is doing for the community. Support it whenever you can. These efforts make the entire community safer and provide you with a cheaper way to pursue your first principle infosec program that won't break the bank.

[50]Holseberg, K., 2022. Our Sharing Model [WWW Document]. Cyber Threat Alliance. cyberthreatalliance.org/about/our-sharing-model (accessed 11/1/22).

Red/Blue/Purple Team Operations: A Tactic for Intrusion Kill Chain Prevention

In one form, red teaming is a safeguard that leaders can deploy to reduce the effects of groupthink. Coined by psychologist Irving L. Janis in 1972, he noticed that many people in group settings will tend not to buck the crowd even if they think the consensus idea is wrong.[51] With red teaming, leadership will carve out resources from within to take the opposite position of the current good idea in an effort to break up the groupthink trend.

William Kaplan, author of *Why Dissent Matters*, calls the red team the Tenth Man.[52] "The Tenth Man is a devil's advocate. If there are 10 people in a room and nine agree, the role of the tenth is to disagree and point out flaws in whatever decision the group has reached." He says that the Tenth Man was born out of an infamous groupthink example: the October 1973 Yom Kippur War (the fourth Arab–Israeli War fought between Israel and a coalition of Arab states).

Israel's military planners experienced a classic intelligence failure when they accepted as a base truth the concept of "Arab Intentions—a preset world view that did not contemplate the possibility of an all-out assault." They were completely wrong. On the sacred Islamic holiday, Yom Kippur, Egyptian and Syrian forces launched an all-out attack against Israel. In the aftermath, according to Kaplan, the Israeli Agranat Commission, established by the Israeli government to investigate the shortcomings of the Israel Defense Forces (IDF), "created two new tools: the position of the Tenth Man, also referred to as the Revision Department, and the option of writing 'different opinion' memos."

---

[51]Janis, I.L., 1972. Victims of Groupthink: A Psychological Study of Foreign-policy Decisions and Fiascoes. Houghton Mifflin.
[52]Kaplan, W., 2017b. Why Dissent Matters: Because Some People See Things the Rest of Us Miss. McGill-Queen's Press - MQUP.

The Roman Catholic Church may have invented the concept of red teaming in 1587 when Pope Sixtus V assigned the job of devil's advocate during the beatification process of St. Lawrence Justinian (1381–1456).[53] The Advocatus Diaboli was to be the opposing force, the red team, to make sure that, according to Ellen Lloyd of Ancient Pages, "[N]o person received the honors of sainthood recklessly and too fast. Every potential weakness or objection to the saints' canonization was raised and evaluated in order to ensure that only those who were truly worthy would be raised to the dignity of the altars."

But there have been many examples in history where leadership of big organizations used red teaming as a tool. President Reagan used the concept as early as 1982 by forming a red team panel designed to anticipate every conceivable way the Soviets might try to go around the arms control treaty.[54] After the 1990 bombing of Pan Am 103, a presidential commission directed the FAA to create a red team to replicate typical terrorist tactics, techniques, and procedures. As chairman of the nine-member Commission to Assess the Ballistic Missile Threat to the United States in 1998, Donald Rumsfeld used a red team approach to examine the same data available to the intelligence community to identify alternative scenarios.[55]

---

[53]Lloyd , E., 2018. Devil's Advocate - Ancient Phrase Traced To The Roman Catholic Church [WWW Document]. Ancient Pages. www.ancientpages.com/2018/11/19/devils-advocate-ancient-phrase-traced-to-the-roman-catholic-church (accessed 11/1/22).

[54]Reagan, R., 1982. ESTABLISHMENT OF NATIONAL SECURITY COUNCIL ARMS CONTROL VERIFICATION COMMITTEE, NATIONAL SECURITY DECISION DIRECTIVE NUMBER 65. The White House.

[55]Rumsfeld, D., 1998. Commission to Assess the Ballistic Missile Threat [WWW Document]. Federation of American Scientists (FAS). irp.fas.org/threat/bm-threat.htm (accessed 12/17/22).

When I was the ACERT commander in 2003, military intelligence had discovered that Chinese government hackers were all over our networks. We lumped together all of that hacker activity under a military umbrella code name, called TITAN RAIN. I love cool-sounding code names. It's one of the reasons I love cybersecurity so much. We have cool names for everything. This time, though, it wasn't an exercise. This was for real. In response, we, the blue team, built a defensive plan to counter the TITAN RAIN offensive campaign plan. Before we deployed it, though, we wanted to test it. We emulated the entire NIPRNET on an Air Force run cyber range in San Antonio, deployed the blue team's defensive plan on it, and told our in-house red team to use TITAN RAIN's tactics, techniques, and procedures to break through. When the red team couldn't get it done, the Army leadership gave us a green light to deploy the blue team's defensive plan on the NIPRNET.

In military exercises, planners typically use two colors to represent both sides: blue for the good guys and red for the bad guys. The origin of the colors isn't a random choice either. We have the Prussian Army to thank for that. According to Peter Attia, "In the early 19th century, the Prussian army adopted war games to train its officers. One group of officers developed a battle plan, and another group assumed the role of the opposition, trying to thwart it. Using a tabletop game called Kriegsspiel (literally "wargame" in German), resembling the popular board game Risk, blue game pieces stood in for the home team—the Prussian army—since most Prussian soldiers wore blue uniforms. Red blocks represented the enemy forces—the red team—and the name has stuck ever since."[56]

[56]Attia, P., 2020b. The importance of red teams. Peter Attia. peterattiamd.com/the-importance-of-red-teams (accessed 12/17/22).

When mainframe computers started to come online in the 1960s, it didn't take long for computer experts to realize that they were vulnerable to abuse. Early designers of mainframes didn't conceive of anything close to a threat model. They were still mostly concerned with getting the ones and zeros moving in the right direction. But that quickly started to change. At maybe the first cybersecurity conference ever, hosted by the System Development Corporation in California in 1965, 15,000 mainframe operators from around the world discussed all the ways in which these new machines could be "penetrated" by unsavory people.[57]

By the late 1960s and early 1970s, elite computer operators were passing around a paper authored by Dr. Willis Ware and others, called the "Willis Paper," that according to William Hunt at the College of William & Mary, "showed how spies could actively penetrate computers, steal or copy electric files and subvert the devices that normally guard top secret information. The study touched off more than a decade of quiet activity by elite groups of computer scientists working for the Government who tried to break into sensitive computers. They succeeded in every attempt."[58] These were the first penetration testers.

In 1971, the U.S. Air Force contracted James Anderson to run Tiger Teams against their Multiplexed Information and Computing Service (MULTICS) operating system, the precursor to UNIX. Anderson's 1972 after-action report described a methodology to penetrate and compromise those systems, which is fundamentally the basis for all penetration testing even today.[59]

---

[57]Dennis, R., 1966. SECURITY IN THE COMPUTING ENVIRONMENT. System Development Corporation for the Defense Documentation Center Defence Supply Agency.

[58]Ware, W.H., 1970. Security Controls for Computer Systems (U): Report of Defense Science Board Task Force on Computer Security. The Rand Corporation.

[59]Anderson, J.P., 1972. Computer Security Technology Planning Study (Volume I). Electronics System Division 1.

In 2020, the big difference between penetration testers and red teamers is that, in general, the penetration testers are supposed to find any flaw in the system, similar to the devil's advocate, and they are allowed to pursue any course of action that presents itself during the test. They are trying to find ways to reduce the attack surface by finding previously unknown weaknesses. In this regard, conducting penetration tests fall under the zero trust strategy umbrella (see Chapter 3). Network defenders aren't trying to stop a specific adversary with a penetration test. They are actively trying to find holes in the deployed defensive posture.

Red teamers, on the other hand, generally follow known adversary attack campaigns. For example, according to the MITRE ATT&CK framework, the adversary campaign known as Cobalt Spider uses 31 attack techniques and 5 software tools to compromise its victims. The red team that attempts to verify that an organization's network is protected against Cobalt Spider can use only those 31 attack techniques and 5 software tools, and nothing else. It's similar to my TITAN RAIN days back in the army. In this exercise, network defenders are specifically looking to make sure that the Cobalt Spider attack campaign won't be successful against their own networks across the intrusion kill chain.

The blue team is the normal day-to-day internal infosec team. In addition to their normal day job of protecting their organization, they take on the additional task of trying to detect and prevent the red team from successfully emulating Cobalt Spider. The red team might be a separate offensive team built in-house supplemented by the CTI team's internal knowledge of Cobalt Spider, or the red team may be an outside contractor who specializes in this kind of service.

Sometimes, network defenders call this opposing force exercise a *purple team* operation, from the red and blue mixed together. By adding this blue team element to the red team operations, the internal infosec team gains a couple of additional benefits. The first big one is that the blue team gets to practice its incident response plans against a real adversary. Then, when the exercise is over, or even during the exercise at the concussion of each phase, they get to ask the adversary what they did in response to the blue team's efforts. You don't get that opportunity in the real world when Cobalt Spider really comes knocking. A second benefit is the individual training opportunity for the newbies and mid-tier analysts on the infosec team. When they normally sit in the SOC all day long watching alerts fly by their screens that were not caught by the SOAR and SIEM tools, they are learning very little. But, you put them on a red team/blue team exercise and just watch how fast their cyber expertise grows. That kind of training is invaluable.

The concept of red teaming has likely been around since at least the 1500s. It hit the IT space in the form of penetration testing in the 1960s and 1970s just as mainframe computers started to become useful for governments and the commercial space. Ever since, we have used penetration tests to reduce the attack surface of our computers and networks in a zero trust kind of way. In the early 2000s, the idea of a combined red team, blue team exercise, or purple team exercise, if you prefer, became popular to test our defenses against known adversary attack campaigns in an intrusion kill chain way. This had the added benefits of exercising our incident response teams and accelerating the training of our newbie and mid-tier analysts in the SOC. Red team, blue team operations are an essential item in the infosec tool kit and will greatly improve our chances of reducing the probability of a material impact to the business due to a cyber event.

Intelligence Sharing: A Tactic for Intrusion Kill Chain Prevention

In J.R.R. Tolkien's classic novel *The Fellowship of the Ring*, Gandalf the Grey, after years of research and analysis, makes a discovery.[60] He realizes that Bilbo Baggins' magic invisibility ring, the one that Bilbo

[60]Tolkien, J.R.R., 2020. The Fellowship of the Ring (the Lord of the Rings, Book 1). HarperCollins.

used to trick Gollum into showing him the way out of the caves underneath the Misty Mountains and the one he used to hide from Smaug inside the Great Hall of Erebor, is in reality, the "one ring to rule them all." This is the singular weapon that the big bad guy, Sauron, could use to conquer all of Middle Earth, but, if the ring is destroyed, would take Sauron off the board. This makes Gandalf the Grey likely the first intelligence analyst ever portrayed in a fantasy novel. I'm just saying.

Gandalf and Elrond (Lord of Rivendell) make the extraordinary decision to share that intelligence with a loose group of frenemies: select members of the White Council, various elf clans, hobbits, dwarfs, and men. This group represents a set of competing interests. The participating members don't hate each other per se, but also don't invite each other to dinner parties either. Let's just say that they agree to disagree on many things. But in this one thing, this singular monumental task—the destruction of Sauron—their interests are completely aligned. It makes total sense to share that key piece of intelligence to facilitate working together to accomplish it.

And that is the perfect analogy to the current state of cybersecurity intelligence sharing today. Even if we compete in the business world on all things, we can come together and cooperate to defeat a common threat. In the business world for example, a set of banks ruthlessly battle against each other in the marketplace. But criminals engaged in cybercrime and cyber fraud don't just impact a single victim bank. When they are successful, they impact the entire industry. It causes customers to lose faith in the system, to be afraid of it, to not spend their money in it. The same is true for nation-states trying to ruin or degrade an enemy by attacking that country's financial system. Those attacks don't just hurt the victim bank and the financial sector; they reverberate across the entire nation. It adds to the general distrust of the entire banking system. That's why it makes total sense for the banking community and the government to share cyber threat intelligence with each other so that they can work together to defeat this common-to-all enemy.

All of that sounds great when you say it fast, but there is friction in the system. Just because we all agree that there is a common threat doesn't negate the trust issues we have with our frenemies. It's tough to hold these loose intelligence sharing alliances together or make them useful. Even Tolkien's fellowship of men, dwarves, elves, and hobbits disbanded at the end of the first book because of trust issues.

The question then is, what is working today in cyber threat intelligence sharing? What is the current state and what are the next steps to making the system more useful?

The Hack Heard 'Round the World At around 8:30 p.m. on November 2, 1988, a 23-year-old Cornell University graduate student named Robert Tappan Morris released the Morris worm. According to the FBI, within 24 hours, 10 percent of the existing 60,000 Internet-facing computers at the time became incapacitated.[61] The Morris worm marked the first global use of a destructive Internet worm, and it was clear that nobody had anticipated that bad guys would use the entire Internet for malicious purposes. Impacted administrators were mostly on their own to deal with the problem because no formal relationships had been established yet to deal with incident response or intelligence sharing.

The First ISACs As mentioned in the "Security Operations Centers" section, the first government CERTs emerged in the aftermath of the Morris worm in 1988. The CERTs represented the first efforts by governments to get cybersecurity information out to the public.

---

[61]Staff, 2018. The Morris Worm [WWW Document]. Federal Bureau of Investigation. www.fbi.gov/news/stories/morris-worm-30-years-since-first-major-attack-on-internet-110218 (accessed 11/2/22).

By the late 1990s, though, many security practitioners began realizing they needed a more robust information sharing framework, something that was bigger than just responding to global incidents like the Morris worm. Y2K was approaching, and it represented another global existential threat not only to the Internet but to business computing in general. According to Investopedia, Y2K referred to the anticipated "widespread computer programming shortcut that was expected to cause extensive havoc as the year changed from 1999 to 2000."[62] Cobol programmers used only two digits to represent dates in the early days of computing, not four, and IT experts expected that millions of lines of business logic code would break on the new year.

In anticipation of Y2K and other factors, U.S. President Clinton established the ISAC system, the information sharing and analysis center framework, when he signed Presidential Decision Directive-63 (PDD-63) on May 22, 1998.[63] He aligned the ISACs specifically around designated critical infrastructure sectors and intentionally didn't mandate specific requirements to encourage innovative information sharing approaches.

> I was in charge of the Pentagon's Army Operations Center (AOC) network during Y2K. The 24/7 AOC is the headquarters of the U.S. Army and every order assigned to units in the field comes from there. As you can imagine, U.S. Army leadership was quite concerned about whether Y2K would completely disrupt Army operations specifically but

---

[62] Halton, C., 2022. The Truth About Y2K: What Did and Didn't Happen in the Year 2000. Investopedia.

[63] Clinton, Bill, 1998. PRESIDENTIAL DECISION DIRECTIVE/NSC-63 [WWW Document]. White House. irp.fas.org/offdocs/pdd/pdd-63.htm (accessed 12/17/22).

perhaps the world in general. In addition to the extensive Army Cobol upgrade program that went on for years before the actual Y2K event, the AOC ran a special watch before and during the event to note if computer systems started failing. We followed the sun so to speak and after years of dire warnings that the world might come to an end on Y2K, nothing happened. That begs the question: did Y2K pundits (which I was one) blow up the existential threat way bigger than it should have been, or did all the Cobol improvement programs prior to the event mitigate the risk? We may never know.

The FS-ISAC Out of all the ISACs that formed in those first years, the Financial Sector ISAC (FS-ISAC) emerged as the most organized and most resourced in the next decade. Leadership from across the banking sector lent their big thinkers and doers to the project.[64] Denise Anderson (as of this writing, the president and CEO of the Health ISAC) was employee number two at the FS-ISAC after the organization hired its first CEO, Bill Nelson. Nelson hired Anderson as a kind of COO to herd all of the cats. According to Anderson, Nelson liked the idea that she was a volunteer firefighter and understood the importance and gravity of first responders.

According to Anderson, the success of the FS-ISAC depended on visionary leaders who believed in the concept of information sharing. They built trust by insisting that their organizations contribute. People like Byron Collie (Wells Fargo and later Goldman Sachs), Jason Healey and Phil Venables (both at Goldman Sachs), and Mark

[64]Howard, R., Anderson, D., Weiss, E., Collie, B., 2022. Intelligence sharing: A Rick the Toolman episode. The CyberWire.

Clancy, Gary Owen, and Errol Weiss (all at Citigroup) led by example and insisted that their organizations shared intelligence with the FS-ISAC membership.

> I know how important leadership by example is. I helped found the Cyber Threat Alliance in 2012, the first ISAO for security vendors. The guiding principle of the Cyber Threat Alliance was that every member had to share intelligence every day, and we kept track of how much. The mandate I gave to my team at Palo Alto Networks was that we would always be the number-one contributor at the end of the day. On the days when Palo Alto Networks was the number-one contributor, I would make fun of the other Alliance members for being contributing slackers. The next day, when they were on top of the leader boards, they would make fun of me.

Traffic Light Protocol Even with Citigroup, Goldman Sachs, and Wells Fargo leading by example, establishing trust between FS-ISAC members was a difficult task. According to both Anderson and Weiss, one of the key innovations that helped was the formalization of the Traffic Light Protocol. The National Infrastructure Security Coordination Centre in the UK (now called the Center for the Protection of National Infrastructure [CPNI]) developed the Traffic Light Protocol (TLP) as a method for labeling and handling shared sensitive information. Bill Nelson and Byron Collie attended a meeting in London at MI5, heard about the protocol, and brought it back to the FS-ISAC.

According to Eric Luiijf and Allard Kernkam in a paper titled "Sharing Cyber Security Information Good Practice Stemming from the Dutch Public-Private-Participation Approach," TLP provides a simple method for labeling and handling shared sensitive information.[65] "One of the key principles of the TLP is that whoever contributes sensitive information also establishes if and how widely the information can be circulated. The originator of the information can label the information with one of four colors.

- *Red*: Restricted to a need-to-know subset of the group
- *Amber*: Adding additional members who need to take action
- *Green*: Everybody in the group
- *White*: Public information

According to Anderson and Weiss, Jim Routh (the CISO at the Depository Trust & Clearing Corporation at the time) was instrumental in formalizing the FS-ISAC Stop Light Protocol. That meant that every communication between members through the FS-ISAC portal had to be labeled with the proper color. By doing so, every FS-ISAC member felt less anxiety about sharing intelligence with the group because they all saw that there were formalized processes for handling sensitive information.

Anderson says that with the FS-ISAC's success of the TLP, the Forum of Incident Response and Security Teams (FIRST) picked up the best practice for their incident response missions. Today, TLP is a standard best practice for most sharing organizations.

Weiss says that, at this point, all ISACs were sharing information on cyber incident response events, best practices around combatting existential threats like Y2K, and general best practices for what everybody else was doing in the space. With the formalized procedures in place to share intelligence with other members (the how) the next question was what were they going to share? This intelligence and information was going to be the reason that members joined.

---

[65]Luiijf, E., Kernkam, A., 2015. Sharing Cyber Security Information - Good Practice Stemming from the Dutch Public-Private Approach, Global Conference on Cyberspace 2015.

Jason Healey and Byron Collie established the foundational FS-ISAC threat intel committee in the early 2000s, a convergence of threat intelligence and SOC operations. This influential group provided the value that all FS-ISAC members wanted.

ISACs and the U.S. Government According to the U.S. government's Cybersecurity and Infrastructure Security Agency (CISA), ISACs "are non-profit, member-driven organizations formed by critical infrastructure owners and operators to share information between government and industry."[66]

CISA coordinates with all the ISACs as described in President Clinton's directive. But, according to the CISA website, certain ISACs get special attention because of their nature.

- *Multi-State Information Sharing and Analysis Center (MS-ISAC)*: The ISAC for state, local, tribal, and territorial (SLTT) governments
- *Communications ISAC*: The ISAC for members from the nation's major communications carriers
- *Financial Services Information Sharing and Analysis Center (FS-ISAC)*: The ISAC for the financial sector
- *Aviation Information Sharing and Analysis Center (A-ISAC)*: The ISAC for the aviation industry

The First Fusion Centers The U.S. Congress passed the Intelligence Reform and Terrorism Prevention Act (IRTPA) on December 17, 2004 to provide regional situational awareness and analysis (including cyber) at both the state and city levels. The nexus for that activity in

---

[66]CISA, n.d. Information Sharing and Awareness [WWW Document]. www.cisa.gov/information-sharing-and-awareness (accessed 11/1/22).

each location is called a Fusion Center.[67] According to the Florida Department of Law Enforcement this year (2022), "Fusion centers were established following the terrorist attacks of September 11, 2001 to connect-the-dots between critical information housed in different agencies and share information and intelligence to aid in protecting communities."[68] As of this writing, 79 fusion centers have been established in the United States.

The First ISAOs Arguably, the FBI founded the first ISAO in 1996, although the community wouldn't have a name for it until two decades later. They called it the InfraGard National Members Alliance, or InfraGard National, and designed it to facilitate information sharing between law enforcement and the private sector.[69] InfraGard isn't a CERT, although it does some of the same things a CERT does, and it isn't an ISAC because it doesn't service one of the U.S. government's critical infrastructure sectors. It's a different thing. The FBI was way ahead of its time in establishing InfraGard by realizing that other communities of like-minded people might want to share intelligence on their communal set of existential threats, in this case cybercrime.

In the early days, and even still today, one of the recurring stumbling blocks in the information sharing space is the fear that the act of sharing any information about cyberattacks would come back to bite the sharing member in the form of lawsuits. Lawyers from victim organizations worry that their name would become public

[67]Collins, S., 2004. Intelligence Reform and Terrorism Prevention Act.
[68]Glass, M., n.d. Fusion Center History [WWW Document]. Florida Department of Law Enforcement. www.fdle.state.fl.us/FFC/FFC/FusionCenterHistory (accessed 11/1/22).
[69]Staff, 2019. Overview [WWW Document]. InfraGard National Members Alliance. www.infragardnational.org/about-us/overview (accessed 11/2/22).

knowledge and subject the brand to customer lawsuits from people who thought the organization didn't adequately protect their personal data. These lawyers weighed the risk of those potential lawsuits against the benefit of sharing the information with the community and found it wanting. It wasn't until much later that sharing organizations realized that the intelligence they needed to share didn't involve anything about the victim but should focus on how the adversary traversed the intrusion kill chain to be successful. In other words, share the hacker's TTPs, not the details about what happened to the victim. By sharing that intelligence with the community, everybody could be better protected.

In 2015, U.S. President Obama signed Executive Order 13691 establishing the ISAO framework that made it legal to share information about cybersecurity incidents without fear of prosecution.[70] ISAOs are sector-agnostic and can be any group of like-minded organizations, like the Cyber Threat Alliance. The Executive Order also established a funding path for an ISAO standards organization. I actually worked as the co-chair to the Security and Privacy Committee to help get it started. As of this writing, there are just over 90 ISAOs officially registered with the ISAO standards body.

Other U.S. Government Sharing Programs According to MITRE's Bruce Bakis and Edward Wang, the Department of Homeland Security (DHS) is the epicenter of the U.S. cyber information-sharing ecosystem.[71] In 2018, U.S. President Trump signed into law the Cybersecurity and Infrastructure Security Agency Act, which

---

[70]Obama, Barack, 2013. Executive Order -- Improving Critical Infrastructure Cybersecurity [WWW Document]. whitehouse.gov. obamawhitehouse .archives.gov/the-press-office/2013/02/12/executive-order-improving-critical-infrastructure-cybersecurity (accessed 12/17/22).

[71]Bakis, B., Wang, E., 2017. Building a National Cyber Information-Sharing Ecosystem. Mitre.

established the Cybersecurity and Infrastructure Security Agency (CISA) inside of DHS.[72] According to the department's official website, CISA coordinates cybersecurity defense for the federal government, acts as the incident response execution arm for the national cyber defense, and owns the responsibility of intelligence sharing. The National Cybersecurity and Communications Integration Center (NCCIC) and the United States Computer Emergency Response Team (US-CERT) work for CISA.

CISA manages four formal information sharing programs, one at the senior leadership level (the Joint Cyber Defense Collaborative) and three at the operator level.

- *Joint Cyber Defense Collaborative (JCDC)*[73]: Established in August 2021 to enhance collaboration with the private sector, one of the six pillars of the Cyberspace Solarium Commission[74] is a group of public and private-sector organizations as well as federal and state, local, tribal, and territorial (SLTTs) government entities designed to bring senior leaders from the government and the commercial sector together to collaborate on global issues. Their first success story was how the group responded to the log4J crisis in 2021 and 2022.[75]
- *Enhanced Cybersecurity Services (ECS)*[76]: Initially intended for communications service providers (CSPs), President Obama's Executive Order 13636 in 2013 expanded the service to the

[72] McCaul, M., 2018. Cybersecurity and Infrastructure Security Agency Act.
[73] Staff, n.d. Joint Cyber Defense Collaborative [WWW Document], n.d. CISA. www.cisa.gov/jcdc (accessed 12/18/22).
[74] Cyberspace Solarium Commission [WWW Document], n.d. www.solarium.gov (accessed 12/18/22).
[75] Riley, T., 2022. CISA's new JCDC worked as intended, witnesses say at Senate hearing on Log4Shell bug. CyberScoop.
[76] Staff, n.d. Enhanced Cybersecurity Services (ECS) [WWW Document]. CISA. www.cisa.gov/enhanced-cybersecurity-services-ecs (accessed 12/18/22).

16 critical infrastructure sectors and to their corresponding customer bases. DHS shares sensitive and classified cyber-threat information with accredited organizations through automated means.

- *Cyber Information Sharing and Collaboration Program (CISCP)*[77]: DHS shares unclassified information through trusted public-private partnerships across all critical infrastructure sectors.
- Th*e DHS Automated Indicator Sharing (AIS) program*[78]: This provides unclassified, bidirectional, machine-to-machine sharing of cyber threat indicators between the NCCIC and the private sector, ISACs, ISAOs, public sector, and international partners and companies.

These are all great mechanisms to share and collaborate on threat intelligence between the U.S. government and the private sector. The criticism of these programs is that the intelligence that the government shares has not been that useful and has mostly been shared manually. The AIS program automated the process with STIX and TAXII, but the quality of the intelligence was so low from the government side that most commercial organizations didn't bother with it. The commercial side of the JCDC is a collection of high-end security and cloud providers (such as AWS, Cisco, Crowdstrike, Microsoft, and Palo Alto Networks; as of this writing, 21 in all), but the information sharing mechanisms are Zoom calls and email. Thirty years after the establishment of the first CERTs, intelligence sharing between the government and the private sector is still mostly manual and ad hoc.

---

[77]Staff, n.d. Cyber Information Sharing and Collaboration Program (CISCP) [WWW Document]. CISA. www.cisa.gov/ciscp (accessed 12/18/22).
[78]Staff, n.d. Automated Indicator Sharing [WWW Document]. CISA. www.cisa.gov/ais (accessed 12/18/22).

The Future of Cybersecurity Information Sharing In terms of the first principle intrusion kill chain strategy, information sharing and intelligence sharing are essential tactics at all levels. At the government, Fortune 500, and security vendor scale, these organizations have the resources to build CTI teams that collect actionable intelligence on adversary behavior in real time every day, across the intrusion kill chain. Following the Counsel of Elrond example at the beginning of the chapter, it just makes sense that these organizations would share this kind of intelligence with everybody else (ISACs, ISAOs, Fusion Centers, MSSPs, CERTS, organizational SOCs, and the general consumer) in an effort to make the entire community safer. The fact that small- to medium-sized organizations don't have the resources to do this themselves emphasizes the point. The haves could help the have-nots. Most agree with this notion as a strategy, but the manual and ad hoc tactics adopted so far have impeded progress. What is required is not a fundamental shift in strategy. What is required is an adoption of modern tactics.

Imagine a future where some government that had the intelligence resources to do it (presumably the U.S. government, but it could be others) tracked all known adversary campaigns across all motivations (crime, espionage, warfare or low-level-cyber-conflict, hactivism, propagandists, or general mischief makers; see Figure 4.2), not just the nation-state activity that the MITRE ATT&CK wiki tracks. Further imagine that they formatted the intelligence with the industry's de facto standard (STIX) and populated a wiki with that intelligence using the Lockheed Martin Kill Chain model, the DOD's Diamond model, and the MITRE ATT&CK framework. They could even just pay MITRE to cover everything since it's an FFRDC. Further imagine that they provided an API to everybody so that the intelligence could be consumed easily and automatically by whomever wanted it (see Chapter 7). Additionally, they could develop a scheme where they paid security vendors, sharing organizations like ISACs and ISAOs, and others, to populate the database from the telemetry they collect from their customers and members. Also, they develop some means to rank order the intelligence as actionable compared to others in a kind of intelligence marketplace. In that way, network defenders consuming the intelligence could have a means to decide which contributions to the database were good and which were to be avoided, and the government could have a means to judge how much to pay.

All of this may seem like a bridge too far both technically and politically, but that's just not true. For technical architecture, models already exist that have been running for a few years now. Both the DHS Automated Indicator Sharing (AIS) program and the Cyber Threat Alliance systems could easily be used to pursue this vision. Other commercial security vendors have versions of this that could work too. Politically, the U.S. government has demonstrated an interest in resourcing information sharing programs since 1998. It's not a question of will and know-how. It's a question of vision.

The one criticism for this vision is that if this new adversary campaign intelligence repository was open to anybody who wanted to access it, that means the bad guys could access it too. It would be easy for them to also consume the intelligence to discover what their potential victims know about how they operate. This would allow them to design schemes to avoid the prevention and detection controls these victims were deploying to block their hacking campaigns. All of that is true enough, but it's not a real threat.

Essentially, that criticism is the old sources-and-methods problem that intelligence organizations have been trying to protect since the biblical days. We don't want our potential enemies to know how we got the intelligence on them, and we don't want them to know what we know about them. They could use it against us. But in this age of DevOps and infrastructure as code, that doesn't matter as much. If the entire infosec community is exchanging intelligence on hacker campaigns in real time on the less than the 500 active campaigns on the Internet on any given day, the burden to find new TTPs that no potential victim has any knowledge about becomes astronomical for any one hacker group to stay ahead of. Even if they are successful once, the community would quickly share that intelligence making the campaign nonreusable. It's expensive enough to build even new tools like malware and exploits. But it's exceedingly expensive to build new attack sequences from scratch after a one-time use.

That said, the intelligence sharing community is a long way from this vision. The bits and pieces are there to put it all together, but somebody has to do it. The commercial sector might do it, but the price for the service would almost certainly eliminate the possibility of small- to medium-sized organizations using it, thus defeating the purpose. I'm not saying that they couldn't find a business model that works for everybody. I'm just saying that I haven't seen one emerge. That means that some government will have to lead the charge, to prime the pump so to speak, and I don't see any organization stepping up to do it.

Conclusion

In this chapter, I summarized the historical beginnings of three of the most important adversary campaign threat models of the last decade: the strategic Lockheed Martin Kill Chain model, the DOD's CTI-specific Diamond model, and the operational MITRE ATT&CK framework and wiki. I made the point that these are not competing models but work in conjunction with each other. The use of these models by government and commercial CTI teams has given us all of those colorful names associated with adversary activity like APT1, Fancy Bear, the Lazarus Group, and Charming Kitten. But I made the distinction that these names don't necessarily represent the people or governments behind the attacks. They represent the attack sequence across the intrusion kill chain that CTI teams have repeatedly seen in the wild. As much as we would like to associate Charming Kitten with the Iranian government, the CTI community's confidence of that attribution should not be high except for some special circumstances. And even if those circumstances are met, for the general-purpose network defender, attribution to a government or a person is not important in terms of first principle strategies and cybersecurity. What is important is attribution of the attack sequence so that all network defenders can install prevention and detection controls within their internal security stack to counter the adversary's attack campaign at every step of the intrusion kill chain. I made the case that there weren't that many adversary playbooks active on the Internet on any given day and that it should be somebody's task (maybe the U.S. government) to keep track of them all and to make all of that intelligence available to the public.

To fulfill the intrusion kill chain strategy for their own organizations, I advocated that network defenders should consider certain first principle tactics to some degree or another.

- Establishing a SOC or at least assigning one or more people the task of performing the functions of a SOC.
- Creating a CTI team or at least assigning one or more people the task of performing the functions of a CTI team within the SOC.
- Excelling at orchestrating the security stack on all data islands with the latest detection and prevention controls across the intrusion kill chain.
- Running purple team exercises where one half of the team (the red team) emulates known adversary attack sequences against the internal network and the other half (the blue team) tries to counter that attack. At each phase of the exercise, the two teams compare notes in order to improve.
- Sharing attack sequence intelligence with peers, official sharing organizations like ISACs and ISAOs, or using security vendors who do that for you.

This entire chapter was all about prevention and detection. In the next chapter, I will talk about what happens if all of this fails. Remember, executing on the intrusion kill chain prevention strategy will not guarantee that you won't have a material cyber event happen. It reduces the probability of one. In the next chapter, we will talk about what to do to survive one: resilience.

5 Resilience

[Resilience is]. . .the ability to continuously deliver the intended outcome despite adverse cyber events.

—Janis Stirna and Jelena Zdravkovic, authors of *Cyber Resilience:—Fundamentals for a Definition*

That which does not kill us makes us stronger.

—Friedrich Nietzsche, German scholar and philosopher

Overview

In this chapter, I present the case for the best definition of resilience. I then describe the four tactics to deploy it: crisis planning, backup and restore operations, encryption, and incident response. Next, I explain that to run a mature resilience program, infosec teams have quite a bit of planning to do, which typically shows up in corporate business continuity and disaster recovery plans. Finally, I will explain how mature programs also practice their plans with the organization's senior leadership team.

What Is Resilience?

As a concept, ASIS International coined the phrase *cyber resilience* as early as 2009, but it was really describing what turned out to be business continuity.[1] I will cover the difference between the two later in this chapter. In 2010, the Department of Homeland Security identified resilience in cyberspace as the "ability to adapt to changing conditions and prepare for, withstand, and rapidly recover from disruption.[2] The World Economic Forum formalized a cyber resilience definition in 2012: ". . .the ability of systems and organizations to withstand cyber events. . . ."[3] Since then, other thought leaders have refined it. U.S. President Obama even signed a presidential policy directive dictating resilience for the country's critical infrastructure in 2013.[4] In 2017, the International Standards Organization (ISO) published this definition: ". . . the ability of an organization to absorb and adapt in a changing environment to enable it to deliver its objectives and to survive and prosper."[5]

Then in 2019, NIST standardized the definition of *cyber resilience* as "the ability to anticipate, withstand, recover from, and adapt to adverse conditions, stresses, attacks, or compromises on systems that use or are enabled by cyber resources."[6] NIST also states that the cyber resilience discussion "is predicated on the assumption that adversaries will breach defenses." This statement is often overlooked

---

[1]Staff, 2009. Organizational Resilience: Security, Preparedness, and Continuity Management Systems . ASIS International.
[2]Staff, 2010. DHS Risk Lexicon 2010 Edition. U.S. Department of Homeland Security.
[3]Staff, 2012. Partnering for Cyber Resilience. World Economic Forum.
[4]Obama, Barack, 2013. Presidential Policy Directive – Critical Infrastructure Security and Resilience [WWW Document]. The White House: President Obama. obamawhitehouse.archives.gov/the-press-office/2013/02/12/presidential-policy-directive-critical-infrastructure-security-and-resil (accessed 12/4/22).
[5]Staff, n.d. Security and resilience — Organizational resilience — Principles and attributes [WWW Document]. ISO. www.iso.org/obp/ui#iso:std:iso:22316:ed-1:v1:en (accessed 12/4/22).
[6]Staff, n.d. Cyber Resiliency [WWW Document]. NIST Glossary. csrc.nist.gov/glossary/term/cyber_resiliency (accessed 12/18/22).

and not understood. Cyber resilience is not about protecting the system and preventing the adversary from breaching your systems. It means assuming the system is or will be breached and figuring out what you need to do to continue your mission after the fact.

But the definition I like best comes from two Stockholm University researchers in 2015. Janis Stirna and Jelena Zdravkovic define it this way: ". . .the ability to continuously deliver the intended outcome despite adverse cyber events."[7] Assume that the bad guys will successfully negotiate the intrusion kill chain, find a weak spot in my zero-trust armor, or, in general, assume that there will be a massive IT failure at some point in the future. Then devise a strategy to ensure that your organization's essential services will still function.

Resilience Examples

> A great example of resilience can be seen in the movies *Terminator* and *Terminator 2*. In the original movie, the terminator was designed for survivability. Much like our systems today, Arnold Schwarzenegger was loaded with various functions to identify, protect, detect, and respond to ensure that he would survive and be able to defend himself. However, upon attack on the terminator, he began to lose functionality. By the end of the movie, his functions were slowly destroyed. He lost his ability to identify, protect, detect, and respond. But he was surviving.

[7]Björck, F., Henkel, M., Stirna, J., Zdravkovic, J., 2015. Cyber Resilience – Fundamentals for a Definition, in: New Contributions in Information Systems and Technologies. Springer International Publishing, Cham, pp. 311–316.

Terminator 2 was built not just to survive but to be resilient. The leaner, smaller terminator could anticipate, withstand, recover from, and adapt to attacks. His body would absorb the bullet and heal if he was shot. In addition, he could morph his body into a sword shape if he needed a sharp weapon. Similarly, cybersecurity today must extend beyond providing for survivability. It must include resilience to ensure the overall functions and mission can be conducted while operating in a contested cyber environment.

Terminator 2 is by far my favorite example of resilience. But, usually, when I give this example to people younger than 30, they tell me they have never seen either of the movies. So it's not always as effective as I hope.

My favorite example of a practical implementation of resilience is what the people at Netflix call *chaos engineering.* I will do a deep dive case study in Chapter 7, but let me provide an overview now. In 2008, the Netflix infrastructure experienced two major IT outages late in the year that prevented the company from delivering DVDs via mail to their customers.[8] At the time, they were transitioning from traditional software development methods to adopting DevOps best practices. As a result, they moved their support infrastructure from on-premises (commonly called on-prem) to the cloud to provide more resilience to their business process in 2011.

A small team of Netflix engineers also built their first resilience module called Chaos Monkey. From the Netflix website, "Chaos

---

[8]Staff, 2018. Chaos Monkey at Netflix: the Origin of Chaos Engineering [WWW Document]. Gremlin. www.gremlin.com/chaos-monkey/the-origin-of-chaos-monkey (accessed 12/18/22).

Monkey is a tool that randomly disables our production instances to make sure we can survive this common type of failure without any customer impact."[9] Let me say that another way: Netflix routinely runs an app that randomly destroys pieces of their customer-facing infrastructure, on purpose, so that their network architects understand resilience engineering deep in their core.

In my typical world, disasters might happen sometime in the future but probably never. At least I hope that they don't. However, in the Netflix world, planned disasters happen daily. Since they deployed the original Chaos Monkey module, the Netflix team has built an entire series of chaos tools designed to increase their confidence in surviving a catastrophic event. The ultimate objective is to ensure customers will not notice that the Netflix infrastructure is going through a disruption, and I can still watch episodes of *The Witcher* uninterrupted as if nothing happened.

There are some network defenders and IT professionals who would categorize what Netflix does as impressive and aspirational. But most of us would categorize what Netflix does as stark raving bonkers. We're not going to bring down our customer-facing infrastructure for a test. It's hard enough to keep the thing up and running without destroying it ourselves. We would be wrong, but that's the current thinking in our community. Netflix has embraced resiliency in its Infrastructure. The bulk of the rest of us just wave our hands at it.

The other resiliency example I like to discuss is the Google site reliability engineer (SRE) teams.[10] In 2004 when Google was nothing more than a search engine, the leadership team made an extraordinary decision. Instead of creating a team of network engineers to manage the infrastructure like every other company on the planet, they

---

[9]Staff, 2018. Netflix Chaos Monkey Upgraded. Netflix Technology Blog.
[10]Beyer, B., Jones, C., Petoff, J., Murphy, N.R., 2016. Site Reliability Engineering: How Google Runs Production Systems. O'Reilly Media.

handed the responsibility to the software development team. The domino effect you get when you hand a task like that to a bunch of programmers is that it fertilizes the seeds for an Internet tech giant to emerge down the road. At the start, the SREs wrote programs to automate those jobs that a network engineer would do manually by logging into a console and typing commands. They were doing DevOps for 6 years before the industry even had a name for it. And by the way, so was Amazon. Amazon's work eventually led to AWS. Over time, that monumental decision made by both companies pioneered the idea of infrastructure as code.

SREs label manual tasks as "toil." They describe toil as anything repetitive, tactical, and devoid of any enduring value. We all know the benefits of automating tasks, but the Google SREs have taken it to the Nth degree. They realize that it is not a panacea, but a force multiplier. Done correctly, it layers a blanket of consistency across the entire organization and, once built, the emerging platform can be easily extended. Google didn't just automate critical tasks. They built an autonomous system that instantiates a framework for resilience. In my personal experience, I can't remember the last time a Google product failed for any length of time. But you know that internally, their systems are failing all over the place. The infrastructure is too big for that not to be true. The fact that I never notice meets the very definition of resilience.

IT Resilience and Infosec Resilience

The Netflix and the Google examples are more aligned with IT operations than security; they're more DevOps than DevSecOps. That's unfortunate. But the SREs of the world have set an excellent example for the security community. Design and deploy the digital infrastructure so that the impact on the organization would be minimal, even if the Fancy Bear hackers penetrated the deployed defensive system. Design it so that even if the BlackByte ransomware hackers take over a segment of my network, my business can continue to provide service. Hence, design the network to anticipate, withstand, recover, and adapt. That's resilience.

Resilience vs. Resiliency Planning

Plans are not strategies nor are they tactics. They are how-to manuals to deploy the tactics necessary to achieve the overall strategy. Remember that resilience is one of our first principle strategies. We are trying to deliver the intended outcome despite adverse events continuously. We want to anticipate, withstand, recover from, and adapt. How we accomplish that will involve deploying one or more tactics, and this chapter covers the most impactful ones.

Executing those tactics requires a great deal of resilience planning. According to NIST's Contingency Planning Guide for Federal Information Systems (SP 800-34 Rev. 1, Published: November 2010),[11] these are the typical kinds of resiliency plans that the U.S. Federal Government will have on hand. See Figure 5.1.

- *Business continuity plan (BCP)*: To sustain business operations while recovering from a significant disruption
- *Continuity of operations plan (COOP)*: To sustain the essential functions at an alternate site
- *Crisis communications plan (CCP)*: To disseminate communications for critical status and rumor control
- *Critical infrastructure protection (CIP) plan*: To protect critical infrastructure components

[11]Swanson, M., Bowen, P., Phillips, A., Gallup, D., Lynes, D., 2010. SP 800-34 Rev. 1, Contingency Planning Guide for Federal Information Systems [WWW Document]. CSRC. csrc.nist.gov/publications/detail/sp/800-34/rev-1/final

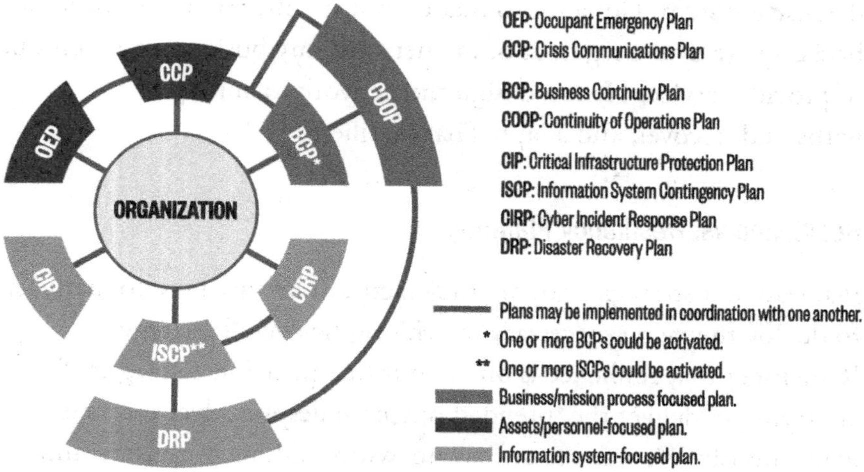

Figure 5.1 Continuity plan relationships[11]

- *Cyber incident response plan (CIRP)*: To mitigate a cyberattack
- *Disaster recovery plan (DRP)*: To relocate information systems to alternate locations
- *Information system contingency plan (ISCP)*: To recover an information system
- *Occupant emergency plan (OEP)*: To minimize loss of life or injury and to protect property damage in response to a physical threat

In the commercial world, planners typically boil NIST's laundry list of required plans down to two: business continuity and disaster recovery. But these two plans incorporate key elements from most of the plans on the NIST list. To simplify, business continuity is the plan for force majeure events the organizations might experience such as fires, active shooters, earthquakes, executive deaths, etc. Disaster recovery is the plan that deals specifically with the digital infrastructure like loss of service from cloud providers, data center power outages, and cyberattacks. So, in that way, disaster recovery plans are a subset of the business continuity plan, and that's where we will plan the resilience first principle strategy.

At the time of this writing, the Global Resilience Federation has published the first version of the Operational Resilience Framework (ORF).[12] Recognizing the interconnections between organizations, providers, and suppliers, the ORF extends the business continuity and disaster recovery plans to the organization's entire ecosystem. This means identifying the minimal viable external products and services required from the organization to identify the operational requirements during an impaired state. Put more plainly, remember the bank run scene in *It's a Wonderful Life*, where all of the banks' customers descended on the bank to withdraw all of their money. This would surely mean the bank would run out of money, most customers would not receive their money, and the bank would have to close permanently. But, thanks to George Bailey's quick thinking, he pleaded with everyone to withdraw what they absolutely needed. By doing so, everyone received what they needed, and the bank could stay in business.

After identifying the operational requirements to meet the customers' minimal needs during an impaired state, the ORF then includes the system's resilience aspect by ensuring the technical capabilities and its dependencies will be available. For example, this might mean recovering only business-critical data versus the entire backup.

When developing a resilience plan, it is imperative to understand the relationships between people, processes, and technologies. Far too often, the business continuity plan is written in a silo and may not

---

[12]McGlone, P., 2022. Operational Resilience Framework (ORF) Released for Public Comment — GRF. GRF.

consider that the system's restore process may take weeks or months to get back online or that the phones, computers, and networks they depend on will have their own timeline and dependencies not considered.

The ORF also blends the enterprise business perspective of resilience with the system's engineering aspect of engineering found in NIST SP 800-160v2 Developing Cyber Resilient Systems: A Systems Security Engineering Approach, which presents a cyber resiliency engineering framework complete with the resilience goals, objectives, techniques, approaches, and design principles.[13] It's one thing to plan for resilience, another to have a resilience plan, and an altogether different thing to have a resilience plan that has been vetted through the enterprise and regularly tested, table-topped, taught, and updated.

> A small pet peeve of mine is how we name things in the infosec community. If we don't do it correctly, the result is years of confusion within the infosec community. I've already cited a few examples in this book where this has happened. One is the confusion around what zero trust means. It doesn't mean to trust nobody. It means limited trust down to the bare essentials (see Chapter 3). The confusion around adversary group attribution versus campaign attribution (Chapter 4) is another. Attribution is about campaigns and not the hackers behind the campaign. A third is the name we use for software-defined perimeter (SDP) (see Chapter 3). SDP eliminates the perimeter. It doesn't establish one. And here we have disaster recovery, which at first reading sounds like a synonym for

[13]Ross, R., Pillitteri, V., Graubart, R., Bodeau, D., McQuaid, R., 2021b. SP 800-160 Vol. 2 Rev. 1, Developing Cyber-Resilient Systems: SSE Approach [WWW Document]. NIST. csrc.nist.gov/publications/detail/sp/800-160/vol-2-rev-1/final (accessed 12/18/22).

business continuity. Further, if you're new to the field, how would you know that disaster recovery is a subset of business continuity? Establishing a well-thought-out name in the beginning of some project, whether it becomes an internationally recognized set of standard best practices or it's just a name for the next internal IT modernization product, will reduce the confusion later when you have to explain it to somebody.

Herding the Cats: Responsibility Assignment Matrices

Once a cyber event turns into an honest-to-goodness incident, the situation will likely no longer be contained in the SOC. Based on the business continuity plan, other business functions may have to kick in. The incident response plan must keep all those decision-makers, stakeholders, and other interested parties up-to-date on who is doing what, who is in charge, and next steps. It's a challenging process and is not limited to cyber issues. Shepherding big and complex projects across multiple organizational units has been a management problem since the early days of business.

It's unclear when but sometime in the late 1940s, Dutch consultant Ernst Hijams, working for a Canadian consulting firm Leethan, Simpson, Ltd., introduced the idea of linear responsibility charting (LRC); this is a graphical representation of who is responsible for each major task in the project, who is in support, who must be consulted, who may be consulted, who reviews, and who has final approval. See Figure 5.2.[14]

[14]Source: Staff, 2014. Linear Responsibility Chart [WWW Document]. SprAid. spraid.onmason.com/project-management/linear-responsibility-chart (accessed 11/12/22).

Linear Responsibility Chart	Nathan Jordan	Richard Patrican	Andrew Cedeno	Dr. Wu	Dr. Reagle
1.0 Understand Customer Requirements	2	1	2	5	5
1.1 Clarify Problem Statement	3	1	1	3	3
1.2 Conduct Research	2	1	1	3	3
1.3 Develop Objectives Tree	2	1	1	4	4
1.3.1 Draft Objectives Tree	2	1	2	4	4
1.3.2 Review with Client	2	1	1	4	4
1.3.3 Revise Objectives Tree	2	1	1	4	4
2.0 Analyze Function Requirements	3	1	1	4	3
3.0 Design Prototypes	2	1	1	4	3
3.1 Draw Paper Sketches	2	1	1	4	3
3.2 3D Drawings on Autodesk	2	1	1	4	3
4.0 Build Prototype	2	1	1	4	3
4.1 Build Basic Mockup	2	2	1	4	3
4.2 Finalize Second Prototype on Autodesk	2	1	1	4	3
4.3 Order Parts	2	1	1	4	3
4.4 Print Final Prototype Using 3D Printer	2	1	1	4	3
4.5 Assemble Device with Ordered Parts	2	1	1	4	3
5.0 Evaluate Alternatives	1	1	1	3	3
5.1 Weigh Objectives	3	3	1	3	3
5.2 Develop Test Protocol	2	1	1	3	3
5.3 Conduct Tests	1	1	1	2	2
5.4 Report Test Results	1	2	2	3	3
6.0 Select Preferred Design	2	1	1	3	3
7.0 Document Design Results	2	1	1	2	2
7.1 Design Specifications	2	1	1	4	6
7.2 Draft Final Report	2	1	2	2	2
7.3 Design Review with Client	2	1	1	4	4
8.0 Project Management	1				
8.1 Weekly Meetings	2	1	1	4	5
8.2 Develop Project Plan	2	1	1	4	4
8.3 Track Progress	2	1	1	4	4
8.4 Progress Reports	2	1	1	4	4

Key 1-Primary Responsibility | 2-Support/Work | 3-Must be Consulted
4-May be Consulted | 5-Review | 6-Final Approval

Figure 5.2 Linear responsibility charting examples[14]

	Frodo	Sam	Gandalf	Aragorn	Elrond
Decide on what to do with the ring	C	I	A	C	R
Create Fellowship	R	C	A	C	R
Get the ring to Mount Doom	R	C	A	C	I
Distract and defeat enemies	I	R	C	R	I

R Responsible
A Accountable
C Consulted
I Informed

Figure 5.3 RACI chart for a Middle Earth fellowship to destroy the one ring[15]

In the early 1950s, as project management evolved, these kinds of project charts became known as RACI charts (for "Responsible, Accountable, Consulted, Informed") or responsibility assignment matrix (RAM) charts. See Figure 5.3.[15]

In 2022, there are more than a dozen different versions on this same theme that emphasize different participation types like "Sign-off required," "Input required," "Control," "Suggest," "Facilitates," "Qualitative review," "Verifier," "Driver," etc. Think of LRCs and RAMs as the generic name for these kinds of charts and RACI (and any of its cousins like DACI, RAPID, PARIS, etc.) as specific types.

The point is that most organizations are likely using one version or the other of LRC charts to project manage a crisis in line with the business continuity plan. Both the business continuity plan and the disaster recovery plan likely have a version documented in the

---

[15]Haworth, S., 2021. RACI Chart Template For Project Managers + Example; How-To [WWW Document]. The Digital Project Manager. thedigitalprojectmanager.com/projects/leadership-team-management/raci-chart-made-simple (accessed 11/13/22).

When I was the commander of the Army CERT, there was a big turf war regarding which Army unit owned the cyber mission. All the services had the same fight, and in many ways, they are still fighting about it. But in my day (early 2000s), the fight was between INSCOM (the U.S. Army's intelligence arm and the command that the ACERT belonged to) and NETCOM (the U.S. Army's communication's arm). The two generals in charge decided that "cyber" would be a joint operation between the two and tasked me and MAJ Larry Hall (my counterpart at NETCOM) to iron out the details. We didn't know what to call it back then, but Larry and I used a version of linear responsibility charting (LRC) to do it. For months, he and I would pass back and forth a spreadsheet with all the "cyber" tasks allocated to one side or the other until leadership on both sides agreed to the allocation. The process was painful but would have been impossible without the LRC.

approved plan. When organizations run exercises to test the plans, the RAM is usually the go-to document to see if everybody is doing what they should be doing. After the exercise, or indeed after a real crisis, the RAM is typically the first document that gets updated.

How to Think About Resilience

Resilience is a different way to think about reducing the probability of material impact due to a cyber event than thinking about preventing an attack in the first place. With zero trust and intrusion kill chain prevention, we are actively taking measures to prevent the bad thing from happening. With resilience, we accept that a bad thing will happen and take actions to survive it.

It's similar to the argument about how governments deal with the problem of an asteroid slamming into the earth. The prevention side would follow a course of trying to deflect the trajectory of the asteroid with some kind of missile. The resilience side would pursue establishing a second planet (maybe Mars) where humans live. The missile option would preserve the human race by preventing the catastrophe from happening. The Mars option would exponentially increase the chances of the human race surviving if a sizable asteroid hit the earth.

For cybersecurity, the tactics available for the resilience strategy have the added benefit of probably costing less to implement compared to the other strategies we are considering in our first principle infosec program. Implementing zero trust, intrusion kill chain prevention, and anything like a mature automation program is not cheap. Resilience, relatively speaking, is. This means that if you work for a small- to medium-sized startup, the first strategy to work on, the strategy that will give you the most bang for the buck, the tactics that will reduce the probability of material impact with the least cost, all fall within the resilience strategy.

As Stirna and Zdravkovic say, build business systems that can continuously deliver the intended outcome despite adverse cyber events. Here are some ways you can do that.

Crisis Handling: A Tactic for Resilience

First things first: the senior cybersecurity practitioner for most organizations is probably not in charge of the overall general-purpose business continuity plan. There are many kinds of potential crises that a commercial company, a government agency, or academic institution might encounter that don't involve a ransomware attack by the likes of BlackByte, or a cyberespionage operation from nation-state operators behind Hurricane Panda. To prepare the organization for a cyber crisis, security leaders must plug themselves into the existing crisis management apparatus as one of its key players. How big the overall organization is and how well-resourced the crisis management team is will dictate the level of formality of the crisis plan. What may not be obvious is that the size of the organization and the maturity of its crisis management team are not as important as simply having a plan—any plan—that makes the leadership team feel comfortable.

And when I say "plan," I don't mean a 100-page document that nobody ever reads. Instead, it's a plan that has been lived with, played with, tweaked, bent, crushed, stomped on, straightened out, ripped up again, thrown out, redone, and iterated on so many times that it's second nature. When the plan goes south during an actual crisis, as it will inevitably do, the important thing is that the team members are so familiar with each other, and the desired outcome is so well understood, that any audibles or improvisations during the event have a decent chance of still leading to the desired result.

When I was in the Army, I worked for a colonel who understood this. He always said it was great to have a plan so that we could deviate from it. As Mike Tyson, the famous heavyweight boxer, so eloquently said, "Everybody has a plan until they get punched in the mouth."[16] What I mean by that is the difference between a group of planners and a group of crisis survivors is that the survivors are crystal clear before the instigating event happens about the desired outcome. It doesn't matter if the plan is 100 pages neatly organized in colored binders coded to each senior leadership member's role or if the plan is a hastily drawn stick diagram on a whiteboard. The survivors are so comfortable with each other and what they all want to get done that any improvisation based on outcomes saves the day.

[16]Nag, A., 2021. "Everybody has a plan until they get punched in the mouth." How did the famous Mike Tyson quote originate? Sportskeeda.

Let's take a look at two case studies to highlight the point; these are two approaches that demonstrate each end of the spectrum of what to do correctly and what not to do: the RSA Security breach of 2011 and the Equifax breach of 2017.

RSA Security: A Case Study in Crisis Communications

In the spring of 2011, intelligence analysts working for RSA Security (an EMC company at the time) noticed that something was amiss with the permissions and behavior for one of their Australian employee accounts.[17, 18] The subsequent investigation revealed a massive cyber espionage operation conducted by the as-yet unnamed Chinese adversary group APT1 (the People's Liberation Army Unit 61398). Mandiant wouldn't anoint them their name until two years later.[19]

APT1 hackers had managed to phish the Australian employee, used his account as a beachhead, and then moved laterally through the RSA Security network, escalating privilege, and looking for the data they wanted to steal. In this case, according to Andy Greenberg at Wired, the seed values for the RSA SecurID token product, the two-factor authentication device were used by "tens of millions of users in government and military agencies, defense contractors, banks, and countless corporations around the world."[17] With those seed values, APT1 could bypass the two-factor authentication system in all of them.

---

[17]Greenberg, A., 2021b. The Full Story of the Stunning RSA Hack Can Finally Be Told [WWW Document]. WIRED. www.wired.com/story/the-full-story-of-the-stunning-rsa-hack-can-finally-be-told (accessed 12/18/22).

[18]Bell, S., 2011. Lessons From the RSA Breach [WWW Document]. CSO Online. www.csoonline.com/article/2129794/lessons-from-the-rsa-breach.html (accessed 12/4/22).

[19]"APT1: Exposing One of China's Cyber Espionage Units | Mandiant." Mandiant.com, 2013.

APT1, through this bold cyber espionage campaign, rendered inert this security device that 760 customers worldwide had purchased, distributed, installed, and maintained to reduce their attack surface for government secrets, financial data, and other sensitive information.

If I were one of those customers, I would've been angry, and I would have been actively seeking RSA Security's biggest competitor to kick the SecurID token product to the curb and install a new system that I could trust. When you're in the business of selling security specifically designed to protect secrets, your own systems where you keep your secrets had better be airtight. I imagine that's what many RSA Security customers were thinking at the time. According to the *New York Times*, some big-ticket customers said publicly that they planned to switch vendors as soon as possible: Bank of America, JPMorgan Chase, Wells Fargo, and Citigroup.[20, 21]

But then, the RSA Security leadership team executed a crisis communication plan to save the company. According to Greenberg, within a week, "One person in legal suggested they didn't need to tell their customers." The CEO at the time, Art Coviello, wasn't having any of that. "He slammed a fist on the table: they would not only admit to the breach, he insisted, but get on the phone with every single customer to discuss how those companies could protect themselves." When somebody on the staff suggested they codename the crisis plan as Project Phoenix, Coviello rejected it. "We're not rising from the ashes. We're going to call this project Apollo 13. We're going to land the ship without injury."

---

[20]Staff, 2011. What did the RSA breach end up costing EMC? [WWW Document]. Help Net Security. www.helpnetsecurity.com/2011/07/28/what-did-the-rsa-breach-end-up-costing-emc (accessed 12/4/22).
[21]Schwartz, N.D., Drew, C., 2011. RSA Security Faces Angry Users Over Breach. The New York Times.

And that's what they did.

They immediately filed a form 8-K with the Securities and Exchange Commission, a report of an unscheduled material event. The next day, according to Greenberg, "Coviello published an open letter to RSA's customers on the company's website" and created a group of 90 staffers who began arranging one-on-one calls with all of their customers. Coviello and his senior staff attended hundreds of these calls personally.

In the end, it worked. In the second quarter earnings call of 2011, EMC reported that their internal incident response cost was about $66 million.[22] By the end of the third quarter, though, according to CSO Online, EMC reported record earnings; so much for the fear of reputation loss due to a cyber event. But, I can make a strong case here to attribute that quick recovery, that resilience, to the crisis communications plan led by the CEO, Art Coviello.

RSA Security (EMC) experienced a black swan event, a phrase made famous by Nassim Taleb in his 2007 book, *The Black Swan: The Impact of the Highly Improbable*.[23] Black swan events are so unlikely that you never expect to be affected by one (like a meteor hitting the earth), but the impact is catastrophic when they do happen. This was EMC's black swan event. By all rights, the company shouldn't have recovered from it. Customers should have left the company in droves. But that's not what happened. Because of Coviello's stated support of his customers and laser focus, most customers stayed with the company after the crisis when they had

---

[22]Staff, 2011. SecurID data breach cost RSA $66 million-so how much did it cost you? [WWW Document]. SecurEnvoy. securenvoy.com/blog/securid-data-breach-cost-rsa-66-million-so-how-much-did-it-cost-you-asks-securenvoy (accessed 12/4/22).

[23]Taleb, N.N., 2010. The Black Swan: Second Edition: The Impact of the Highly Improbable: With a new section: "On Robustness and Fragility." Random House Trade Paperbacks.

plenty of reasons to leave. RSA Security didn't have a crisis plan before the incident, but after the CEO took charge, he set the direction, and his team executed. He was so clear on the desired outcome (Project Apollo versus Project Phoenix) that all internal company energy focused on it and succeeded beyond what anybody would have predicted.

Consider the opposite end of the spectrum: the Equifax breach of 2017.

Equifax: A Case Study in Crisis Communications

On March 10, 2017, Chinese hackers (members of the 54th Research Institute, a component of China's People's Liberation Army) established a beachhead within the Equifax networks.[24] The Equifax internal security team didn't discover the intrusion until more than three months later at the end of July. Immediately, they hired Mandiant as an outside incident response team. Mandiant eventually discovered that Equifax had lost the personally identifiable information (PII) to some 60 percent of all Americans (143 million U.S. consumers).[25]

The Equifax CEO, Rick Smith, decided to sit on that information for more than a month but eventually went public on September 7.[26] He announced what has become the traditional handwave of support to his customers for public breach

[24]Staff, 2020. Chinese Hackers Charged in Equifax Breach [WWW Document]. Federal Bureau of Investigation. www.fbi.gov/news/stories/chinese-hackers-charged-in-equifax-breach-021020 (accessed 12/4/22).
[25]Staff, 2017. The Equifax Credit Breach Timeline: What Happened? The Eichholz Law Firm. www.thejusticelawyer.com/blog/the-equifax-credit-breach-timeline-what-happened (accessed 12/4/22).
[26]Weidlich, T., 2017. Equifax Engages in Almost Wholly Reactive Crisis Communications [WWW Document]. prcg. prcg.com/blog/equifax-engages-almost-wholly-reactive-crisis-communications (accessed 12/4/22).

announcements: free credit monitoring, a website for information, and a call center for customer questions—you know, thoughts and prayers but nothing of value. And he kept piecemealing the information to the public in dribs and drabs over weeks. It felt as if, from the start, that Smith was making it up as he was going along. The message was at best confusing and at worst opaque and misleading.

Three days later, customers discovered they could get the "coveted" free credit monitoring service, but only if they agreed they wouldn't sue the company later. By September 15, Smith fired the CIO (Susan Mauldin) and the CSO (David Webb).[27] On September 21, the breach information website was still not ready, so the company started directing customers and journalists to a white-hat phishing site specifically intended to test the company's security response. By September 26, the Equifax board fired the CEO.[28] In March of the following year, the Securities and Exchange Commission secured the indictment of Jun Ying, the replacement CIO, for using the not-as-yet public breach information to sell his vested Equifax stock options.[29] It had come to seem that the entire Equifax culture was made up of opacity and used-car-salesman chicanery. The leadership team didn't prioritize protecting the PII that they had collected on over half the American population and thus didn't have a disaster recovery plan in place before the incident. If they had a business continuity plan or a crisis communications plan, either it was weak or they chose to ignore it.

---

[27]Popken, B., 2017. Equifax Execs Resign; Security Head, Mauldin, Was Music Major. NBC News.
[28]Arnold, C., 2017. Equifax CEO Richard Smith Resigns After Backlash Over Massive Data Breach. NPR.
[29]Staff, 2018. Former Equifax employee indicted for insider trading [WWW Document]. Department of Justice. www.justice.gov/usao-ndga/pr/former-equifax-employee-indicted-insider-trading (accessed 12/18/22).

During that period between the breach and Smith's firing, many outside observers agreed that Smith bungled the communications plan.[30, 31]

- He waited six weeks before he announced.
- He chose not to reach out to customers specifically, instead setting up a website, which wasn't ready for weeks after the announcement.
- He offered free credit monitoring but required enrollees to waive their right to sue.
- He changed his mind later, but customers had to send Equifax written notice of their decision within 30 days. But the written opt-out language from its general terms of service was wrong.
- He initially charged customers impacted for the service of freezing credit.
- Equifax assigned easy-to-guess PINs to people who froze their credit.

In the end, at least four executives lost their jobs, and the U.S. House Digital Commerce and Consumer Protection subcommittee hauled Rick Smith in to explain himself. Then, in May 2019, Equifax reported that the incident response cost was roughly $1.4 billion plus legal fees.[32]

---

[30]Staff, 2017. Equifax: An Epic Fail In Crisis Communications [WWW Document]. Strategic Vision PR Group. www.strategicvisionpr.com/equifax-epic-fail-crisis-communications (accessed 12/4/22).
[31]Wiener-Bronner, D., 2017. Equifax turned its hack into a public relations catastrophe [WWW Document]. CNNMoney. money.cnn.com/2017/09/12/news/companies/equifax-pr-response/index.html (accessed 12/4/22).
[32]Schwartz, M., 2013. Equifax's Data Breach Costs Hit $1.4 Billion [WWW Document]. BankInfoSecurity. www.bankinfosecurity.com/equifaxs-data-breach-costs-hit-14-billion-a-12473 (accessed 12/18/22).

Like RSA Security, Equifax's black swan event didn't kill the company either but for a completely different reason. Clearly its crisis communication plan was disastrous compared to RSA Security, but the 143 million American victims were not Equifax's customers. According to Lily Newman at Wired, Equifax and its two other competitors (Experian and TransUnion) are commodity consumer data sellers.[33] This means the victims had no choice about which of these companies held their data. In other words, the victims didn't pay Equifax for products and services rendered. According to Kate Fazzini at CNBC, "Equifax is a credit bureau gathering and collating data about each U.S. citizen for the purpose of selling it to creditors and lenders. They collect the information from various sources (some paid and some free), and then they use algorithms to calculate a credit score."[34] Unlike RSA Security, Equifax didn't have to appease angry customers.

Equifax's stock price (EFX) dipped by 13 percent after the public announcement, but by March 2020 it had rebounded and continued to grow. According to Dennis Cannon at the Rice-Properties website, Equifax today has more than 10,000 employees worldwide and generates $3.1 billion in annual revenue.[35] So, the company survived, but the leadership team didn't.

Desired Outcomes

The desired-outcomes idea leads us back to the atomic cybersecurity first principle: reduce the probability of material impact. Here's the

---

[33]Newman, L.H., 2018. Equifax's Security Overhaul, a Year After Its Epic Breach. WIRED.

[34]Fazzini, K., 2019. The great Equifax mystery: 17 months later, the stolen data has never been found, and experts are starting to suspect a spy scheme. CNBC.

[35]Cannon, D., 2022. What happened to Equifax after the data breach? [WWW Document]. Rice-Properties. rice-properties.com/qa/what-happened-to-equifax-after-the-data-breach.html (accessed 12/18/22).

thing. During a cyber crisis, your black swan event, resilience is the only strategy that matters now. If you're in a cybersecurity crisis, it means your other first principle strategies failed. None of them prevented the crisis from happening. So, now what? We can talk about what went wrong with these strategies after the crisis. In the meantime, where should leaders focus?

Going back to the Stirna and Zdravkovic definition, crisis leaders should concentrate on continuing to deliver whatever service they offer to their most valuable customers. In the RSA Security case in 2011, that meant senior leadership, including the CEO, talking to customers individually, apologizing for the mistake, and providing valuable assistance in helping each customer respond to the incident. Check! For Equifax in 2017, I'm not sure what it was trying to do.

Reviewing the literature on both attacks, it's unclear that either of the companies had a formal crisis plan before their black swan event. Instead, the difference in outcomes stems from Coviello's leadership setting the desired outcome and the plan to get there from the start: "We're going to land the ship without injury." Essentially, he drew a stick figure plan on a whiteboard and ensured that his team executed. In contrast, Equifax's Smith was all over the map with inconsistency and a plan that changed significantly throughout the period.

Executives Are Busy: Exercise Them Efficiently

Ensuring that the executive leadership team is on the same page regarding desired outcomes before a cyber crisis is difficult. So, how do you do it? As violinist Mischa Elman said, when two New York City tourists asked him how to get to Carnegie Hall, he replied, "Practice."[36] Whether you have a 100-page strategic plan or a

[36]Carlson, M., 2020. The Joke [WWW Document]. Carnegie Hall. www .carnegiehall.org/Explore/Articles/2020/04/10/The-Joke (accessed 12/18/22).

whiteboard stick figure plan, walking the senior leadership team through various scenarios to get their reactions and reaffirm the desired outcomes is key.

It's my experience that large organizations execute at least one formal scenario exercise a year. Some do several where they dust off the plan, bounce a scenario off it (like ransomware, cyber espionage, or cyber hacktivism), and get the senior leadership team's reaction to it. The priority is to make them aware of the various resilience tactical measures you already have in place that might mitigate the event, such as incident response, backups, and encryption. During the exercise, gaps will be found in your tactics that you hadn't thought of before, which is totally acceptable and desired. Indeed, it's one of the main reasons to run the exercises. More important, though, you will get your senior leadership team's reactions to those gaps and their desire to close them.

In every one of these exercises in my career, I have always learned something new. Either the plan was not clear enough, the plan was wrong about how to handle some detail, or some senior executive objected to what we were trying to do with the plan. The point of these exercises, however, is not to run the leadership team through every possible scenario. The point is to get them all making decisions that will support the desired outcome regardless of the given scenario and regardless if the stated plan is tossed out as soon as we get punched in the mouth. In other words, practice not the scenario, but the outcome.

These scenario exercises don't have to be that formal. The senior leadership team is busy. Getting them to commit to an afternoon of exercise play once a year is a tremendous act of scheduling deconfliction, convincing them that this is a good use of their time, and making do when some have to drop out at the last second because a fire pops up that requires immediate attention. Even if the CEO is totally committed to the exercise, which is not always a given, things happen. But there are simpler approaches.

One that I have used with some success in the past is an extended lunch (maybe 90 minutes) with the senior leadership team. The purpose is to drop a scenario on the table during the meal, remind everybody the desired outcomes are based on the current plan and previous scenario lunches, and get their reaction. As they discuss what they would be doing during each phase of the scenario, the exercise crisis team leader would be interjecting what the rest of the company would be doing based on the current plan using the responsibility assignment matrix.

The beauty of this approach is that even senior executives like a free meal, and this is not a huge time commitment for them. And it's informal. People are more likely to throw ideas around when you are all sharing the same salad. Further, this is a good approach for small- to medium-sized organizations as well.

Feel free to invite outside parties to the exercise too, like agents from your local FBI field office and even your auditor team. In the FBI case, you don't want to be meeting your representatives for the first time during an actual crisis. The exercise gives your entire organization a chance to get to know them and to learn what services they might be able to offer during the real thing. For the auditor case, the exercise allows you to show the team in a nonadversarial environment how your organization follows the plan they audited. It's adversarial when they do the actual audit, but in the exercise, it's a nod for inclusion as part of the team and their observations and suggestions can help make the plan better. Lastly, if the organization ever faces a lawsuit because of some cyber event, the FBI and auditors participation can help defend against it.

To have any hope of successfully executing our resilience strategy, practice makes perfect. Give your senior executives a lot of chances to make decisions that further the desired outcome before the actual black swan event happens. As the saying goes, you don't want them to be thinking about this stuff for the first time during a real crisis.

You want them comfortable making the right calls in these crisis situations. And that's what cybersecurity crisis handling gives you.

Backups: A Tactic for Resilience

About 15 years ago, I set up the backup scheme for the Howard family data set. Digital was just starting to become mainstream, and we had all of these electronic artifacts scattered across mobile phones, digital cameras (remember those?), and the family home computer. Between five people (the wife, the two daughters, and one son), it was starting to get out of hand. I realized some of these items, like precious videos of my daughters leaping across the stage in their dance studio production of the *Lion King* and 20 years of tax files, just to name two, might be worth spending the time to get organized in one place and then backing the data up so that one catastrophe didn't wipe everything out.

As an aside, by the time the family wrapped the production of the *Lion King*, we had spent enormous resources in terms of the purchase of costumes, dance rehearsal time, and backstage prep time. And make no mistake, it was a full-court press on family participation. The two daughters were in something like a thousand numbers combined, Mom was the backstage coordinator, and my son and I were security (which meant we spent a lot of time directing traffic in the local high school parking lot). At the end of the production, we treated the entire family to a Disney World trip for a job well done. And there we were in the middle of Disney's Animal Kingdom, at the intersection of the Pangani Forest Exploration Trail and the Wildlife Express Train, when a bunch of Disney street performers began singing and dancing to the *Lion King* soundtrack and asking patrons to join. And oh my god, this was going to be the perfect Kodak moment. Right? My two daughters had just spent the last six months perfecting the aforementioned thousand Lion King dance numbers. They were going to kill this. Video camera in hand, I started recording. Alas, to my great frustration, all I got were two embarrassed teenagers swaying back and forth as awkward as if they just learned to walk and chew gum last Tuesday. They weren't even swaying in time with the music.

I think that's my all-time favorite video of my two daughters and their dancing career. Clearly, I needed to make sure that no computer catastrophe would cause me to lose that video and all the other digital detritus that we had collected over the years. I went to work.

Not only did I build a scheme that would automatically upload a copy of all of our files to one of the early cloud providers, I also built a local RAID array for my home system. If any one disk in the array failed, I could remove it and stick in a brand new one. Nobody would be the wiser. This system was foolproof. I had backups of backups.

About a year later, the inevitable catastrophe happened. The hard drive for my home computer failed, and I couldn't get it to come back online. My wife gave me that panicked, "What about all of my files" look. Smugly, I just looked back at her saying, "Not to worry. I have backups." After building a new computer, I went to my cloud provider to restore the data. Much to my horror, none of the data was there. I couldn't believe it. There wasn't a single video, picture, or TurboTax file anywhere in the cloud. And that's when my own panic started to creep in. But then I remembered the RAID array. That was my backup to my backup plan. I could restore from there.

All I can say is I had a great plan and failed completely in execution. Oh, I had a cloud backup system in place and routinely checked that the system was saving all of my files there. And I had a RAID array where I made sure to make a backup copy of the backup files. My failure stemmed from where I told the two systems to back up. Apparently, I configured it so that every day, my backup system copied an empty directory and not the directory where everything was stored. Every week or so I would check to ensure the system was working, and every week I would get the green light, with everything A-OK.

I'm embarrassed to admit that to get my files back, I had to pay the Geek Squad down at the local Best Buy to recover the corrupted files on the home computer. The experience was, shall we say, humbling, and 15 years later, that's the one story my wife loves to tell to family and friends when they start asking questions about my storied cybersecurity career. It goes something like this. "Ya, let me tell you about my husband and his big fancy pants cybersecurity career when he lost all of the family data for the past 20 years."

So, in the immortal words of Bill Murray in one of my favorite movies, *Caddy Shack*, "I got that going for me." The lesson learned here is that if a plan is not exercised, it is almost guaranteed to fail.

Backups As a Strategy Against Ransomware

It's interesting to note the evolution of ransomware over the last decade. When ransomware first started, the target victim was the home user. Cybercriminals would compromise Grandma's computer, encrypt the hard drive, call her on the phone, and tell her that if she wanted her cherished pictures of cats and grandkids back, she would have to pay $500 in bitcoin.

The back-end business systems these ransomware groups developed to make this model work was, and is, astonishing. Call-center employees, mostly working out of Russia, would call the grandmas of the world, explain what they did to her computer (encryption), articulate what she needed to do to fix it and what it would cost her, walk her through creating a bitcoin account, handhold her through the process of transferring money into her bitcoin account from her bank, and then show her how to transfer those bitcoins into the ransomware gang's bitcoin wallet, all in a second language.

The preferred target victim changed sometime in 2017. Nicole Perlroth, *New York Times* journalist and author of Cybersecurity Canon Hall of Fame Candidate *This Is How They Tell Me the World Ends*, said that after the North Koreans launched WannaCry in the summer of 2017 and one month later the Russians launched NotPetya, the ransomware gangs realized that there was a much more lucrative revenue stream to tap into: the corporate world.[37] Instead of working hard for a $500 payout from Grandma, the average ask, as of this writing, is north of millions of dollars from the corporate world.

The FBI said in 2021 that they were tracking at least 100 unique ransomware groups.[38] That tracks with the back-of-the-envelope forecast that we did in Chapter 4 for all CAMM groups (criminals, activists, and mischief makers); it's slightly higher but in the same ballpark. That's not a lot of criminal gangs, but the price tag to you if your organization gets caught in the crosshairs is high. According to a

---

[37]Perlroth, N., 2021. This Is How They Tell Me the World Ends: Winner of the FT & McKinsey Business Book of the Year Award 2021. Bloomsbury Publishing.

[38]Collier, K., 2021. FBI tracking more than 100 active ransomware groups. NBC News.

study that Sophos did in 2021, "The average cost to recover from the most recent ransomware attack in 2021 was $1.4 million."[39] But we have seen the costs to recover from a ransomware attack go much higher. According to Andy Greenberg in his Cybersecurity Canon Hall of Fame book *Sandworm*, the total recovery costs for the 2017 NotPetya attacks for all the victims combined topped out at $10 billion.[40]

As the new corporate model evolved, ransomware criminals found at least four ways to generate revenue from their new victims.

1. Payment to unencrypt the data. This doesn't mean they intend to give you the key that will unlock everything, just that they intend to charge you for it.
2. Payment to not make the stolen data public. Again, this doesn't mean they won't eventually do it, just that they will charge you for the service anyway.
3. Payment to not sell the stolen data to competitors (slightly different than a public release).
4. Even after receiving payments on revenue streams 1–3, sell the stolen data anyway to whomever wants it.

Encrypting your material data (see the next section) protects you from revenue streams 2–4. If your material data is encrypted, it's not worth anything to outside parties because they won't be able to read it. But that leaves us with revenue stream 1. Encryption doesn't work here because the ransomware criminals will just encrypt your already encrypted data. They don't have to read it to make it unusable to the

---

[39]Adam, S.S.A., 2022. The State of Ransomware 2022 [WWW Document]. Sophos News. news.sophos.com/en-us/2022/04/27/the-state-of-ransomware-2022 (accessed 12/18/22).
[40]Greenberg, A., 2020. Sandworm: A New Era of Cyberwar and the Hunt for the Kremlin's Most Dangerous Hackers. Anchor.

victim organization. The only way to protect against revenue stream 1 is a one-two punch of backing material data up and being proficient at restoring that data when a crisis emerges. Like encryption, that's a lot easier to say than it is to do.

For most of us, our data is scattered across multiple data islands (mobile devices, SaaS applications, data centers, and hybrid cloud environments). There is no easy button anywhere that will back up your material data on all of these islands and magically restore it all if some catastrophe happens. You have to build that system, refine it, and exercise it. One way to reduce the complexity, though, is to concentrate only on material data. Network defenders don't have to back up and restore all of the data that your organization generates, just the data that's material to your business. This focus can drastically reduce the problem set, but depending on your organization, the complexity of this first principle task could range from slight to chaotic. Still, as a general rule, let's not waste resources on things that we don't need.

Further, in this age of infrastructure as code, don't forget that the software that you are using to run your critical business systems is also data. Ransomware crews can corrupt that collection as well as your customer database. When I say critical data, I mean all of it—all of the data that lubricates the system and all of the software that uses that data to keep the business running, the commercial applications that you pay for, the code you develop in-house, and the open-source software that you pull down from GitHub.

To back up all of that material data, tactics generally come in three forms: centralized backup platforms, one-off decentralized backup systems, and internal automation as part of the critical business application (DevOps). Many organizations use a hybrid approach, with bits and pieces from all three.

Option 1: Centralized Backup Platforms for All Data Islands

According to the June 2021 Gartner quad chart on enterprise backup and recovery platforms, there are a number of companies that offer these kinds of backup services.[41] Most claim the capability of backing up and restoring files and software stored in virtual workloads (such as VMware and Hyper-V), hybrid cloud environments (such as Google, Amazon, and Microsoft), specific SaaS applications (such as SAP and Exchange), and storage devices (like NetApp and Nutanix). You can install them in the cloud or run them from your own data centers. With this kind of model, one organization within your business is responsible for maintaining the system. In other words, one business unit, say, the IT shop, would keep the blinky lights blinking. Other business units would provide input into the specific backup policies. These systems are not cheap, though, and probably reserved for the larger organizations that can afford them. For the small- and medium-sized organizations, network defenders will have to be more prudent.

Option 2: One-Off Decentralized Backup Systems

By decentralization I mean that you might consider backup and restoration solutions designed for the specific material data sets that you are worried about. If your company's intellectual property secret sauce is stored in an Amazon cloud instance, for example, you might consider using its backup solutions for that instance. The same goes for all the other cloud services. For your data centers, if you are using a commercial storage device, you might consider using its disaster

[41] Mellor, C., 2021. Gartner dumps IBM from 2021 enterprise backup'n'recovery MQ leader corner. The Register.

recovery service. They all have some version of this. The point is that instead of having just one backup and restore platform that handles the tasks for all material data stored across all data islands, you would run specific backup and restore solutions for each material data set. This is more complex because you have to manage multiple vendor solutions. More things can go wrong. But for small to midsize organizations, this might be more affordable.

Option 3: DevOps (DevSecOps) for Each Application

The DevSecOps plan would be to include backup and restore capability whenever you roll out a new application as infrastructure as code. This is how the big companies (such as Google, Netflix, and Salesforce) do it. From the Cybersecurity Canon Hall of Fame book *Site Reliability Engineering: How Google Runs Production Systems,* deploying backup systems is part of the task.[10] Google's SREs apply computer science and engineering to "the design and development of computing systems." In other words, they are looking to build reliable solutions, and backups and restore operations are a key part of it. "Traditionally, companies protect data against loss by investing in backup strategies. However, the real focus of such backup efforts should be data recovery, which distinguishes real backups from archives. As is sometimes observed: no one really wants to make backups; what people really want are restores."

Fortune 500 companies have development resources to do this, but even startups building the new SaaS applications are infrastructure-as-code companies. They have development resources on hand to take on this task. Senior leadership just needs to direct them to do it as part of the service the product offers to the customers. The organizations that might have trouble with this option are older companies that are in the range of small to medium in size and have yet to embrace the DevOps model (see Chapter 7) or even the cloud model. They will likely be stuck with the first two options.

How Do You Get to Carnegie Hall? Practice

As with the crisis handling tactic, the only way to become proficient at backup and recovery operations is to practice. Like Google SREs, remember that you're not done before you have actually practiced the restoration process and you're sure that you can deliver the intended outcome with the new, reinstated data. This is the thing that you have to iterate on. You have to be so good at this that it becomes second nature. When the crisis comes, you don't want to be figuring out how to do it on the fly. And, if you have confidence in your ability to restore, when the discussions of "Do we pay the ransom?" comes up on the leadership team, the answer becomes an easy no because you have demonstrated to them over and over again that you can restore the systems yourself.

Encryption: A Tactic for Resilience

Every time I revisit this subject of encryption, I feel like I have to relearn the definitions again. My senior moment brain can't seem to keep them all straight. In a nod to one of my favorite superhero movies of all time, *Spiderman into the Spiderverse*, when all the multidimensional spider people take turns explaining their origin story by saying, "All right, let's do this one last time," let's do this one more time for cryptography.

- *Cryptography*: (Rhymes with photography.) This is the art and science of code making.
- *Encryption*: Converts plain text into an unrecognizable form using the ciphers that the cryptographers make. For the purposes of this book, I'm including techniques like data masking and database tokenization as ways to hide data from prying eyes.
- *Signing*: Uses trapdoor or mathematical one-way functions from cryptography for nonrepudiation. In other words, signed

message or file authors can't deny that they signed it, and it's mathematically improbable for a third party to forge a signature.

- *Keys*: A string of characters used within a cryptographic function to transform plain text into cipher text, or back. Like a physical key, it locks data so that only someone with the right key can unlock it.
- *Cryptanalysis*: The reverse of cryptography. It's all the things you do to break the codes (like Alan Turing using Bayes' rule to break the German Enigma coding machines in WWII; see Chapter 6).
- And just to make things more confusing, cryptology captures both disciplines: cryptography and cryptanalysis.

As an aside, for the computer gamers out there, if you think you might like to try your hand at cryptology, there is a lovely little first-person computer game called *CYpHER* where you walk through a museum of cryptology and solve the multiple puzzles provided in various forms of cryptanalysis.

- Steganography
- Transposition
- Mono alphabetic substitution
- Poly alphabetic substitution
- Mechanized cryptography
- Digital cryptography

I got as far as the first puzzle before I got stumped, but hey, this might be your thing.

The cryptography idea has been around since the world was young. According to the Thales Group, the Spartans around 600 BC used a device called a scytale to code plain text into encrypted messages.[42] For their Spartan friends to decode the messages on the other side, they needed an identical scytale in terms of width and length. By 60 BC, the Romans used a simple substitution cipher where they encoded messages by shifting the letter by some agreed-upon number. For example, if the number was 3, the plain text of the letter *A* becomes an encoded letter *D*, the plain-text *B* becomes an encoded *E*, and so forth. Fast-forward to 1553 AD, Giovan Battista Bellaso introduced the idea of a secret key or password that two parties would need to encrypt and decrypt messages. In other words, if Fred and Ginger want to exchange secret messages, they both would have to have the secret key. Fred would encode the message with the key, and Ginger would decode it with the same secret key.

By 1917, an American named Edward Hebern had invented an electro-mechanical machine in which the key was embedded in a rotating disc.[43] The next year, 1918, German engineer Arthur Scherbius invented the Enigma machine using more than one rotor, and the German military adopted it to send coded transmissions during WWI and WWII (see Chapter 7 for a detailed description of how the Enigma machine worked).[44]

---

[42]Staff, n.d. A brief history of encryption (and cryptography) [WWW Document]. Thales Group. www.thalesgroup.com/en/markets/digital-identity-and-security/magazine/brief-history-encryption (accessed 12/4/22).
[43]Staff, 2020. Hebern Cryptographic Rotor Machine [WWW Document]. Crypto-IT. www.crypto-it.net/eng/simple/hebern-machine.html?tab=0 (accessed 12/18/22).
[44]Perera, T., 2016. ENIGMA Technology and the History of Computers [WWW Document]. Enigma Museum. enigmamuseum.com/enigma-computer (accessed 12/18/22).

By the 1970s, IBM invented a block cypher.[45] Instead of using multiple letters as the Enigma rotors did, the key is an entire block of text. The U.S. government adopted this model, the IBM Data Encryption Standard (DES), in 1973 and used it until it was broken in 1997.[46]

In 1976, Whitfield Diffie and Martin Hellman created the Diffie-Hellman key exchange, making it possible to send encrypted messages without having to share a secret key beforehand. This was huge.[47] It's called *asymmetric encryption*, and it's the main idea behind all modern secure web transactions. There is a public key that anybody in the world can use to encrypt a message to Ginger. But Ginger is the only one that has the secret key that can decrypt any messages sent to her with the public key. The two keys (public and private) are mathematically linked, but it's computationally impossible to use the public key to read the encrypted message.

The next year (1977), the team of Ron Rivest, Adi Shamir, and Leonard Adleman (RSA) created the first working algorithm of the Diffie-Hellman key exchange. By 2000, the Advanced Encryption Standard (AES) replaced DES as the standard by being faster and having the ability to use much longer keys.

Data at Rest and Data in Motion

We use encryption in two ways: data at rest and for data in motion. Data at rest is stored on some hard drive somewhere. Nobody is moving it, and nobody is processing it. It's just sitting there for some

---

[45]Staff, n.d. Block Ciphers Modes of Operation [WWW Document]. Crypto-IT. www.crypto-it.net/eng/theory/modes-of-block-ciphers.html (accessed 12/18/22).

[46]Simmons, G.J., 2009. Data Encryption Standard. Encyclopedia Britannica.

[47]Levy, S., 2001. Crypto: How the Code Rebels Beat the Government—Saving Privacy in the Digital Age. National Geographic Books.

future purpose. Data in motion is being moved between point A and point B, as it is when a website delivers content to a user or an email message travels from sender to receiver. It's also when we are processing it somehow like when we search through a database or when we are running machine learning algorithms on a data set.

When you say it like that, it makes complete sense that you would encrypt both data at rest and data in motion. How hard could it be? But that's how they get you. After you think about it for more than two seconds, you realize that the permutations for all of the things that have to be signed and encrypted grow exponentially. For every physical device that touches those data islands, for every workload that operates in a cloud environment, for every person who uses those devices and workloads, and for every transaction between people and technology, there is potential for some kind of cryptographic transformation.

When I say cryptographic transformation, that means that somewhere in the process, some algorithm is generating a key, applying a key, saving a key, using a key, changing a key, or decommissioning a key for every transaction, every device, and every person across all of your data islands. The unremitting volume and pace of these essential digital operations is enough to make security executives curl up into a fetal position in the SOC murmuring to themselves, "I hope it all works. I hope it all works." Gartner's David Mahdi and Brian Lowans, in a paper they wrote in 2020, said that security executives "struggle to understand the capabilities and limitations that encryption key management (EKM) solutions provide, and how to properly configure them."[48] They implied that most of us don't have a comprehensive encryption policy nor a global plan. They speculated that at best our approaches are piecemeal and

---

[48]Mahdi, D., Lowans, B., 2020. Gartner Report: Develop an Enterprisewide Encryption Key Management Strategy or Lose the Data, Fortanix.

on a case-by-case basis as opportunities arise. They noticed that in most cases, the encryption process and policy are not organizational imperatives.

The good news is that we can reduce the problem size by dealing only with material data. Unfortunately, that doesn't reduce the complexity. Orchestrating encryption solutions for your material data across all of those data islands with all of those permutations is still intricate, knotty, and, dare I say, labyrinthine. The scary part is that most of us have been trying to do it ourselves manually. And because of the diverse array of data silos across all of the data islands, investment in multiple encryption products is required. We design our own homegrown software tools using collections of open-source and commercial software. We might even attempt to tie into some of the cloud key management SaaS services from the likes of Google, Microsoft, and AWS. There hasn't been any sort of comprehensive encryption platform that works across all data islands. But that soon may be changing. According to Mahdi and Lowans, enterprise key management is on the Gartner slope of enlightenment but 5 to 10 years away from the plateau of productivity.

The First Principle Encryption Tactic Is Recursive

A subtle point here is that whatever systems and processes you are using to encrypt your organization's data, those systems and processes by definition become material in a recursive kind of way. You use the encryption system to protect your sensitive data, but because the encryption system is critical to the process, it's also material to the organization. If a bad guy compromises your encryption system in some way, then everything you're trying to protect with it is compromised.

A case in point is the SolarWinds backdoor attack that started in December 2020.[49] It's probably the most famous supply chain attack in recent memory, but the damage to its victims didn't come from the injected backdoor of the SolarWinds platform. That was just the hackers behind the UNC2452 campaign establishing the beachhead on the more than 18,000 victims. The damages came later for roughly 40 victims as the hackers moved laterally within their networks looking for administrator credentials. UNC2452 hackers compromised the cloud token authorization process that allowed them to generate keys that give them legitimate access to cloud resources. In case you're keeping score at home, that's bad.

As such, reducing the probability of this kind of attack against your encryption system is accomplished by following the same first principle strategies that we use to protect all our other material assets.

For Zero Trust (See Chapter 3)

- Centralized key management. Don't leave this process in the hands of the individual teams that need it. It will never be their first priority.
- Limit the number of administrator accounts that can generate keys to the absolute minimum.
- Watch those accounts like a hawk.
- Add quorum authorization, i.e., not just one account required to authorize key generation, but several.

[49]Staff, 2022. Here Are 24 Reported Victims Of The SolarWinds Hack (So Far) [WWW Document]. PanaTimes. panatimes.com/here-are-24-reported-victims-of-the-solarwinds-hack-so-far (accessed 12/4/22).

For Intrusion Chain Prevention (See Chapter 4):

- As of this writing, the MITRE ATT&CK framework describes the Weak Encryption (ID T1600) technique as adversary groups compromising "a network device's encryption capability in order to bypass encryption that would otherwise protect data communications."
- APT32, a suspected Vietnamese state-sponsored adversary campaign and the UNC2452 campaign, are at least two that use this technique. Blocking the entire attack sequence across the intrusion kill chain for these two campaigns, and any other that uses the technique in the future, would be prudent.

Resilience (This Chapter)

- A fully deployed encryption system is the plumbing for delivering the must-have "magic" that your customers demand. If the plumbing fails, you can't deliver the magic.
- Design the encryption system to survive a catastrophic failure in the same way you have already designed the resilient system for delivering the magic.

Risk Forecasting (See Chapter 6)

- Include in your model a way to account for deploying your first principle strategies against the encryption system. (This will make more sense when you read Chapter 7.)
- Your probability of material impact should go down for each step that you deploy. In other words, what's the probability without any safeguards? What's the probability of a partially deployed zero trust program? What's the probability of a fully deployed zero trust program? Incorporate this same step-by-step process for the intrusion kill chain strategy and the resilience strategy.

- Be sure to weigh the cost of each step as you go to see if it is justified against the risk culture of your board and your senior leaders.

In the earlier section on backup and restores as a first principle tactic, I said that encryption was the best way to reduce the impact of a ransomware attack for three of the four revenue streams.

- Payment to not make the stolen data public.
- Payment to not sell the stolen data to competitors (slightly different than a public release).
- Even after receiving payments on all revenue streams, sell the stolen data anyway to whomever wants it.

It's also the best first principle tactic to combat any kind of cyber espionage (corporate or government secrets). You can't steal secrets if you can't read them.

Backup and encryption operations are passive resilience first principle tactics. What I mean by that is that security leaders deploy them before the cyber event happens to protect the organization from any kind of cyberattack in the future. The tactic required when the attack is actually happening right now is incident response.

Incident Response: A Tactic for Resilience

It was the early days of the Internet (late 1980s): no AOL, no World Wide Web, no always-on Internet connection at your house. If you wanted to connect, you most likely drove into the office at your university or your military base. If you connected from home, you used a dial-up modem over your existing phone line to make the connection to one of the only 60,000 computers on the Internet at the time. By contrast, some experts estimate the number of Internet-connected devices will reach 75 billion by 2025. The internet wasn't a thing yet for the masses, but it was vitally important for government and research institutions.

> At the witching hour on November 3, 1988, I was working late in my Navy-housing apartment trying to get a program working for my data structures class at the Naval Postgraduate school in Monterey, California. The deadline for the assignment was just three hours away, but I couldn't get my 2,400 baud modem to connect to the university's modem bank, and I was starting to panic. Little did I know that, just after midnight, a 23-year-old Cornell University graduate student named Robert Tappan Morris would bring the Internet to its knees. He had launched the first ever Internet worm, and for at least some days after, the Internet ceased to function as UNIX wizards of all stripes across the globe worked to eradicate the worm from their systems.

As I mentioned in Chapter 4, the Morris worm caused the Defense Advanced Research Projects Agency (DARPA), a science and technology organization of the U.S. Department of Defense, to sponsor Carnegie Mellon University to establish the first Computer Emergency Response Team/Coordination Center (CERT/CC) to manage future cybersecurity emergencies. But it also sparked a discussion in the newly forming network defender space about how to respond to a cyber incident within your organization. At the Naval Postgraduate School, where I was during the event, the response consisted of faculty members who could spell UNIX correctly three times out of five running around the hallways with their hair on fire shouting esoteric computer slang at each other like *sendmail, rsh attacks, telnet,* and *finger*. Perhaps there might be a better way.

Enter my all-time computer science hero, Dr. Clifford Stoll. If there were baseball cards for computer science giants, my collection would include Grace Hopper, Alan Turing, and multiple copies of Doctor Stoll. His Cybersecurity Canon Hall of Fame book *The Cuckoo's Egg* was one of the first, and still one of the most influential, cybersecurity books ever published.[50] One of the reason's his book remains influential more than 30 years later is that he almost single-handedly invented incident response. The best practices he developed haven't changed that much in the years since.

Dr. Stoll was an astronomer at the University of California at Berkeley in 1986, not a security guy by any means. But he was asked to help out in a UNIX lab on campus and track down an accounting error in the student body computer records. Back then, universities charged their students for computer time, and each month, the sum of the accounting records for all the Berkeley student computer users was off by 75 cents and nobody could figure it out. His investigation to fix the error led to the discovery of the first public cyber espionage campaign run by the Russians using East German hacker mercenaries to break into U.S. university systems in order to break into U.S. military systems. Back then, we didn't really have any security per se. The Internet was basically connected with strings and cans.

Because of his astronomer background, he treated the entire exercise like a science experiment. He developed hypotheses, built experiments to test his hypothesis, and wrote

[50]Stoll, C., 1989. The Cuckoo's Egg: Tracking a Spy Through the Maze of Computer Espionage. Simon and Schuster.

everything down in a logbook. In 1988, he published a paper from his logbook in the journal *Communications of the ACM*,[51] which eventually turned into the book he published in 1989. If you haven't read this book yet, stop what you are doing right now and get it done. Dr. Stoll is, how would you say it, eccentric. His kookiness pervades the entire book, and his joy for life is palpable. Even if you aren't a techie, you'll love it. I promise, you will be delighted, and in the process, you will witness the birth of incident response as a network defender best practice.

I read his book over a weekend when I should have been working on my master's thesis. Back then, authors put their email addresses in their book, and when I finished reading it, I sent a long fan-boy note to Dr. Stoll praising it. I got a nice response note from him 15 minutes later, and I have been a fan ever since.

The NIST Guides on Cybersecurity and Incident Response

The executive summary for the National Institute of Standards and Technology (NIST) 2012 publication "Computer Security Incident Handling Guide: Special Publication 800-61 Revision 2," runs three pages.[52] Only a U.S. government publication would consider three pages an executive summary. Let me simplify what it says.

---

[51]Stoll, C., 1988. STALKING THE WILY HACKER. COMMUNICATION OF THE ACM 31.

[52]Cichonski, P., Millar, T., Grance, T. and Scarfone, K. (2012). Computer Security Incident Handling Guide : Recommendations of the National Institute of Standards and Technology. [online] doi:10.6028/nist.sp.800-61r2.

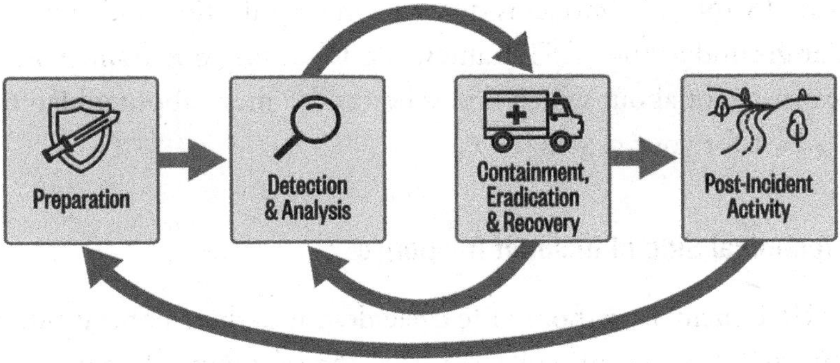

Figure 5.4 Incident response life cycle[52]

Federal law requires that federal agencies establish incident response capabilities and report incidents to the U.S. Computer Emergency Readiness Team (US-CERT). The authors distinguish between cyber events (an observation derived from network device telemetry) and incidents (a violation or imminent threat of violation of computer security policies). Network defenders derive incident response capabilities from analyzing the incident response life cycle (see Figure 5.4).

- *Preparation*: Devise a plan on how to respond to cyber issues.
- *Detection and analysis*: Develop cyber-detection capabilities and analysis skills for early detection.
- *Containment, eradication, and recovery*: Once discovered, don't let adversaries move elsewhere in your network. Destroy their capability to burrow in undetected somewhere else and connect back out. Recover the systems that were affected.
- *Post-mortem*: Review what you did. Make improvements to the plan for the next time.

It's worth noting that the other industry-recognized incident response framework is from a commercial security vendor training and certification company called SysAdmin, Audit, Network, and

Security (SANS). Its model is different in organization and covers similar ground as the NIST framework. Choosing one framework or the other is not about which one is better. It's more about which one works best for your organization.

The Technical Side of Incident Response

The NIST incident response life cycle describes the technical side of monitoring cyber events collected from the telemetry of your deployed security stack and developing those into cyber incidents if the evidence warrants it. If your organization fits on the size spectrum between medium and Fortune 500 organizations, your incident response team is likely managed by your security operations center (SOC). You might have a dedicated team specifically for this function, or it might be an ad hoc team thrown together for a specific event. If you have a cyber intelligence team (see Chapter 4), they are likely part of the incident response team. If your organization is on the other side of the size spectrum (between startup and medium-sized organizations), your incident response team is likely your IT department dropping what they normally do during the day to run this potential cyber incident to ground.

In terms of first principles, the SOC team monitors the telemetry of each deployed tactic for zero trust (Chapter 3), intrusion kill chain prevention (Chapter 4), and resilience (this chapter) looking for signs of a cyber event. As initial evidence accrues, the SOC turns the case over to the incident response team to develop the evidence further. Most times, it doesn't materialize. Most times it's a false alarm. But when it does, that's when the entire crisis action plan begins. But the practice of elevating a cyber event into a cyber incident is more of an art than it is a science.

For example, I mentioned in Chapter 4 that as of this writing, the MITRE ATT&CK® framework lists the adversary campaign known as Cobalt Spider with 31 attack techniques and 5 software tools.

If the SOC notices one of those techniques in the network, that's a cyber event. That could represent anything, though: a false positive, the first indicator that some hacker group is operating in and around our data islands, or perhaps the first signs of the Cobalt Spider hackers specifically. We don't know yet. On the other hand, if the SOC notices all 31 techniques and all of the software tools, the hackers behind Cobalt Spider are definitely in the network, and the incident response team should be handling it like a cyber incident. The tricky part is the fuzzy piece in the middle. At what point in the evidence collection process does the incident response team upgrade a cyber event into a cyber incident? Three techniques and one software tool? Ten techniques and three software tools? It's usually a gut call but an important call all the same because as soon as the event becomes an incident, coordination is no longer contained within the SOC but must now start spreading to the other members of the organization via the crisis plan I mentioned earlier.

According to NIST's 2018 "Framework for Improving Critical Infrastructure Cybersecurity," an update to the original 2014 publication, NIST authors developed their cybersecurity risk management guidance to improve the U.S. government's critical infrastructure.[53] That said, the guidance is universal enough that it can be applied "by organizations in any sector or community. The Framework enables organizations—regardless of size, degree of cybersecurity risk, or cybersecurity sophistication—to apply the principles and best practices of risk management to improving security and resilience." It's essentially an incident response manual.

The guidance became an instant hit and infosec professionals use it as a kind of maturity model for five key functions: Identify, Protect, Detect, Respond, and Recover. See Figure 5.5.

[53]Barrett, M.P., 2018. Framework for Improving Critical Infrastructure Cybersecurity Version 1.1 [WWW Document]. NIST. www.nist.gov/publications/framework-improving-critical-infrastructure-cybersecurity-version-11 (accessed 12/18/22).

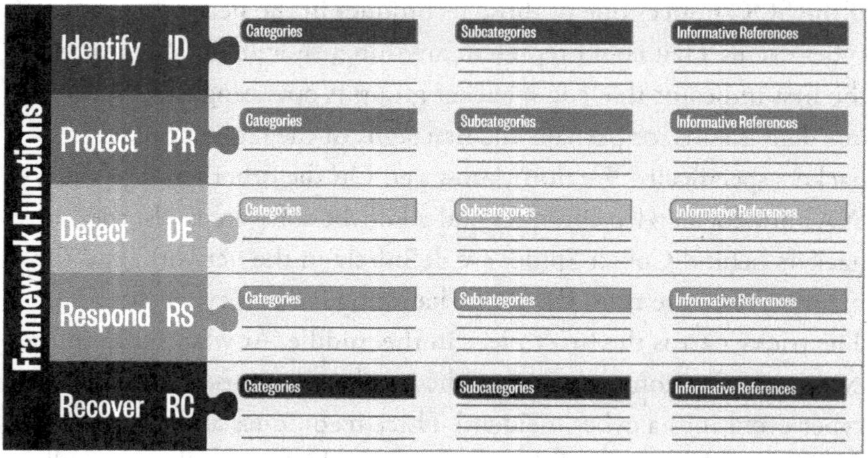

Figure 5.5 Framework core structure[53]

It is a foundational document. The analysis and research that went behind it is strong and the work product, the Identify-Protect-Detect-Respond-Recover Framework, is a more than useful model to frame the cybersecurity space in general and to specifically measure how mature your organization is with respect to these functions. It's worth the time and effort to match your defensive posture against these stated elements.

But it's not a strategy nor an atomic first principle. Even if your organization is the most mature on this scale compared to all the other organizations in the world, what did you accomplish? What do you tell your boss when this happens? The most you can say is that you have checked off many of the items on a government-recommended best practice list. Your boss will likely respond, "Well, how does that help me? What do I get after we spent all that money to accomplish that?" By itself, the framework doesn't help you make the case that the effort was worth the investment in terms of people, process, and technology.

However, if you reframe the discussion around first principles and how we are trying to reduce the probability of material impact due to a cyber incident, that changes the discussion. You tell the boss that one of our key strategies to reduce that probability is resilience and that each tactic listed in the Critical Infrastructure Cybersecurity framework is a resiliency tactic that will reduce that probability by a certain amount (I'll show you how to calculate the amount in Chapter 6). With that information in hand, leaders can make resource decisions about cybersecurity risk compared to all the other risks that they are juggling for the business.

Incident response has been around the security community since the early days (Dr. Stoll in 1988). The NIST guides, "Computer Security Incident Handling Guide" and "Framework for Improving Critical Infrastructure Cybersecurity," established the best practice tactics for executing the task. The bottom line is that network defenders can use the resiliency tactics associated with Identify-Protect-Detect-Respond-Recover to reduce the probability of material impact to our organizations. It's an essential tactic too because we can't launch the crisis plan until somebody in the organization tells us that we have a potential cyber incident in the making. The incident response team is the organization that does that.

Conclusion

In this chapter, I presented the case for the best definition of what a resilience strategy is. Using that as a logical follow-on to our ultimate cybersecurity first principle, I explained four tactics that will have the greatest impact on reducing the probability of material impact: crisis planning, backup and restore operations, encryption, and incident response. In the next chapter, I'm going to demonstrate how to calculate the impact of all of these tactics, not just for resilience but for all of the first principle strategies.

6 Risk Forecasting

How predictable something is depends on what we are trying to predict, how far into the future, and under what circumstances.

—Philip Tetlock

"Essentially all models are wrong, but some are useful."

—George Box

Overview

Out of all the capabilities in the infosec community that have improved over the years, the one essential skill that has barely moved forward is calculating cyber risk. Specifically, how do we convey cybersecurity risk to senior leadership and to the board?

In my early network defender days, whenever somebody asked me to do a risk assessment, I would punt. I would roll out my "qualitative heat map" (a fancy name for a color-coded spreadsheet where all the risks are listed on the x-axis and my three levels of potential impact—high, medium, and low—are plotted on the y-axis) and call it a day (see Figure 6.1).[1] Along with many of my peers, I would tell myself that predicting cyber risk with any more precision was impossible; that there were too many variables; that cybersecurity was somehow different from all other disciplines in the world; that it couldn't be done.

[1]Sketchbubble (2022). Risk Heatmap. [online] Sketchbubble.com. www.sketchbubble.com/en/presentation-risk-heatmap.html (accessed 10/30/22).

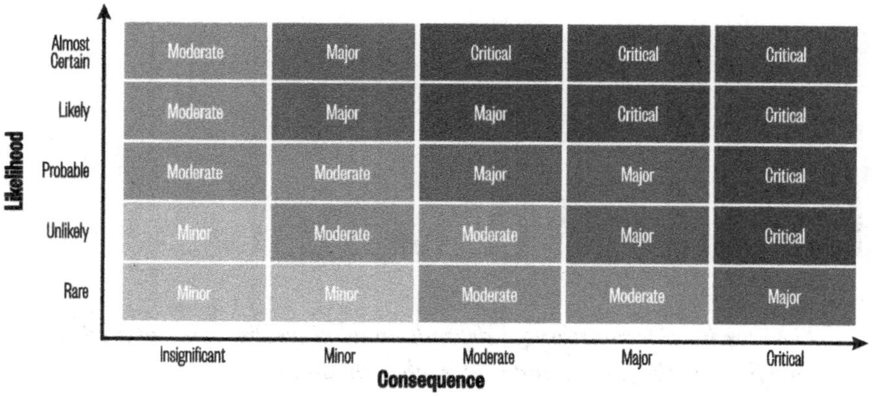

Figure 6.1 A typical qualitative heat map

We were wrong, of course.

The Cybersecurity Canon Project is full of Hall of Fame and candidate books that talk about how to calculate cyber risk with precision.

- *How to Measure Anything in Cybersecurity Risk*, by Douglas W. Hubbard and Richard Seiersen[2]
- *Measuring and Managing Information Risk: A Fair Approach*, by Jack Freund and Jack Jones[3]
- *Security Metrics: A Beginner's Guide*, by Caroline Wong[4]
- *Security Metrics: Replacing Fear, Uncertainty, and Doubt*, by Andrew Jaquith[5]

[2]Hubbard, D.W., Seiersen, R., 2016. How to Measure Anything in Cybersecurity Risk. John Wiley & Sons.
[3]Freund, J., Jones, J., 2014. Measuring and Managing Information Risk: A FAIR Approach. Butterworth-Heinemann.
[4]Wong, C., 2011. Security Metrics, A Beginner's Guide. McGraw-Hill Prof Med/Tech.
[5]Jaquith, A., 2007. Security Metrics. Pearson Education.

These are all great primers regarding how to think differently about precision probability forecasting. I highly recommend them. If this subject is new to you, they will change your view of the world. But my problem with all of them is that I kept waiting for the chapter at the end entitled, "And Here's How to Do It" or, better, "Building the Risk Chart That You Can Take to the Board." None had it or anything close to it. That part was always left as an exercise for the reader. So I am going to do it here.

In this chapter, I'm going to walk you through that exercise. This is the chapter that should have been at the end of those other books. I will cover two case studies. The first is an outside-in analysis of Marvel Studios. I chose Marvel Studios for two reasons. First, I'm a comic book nerd. Second, and, more important, Marvel Studios is a typical midsize company in terms of revenue; it's something most of us can use as a stand-in for our own organizations. It's outside-in because I will not take into account how Marvel Studios protects itself in terms of first principles (an inside-out analysis). It's an analysis of the probability that any company like Marvel Studios in terms of size and revenue will experience a material cyber event.

The second case study will be both an outside-in and inside-out analysis of Microsoft's fictional company called Contoso. Microsoft uses Contoso in its marketing materials to demonstrate how to use its products. But it provides enough detail in its IT architecture that it's possible to make some assertions about their cybersecurity posture. It will enable us to look at both the outside-in forecast and an inside-out forecast.

Before the case studies, though, I need to explain the tools required to do these kinds of calculations: superforecasting techniques, Fermi estimates, black swan problems, and the Bayes rule.

Superforecasting, Fermi Estimates, and Black Swans

The book that changed my mind about risk forecasting, the fact that it could be done, is called *Superforecasting: The Art and Science of Prediction*, by Philip Tetlock and Dan Gardner, another Cybersecurity Canon Project Hall of Fame candidate book.[6]

Dr. Tetlock is quite the character. He's inclined to scream and shake his raised fist at the TV because the talking heads have no idea what they are talking about. He would watch news programs like CNN, FOX, and MSNBC, where the host would roll out famous pundits to give their opinion on some topic because, once in their lives, they had predicted something accurately. It didn't matter that all the predictions they'd made since were wrong. The news programs would still bring them on as if they were Moses coming down from Mount Sinai to present the Tablets of Stone.

Dr. Tetlock thought that they should have to keep score. I always thought that when pundits came on, the viewer should see their batting average rolling across the chyron on the bottom of the screen: "These pundits have made 3 correct predictions out of 100 tries in the last year. Maybe you shouldn't listen too closely to what they have to say." Dr. Tetlock was so taken by this prediction score idea that he ran a scientific study of the concept and tested his theory that most pundits are awful forecasters.

Working with the Intelligence Advanced Research Projects Agency (IARPA), he devised a test using three groups: the intelligence community, the academic community, and a group I call the Geezers-on-the-Go. Now, the Geezers-on-the-Go were not all old people; they were just regular people with time on their hands who liked to solve

[6]Tetlock, P.E., Gardner, D., 2015. Superforecasting: The Art and Science of Prediction. Crown.

puzzles. According to the *Washington Post*, Tetlock then had them forecast answers to more than 500 really hard questions like these:

- Will the Syrian president, Bashar Hafez al-Assad, still be in power in six months' time?
- Will there be a military exchange in the South China Sea in the next year?
- Will the number of terrorist attacks sponsored by Iran increase within one year of the removal of sanctions?

Out of the three communities, the Geezers-on-the-Go outperformed the control group by 60 percent. They beat the academic teams from 30 percent to 70 percent depending on the school (MIT and the University of Michigan were two) and outperformed the intelligence community groups that had access to classified information. But Tetlock also discovered a subset of the Geezers-on-the-Go, a group he called "Superforecasters." By the end of the 4-year tournament, these Superforecasters had outperformed the Geezers-on-the-Go by another 60 percent and could also see further out than the control group. "Superforecasters looking out 300 days were more accurate than regular forecasters looking out 100 days."

This is what changed my mind. Dr. Tetlock demonstrated that it is possible to forecast probabilities on future problems where there isn't much data, the problem domain is complicated, and the number of variables to consider are astronomical. Cybersecurity risk forecasting checks all of those boxes. Cyber risk needs superforecasters.

Superforecaster Superpowers

Superforecasters don't have extreme mutant abilities. They are intelligent for sure, but not overly so. This isn't a collection of

Professor X's from the *X-men* comic book. They aren't all card-carrying members of Mensa, and they're not math nerds either. Most of them perform only rudimentary math calculations when they make their forecasts. But by following a few key guidelines, they outperform random Kentucky windage guesses by normal people like me. Here are six of the most impactful rules:

1. **Forecast in terms of quantitative probabilities, not qualitative high-medium-lows:**

   Get rid of the heat maps. Embrace the idea that probabilities are nothing more than a measure of uncertainty. Use real numbers.

2. **Practice:**

   Do a lot of forecasts and keep score using something called the Brier score (invented by Glenn W. Brier in 1950). The score is on two axes: Calibration and Resolution. Calibration is how close to the line your forecast is (are you over confident or under?) Resolution is that when you predict something is going to happen, it does.

3. **Embrace Fermi estimates (outside-in first, then inside-out forecasts):**

   Outside-in is looking at the general case before you look at the specific situation. For example, an outside-in estimate considers the probability of a material cyberattack against any organization without a review of a specific victim's defensive architecture. What are the odds that any company will be materially affected? An inside-out estimate considers a specific case based on the company's defensive posture. What's the probability that hackers will cause material damage to a company that has a mature zero trust program deployed? Both have merit, but Tetlock says to start with the outside-in forecast and then adjust up or down from there with the inside-out forecast. For example, if your outside-in forecast says that there is a 20 percent chance of material impact due to a cyberattack this year for all U.S. companies, that's the baseline. Then, when you do the inside-out assessment by looking at how well your organization is deployed against our first principle strategies, you might move the forecast up or down depending.

4. **Check your assumptions:**

   Adjust, tweak, abandon, seek new data and hypotheses, and adjust your forecast from there.

5. **Use dragonfly eyes:**

   Consume evidence from multiple sources. Construct a unified vision of it. Describe your judgment about it as clearly and concisely as you can, being as granular as you can.

6. **Forecast at a 90 percent confidence level:**

   As you adjust your forecast, remember that you want to be 90 percent confident that it reflects reality. That means you should be 90 percent confident that the true value falls within your forecasted range. If you're not, then you need to adjust up or down until you are.

The point to all of this is that it's possible to forecast the probability of some future and mind-numbingly complex event with enough precision to make decisions. If the Geezers-on-the-Go can accurately predict the future of the Syrian president, surely a bunch of no-math CISOs like me can forecast the probability of a material impact due to a cyber event for their organizations within a reasonable margin of error. That's cybersecurity risk forecasting.

People Don't Think in Terms of Probabilities but Should

Tetlock spends time talking about how the U.S. government hasn't done this kind of thinking in the past. You and I would call them massive intelligence failures.

- **WMD in Iraq:**
  Twenty years of war on the "slam dunk" CIA assertion that these weapons existed in Iraq. Spoiler alert: they didn't.
- **Vietnam War:**
  Ten years of war on the widely held belief that if South Vietnam fell, the entire world would fall to communism like dominoes. Leaders didn't just think there was a chance this would happen. They thought it was a sure thing.
- **Bay of Pigs:**
  President Kennedy's political disaster when the planners didn't consider the probability of success/failure when the plan changed at the last minute.

Is Osama Bin Laden in the Bunker?

Tetlock describes a scene in one of my favorite movies, 2012's *Zero Dark Thirty* starring Jessica Chastain.[7] The CIA director, Leon Panetta—played by the late great James Gandolfini—is in a conference room asking his staff for a recommendation on whether or not Osama Bin Laden is in the bunker. He's looking for a yes or no answer. One of his guys says that he fronted the bad recommendation about WMD in Iraq, and because of that failure, they don't deal in certainties anymore. They deal in probabilities. That is the right answer, just not a very satisfying one. They go around the room and get a range of probabilities from 60 percent to 80 percent. Chastain breaks into the conversation and says that the probability is 100 percent. "OK fine, 95 percent," she says, "because I know certainty freaks you out. But, it's 100 percent." That's the wrong answer by the way. The probability was never a 100 percent no matter how sure she was with her evidence.

[7]Zero Dark Thirty, 2012. Columbia Pictures.

It's clear that as humans in our everyday lives, we don't really understand probabilities. Even if we do, they're not satisfying. We'd much prefer a yes or no answer. Will the company have a material breach this year? Telling CEOs yes or no is much more palatable to them than saying there is a 15 percent chance. What do they do with a 15 percent chance anyway? That answer is harder to deal with, demands an effort to parse, and requires thinking, strategy, and flexibility. By the way, I will tell you exactly what to do with that 15 percent chance later in this chapter. A yes/no answer, on the other hand, is nothing more than an if-then-else-clause like in a programming language. If we're going to get breached this year, then spend resources to mitigate the damage; else, spend that money on making the product better or increasing sales. Easy.

Unfortunately, no matter how much we desire to live in a fantasy world full of binary answers (yes/no), the real world doesn't work that way. In Neal Stephenson's science fiction novel *Seveneves*, his Neil deGrasse Tyson character, Doc Dubois, explains how he calculates rocket trajectories through a debris field. "It is a statistical problem. On about day 1 it stopped being a Newtonian mechanics problem and turned into statistics. It has been statistics ever since."[8] Exactly. Calculating cyber risk has never been Newtonian either. It's always been stochastic no matter how much we desire to simplify the calculation into easy-to-read heat maps. In the infosec community, we just didn't treat it that way.

It might be more useful to reframe how we think about probabilities. If you're like me, your own statistics experience came from the Probability & Statistics 101 course we all had to take in college. I don't remember a lot from that course, but I do remember one problem in particular where we had to calculate the probability that a blue marble would be the next marble poured out from an urn

---

[8]Stephenson, N., 2016. Seveneves. Borough Press.

filled with colored marbles. Yes, that's a great introduction to the probability concept, but that coursework represents only a small sliver of what probabilities really are.

A more useful description in the cybersecurity context comes from Dr. Ron Howard, the father of decision analysis theory (no relation to yours truly).[9] His entire field of study is based on the idea that probabilities represent uncertainty when making a decision, not the number of marbles in our urn collection.

Probability is not necessarily found in the data, meaning that you don't have to count all the things in order to make an uncertainty forecast using probability. He says that "only a person can assign a probability, taking into account any data or other knowledge available." Counting marbles tumbling out of urns is one way to take account of data, but Howard's great insight is that "a probability reflects a person's knowledge (or equivalently ignorance) about some uncertain distinction." He says, "Don't think of probability or uncertainties as the lack of knowledge. Think of them instead as a very detailed description of exactly what you know."

Tetlock interviewed the real Leon Panetta about that internal CIA meeting and the subsequent meeting Panetta had with President Obama about the decision to send the special forces into Pakistan to get Osama Bin Laden. When the President went around the room with his staff, he also got a range of probabilities. His conclusion, though, after reviewing those recommendations, was that his staff didn't know for sure. Therefore, it was simply a 50-50 chance, a toss-up, on whether Osama Bin Laden was in the bunker, which is the wrong conclusion. It was probably much stronger. He ultimately made the right call, but he could just as easily have erred on the side of caution.

---

[9]Howard, R.A., Abbas, A.E., 2015. Foundations of Decision Analysis. Pearson College Division.

Fermi Estimates Are Good Enough

The Italian American physicist Enrico Fermi was a central figure in the invention of the atomic bomb. He was renowned for his back-of-the-envelope estimates.[10, 11] With little or no information at his disposal, he would often calculate a number that a subsequent measurement revealed to be impressively accurate. He would famously ask his students things like "estimate the number of square inches of pizza consumed by all the students at the University of Maryland during one semester," and he forbade his students from looking up any information. He encouraged them to make back-of-the-envelope assumptions first. He understood that by breaking down the big intractable question (like how many inches of pizza consumed) into a series of much simpler answerable questions (like how many students, how many pizza joints, how many inches in a slice, how many slices a day, etc.), we can better separate the knowable and the unknowable. The surprise is how often good probability estimates arise from a remarkably crude series of assumptions and guesstimates. More on this in a bit.

Frederick Mosteller, a groundbreaking eminent statistician in the 1950s–1970s, said, "It is the experience of statisticians that when fairly 'crude' measurements are refined, the change more often than not turns out to be small. Statisticians would wholeheartedly say make better measurements, but they would often give a low probability to the prospect that finer measures would lead to different policy."[12] That means a network defender's desire to have more

---

[10]Staff, n.d. Fermi Problems: Estimation [WWW Document]. TheProblemSite.com. www.theproblemsite.com/reference/mathematics/estimation/fermi-problems (accessed 11/9/22).
[11]Braun, B., 2011. Fermi Estimations [WWW Document]. BryanBraun. www.bryanbraun.com/2011/12/04/fermi-estimations (accessed 11/9/22).
[12]Mosteller, F., Moynihan, D.P., 1972. On Equality of Educational Opportunity: Papers Deriving from the Harvard University Faculty Seminar on the Coleman Report. Wiley.

precision with their risk forecasts is invalid. For resource decisions we need to make in terms of people, process, and technology, rough estimates are probably good enough.

Black Swans and Resilience

Tetlock also describes criticism of his Superforecasting approach from his colleague, Nassim Taleb, the author of *The Black Swan: The Impact of the Highly Improbable* published in 2007.[13] Taleb says that forecasting is impossible because history is controlled by "the tyranny of the singular, the accidental, the unseen, and the unpredicted." According to *New York Times* journalist Gregg Easterbrook, Taleb argues that "experts are charlatans who believe in bell curves, in which most distribution is toward the center—ordinary and knowable. Far more powerful, Taleb argues, are the wild outcomes of fractal geometry, in which anything can happen overnight." Taleb says that "what matters can't be forecast and what can be forecast doesn't matter. Believing otherwise lulls us into a false sense of security."[14] Acknowledging the argument, Tetlock says, "The black swan is therefore a brilliant metaphor for an event so far outside experience we can't even imagine it until it happens."

Case in point, if we do some first-order, back-of-the-envelope calculations (Fermi estimates), we know that in 2021 the Identity Theft Resource Center tallied 1,862 publicly reported data breaches.[15]

---

[13]Taleb, N.N., 2010. The Black Swan: Second Edition: The Impact of the Highly Improbable: With a new section: "On Robustness and Fragility." Random House Trade Paperbacks.

[14]Easterbrook, G., 2007. The Black Swan: The Impact of the Highly Improbable - Nassim Nicholas Taleb - Books - Review [WWW Document]. The New York Times. www.nytimes.com/2007/04/22/books/review/Easterbrook.t.html (accessed 12/18/22).

[15]Fowler, B., 2022. Data breaches break record in 2021. CNET.

5,000 Successful cyber campaigns in 2021
~6,000,000 U.S companies in 2021

5,000 successful campaigns / 6,000,000 U.S. companies = .0008

The probability that any company in the U.S would have a material cyber incident in 2021 = .0008
The probability is **practically** zero.

Figure 6.2 Math Problem 1: generic outside-in Fermi estimate

Assuming that not all data breaches were reported, let's round up and assume about 5,000 total successful cyberattacks to U.S. companies in 2021. Assume also that there are about 6 million commercial companies in the United States (I show how I estimated the number later in the chapter.) Doing the outside-in forecast, there was a 5,000/6 million chance of a U.S. company getting breached in 2021, or about 0.0008 (see Figure 6.2). That's a really small number. I'm going to refine that forecast later, but for now, just go with it. It's our first estimate of the probability of a material cyberattack against a generic U.S. company.

By definition, the experiences of those 5,000 companies were black swan events, significant impactful events on something that was not very likely to happen at all.

Tetlock's response to Taleb is that there are probably a set of estimate-problems that are too hard to forecast, but he says that they are largely due to the fact that the forecasting horizon is too long. For example, it's tough to forecast who will win the U.S. Presidential election in 2028 (5 years from the time of this writing), but you could come very close with the U.S. Presidential election of 2024 (1 year from the time of this writing). In the cybersecurity space, it's tough for a network defender to predict if the organizations will be materially impacted by a cyber incident at any point in the future, but you could likely have a good enough forecast to make resource decisions (people, process, and technology) if you restrict the forecast to 2 to 3 years in the future.

That said, even if you have high confidence in your prediction that some event might happen, it doesn't make it a lock. Just look at the predictions some pundits were making about the U.S. Presidential election of 2016. Prior to election night, Nate Silver and his 538 web team forecast that Secretary Clinton had a 71.4 percent chance to win.[16] The democrats were feeling confident. When she didn't win, many pointed to the polls saying that they got the election prediction wrong. They didn't get the election wrong. They had high confidence based on many factors that she had a 70 percent chance. But that also means that she had a 30 percent chance to lose; 30 percent is not nothing. In fact, a 30 percent probability event is something that is still likely to happen. The shock that Democrats expressed is another example of how most people don't understand probabilities, even some political pundits who live for polling data.

Taleb's solution to black swan events is to not attempt to prevent them but to try to survive them. He says resilience is the key. For example, instead of trying to prevent a giant meteor from hitting the earth, the question is how would you survive one (maybe establish a colony on Mars to ensure that the human species would survive)? In the cybersecurity context, instead of preventing Panda Bear from breaching your organization, what would you do to ensure that your organization continues to deliver its service during and after the attack? That sounds a lot like our cybersecurity first principle strategy of resilience (see Chapter 5).

That said, this is not a binary choice. You don't have to pick one, prevention, over the other, resilience. You can do both.

---

[16]Silver, N., 2016. 2016 Election Forecast [WWW Document]. FiveThirtyEight. projects.fivethirtyeight.com/2016-election-forecast (accessed 12/18/22).

Changing My Mind

I've been trying to get my mind around how to do risk assessment with more precision for more than 5 years now. I've read the books, interviewed many of the associated authors, published a couple of papers, and even presented those papers in consecutive years at security conferences (one with Richard Seiersen, an author of one of the books).

My initial thought when I started all of this was that the main reason calculating risk was so hard for the infosec community was that it involved some high-order math, a skill that was beyond most senior security practitioners. I became convinced that to have enough precision to convince senior leadership that my risk calculation was valid, I was going to have to demonstrate my prowess with things like Monte Carlo simulations and Bayesian algorithms. And then I was going to have to explain what Monte Carlo simulations and Bayesian algorithms were to these same senior leaders who were having a hard enough time understanding why our annual firewall subscription was so expensive. This seemed like a bridge too far.

After years of looking into how to do that, I've come up with a different approach, one that goes just far enough to be useful but not so far to be esoteric and confusing. I've become a fan of Fermi and Mosteller. According to Nagesh Belludi, "Fermi believed that the ability to guesstimate was an essential skill for physicists."[17] I would say that the skill applies to any decision-maker, but especially decision-makers in the tech and security worlds where the scale of our problems is so enormous and significant. Getting a precise estimate is hard and time-consuming, but getting an estimate that's in the right

---

[17]Belludi, N., 2017. The Fermi Rule: Better be Approximately Right than Precisely Wrong [WWW Document]. Right Attitudes. www.rightattitudes.com/2017/08/28/the-fermi-rule-guesstimation (accessed 11/9/22).

ballpark in terms of order of magnitude is relatively easy and will probably be sufficient for most decisions. Even if it's not, you can always decide to do the more precise estimate later.

Case in point, here at N2K and the CyberWire (where I work as a podcaster and CSO), we did an inside-out evaluation of our internal first principle cybersecurity posture in 2022. We evaluated our defenses in terms of zero trust, intrusion kill chain prevention, resilience, and automation. Once complete, we briefed the boss (Peter Kilpe) on our findings and gave him our estimated probability of material impact due to some cyber event in the next year. I then asked him for permission to do a deeper dive on the issue in order to get a more precise answer. His answer to me was spot on.

He looked at the level of effort (and cost) this deeper dive was going to take, not only for the internal security team but for the entire company and especially for him. Frankly, it was going to be high. He then asked this question: "What do you think the difference is going to be between this initial inside-out estimate and the deeper dive?" I didn't think the deeper dive estimate was going to be that far away from the inside-out estimate, maybe a couple of percentage points up or down, but certainly within a 10 percent margin of error. He then said that if that was the case, he didn't need the deeper dive to make decisions about any future resource investment for CyberWire's defensive posture. The initial estimate was good enough.

Quite so. QED.

Bayes Rule: A Different Way to Think About Cybersecurity Risk

Dr. Tetlock makes the case, and I agree with him, that it's possible to forecast answers to highly complex questions, queries that seemingly no one could possibly answer because there is no prior data or history of occurrence, with enough accuracy to make meaningful decisions in the real world. Specifically, I believe we can use superforecasting techniques to estimate the probability of material impact to our own organizations due to a cyberattack in the next three years.

Superforecasting techniques in general and specifically Fermi, outside-in, back-of-the-envelope calculations are two legs to the cybersecurity risk forecasting stool. The third leg is something called the Bayes rule. It's the mathematical foundation that proves that superforecasting techniques and Fermi estimates work. The great news is that CISOs like me don't have to actually perform higher-order math to make it work for us. We just have to understand the concept and apply it to our day-to-day risk assessments. We can use basic statistics in the general case and expert opinion from our internal staff to get an initial estimate. We can then modify the forecast based on how well our organizations do in adhering to our set of cybersecurity first principles. Before I show you how to do that, though, let me explain Bayes' theorem.

Bayes' Theorem

The Bayesian interpretation of probabilities comes from Thomas Bayes, who penned the original thesis in the 1740s.[18] But what is not commonly known is that nobody would have heard about the idea if

[18]Bayes, T., 1763. LII. An essay towards solving a problem in the doctrine of chances. By the late Rev. Mr. Bayes, F. R. S. communicated by Mr. Price, in a letter to John Canton, A. M. F. R. S [WWW Document]. royalsocietypublishing.org/doi/epdf/10.1098/rstl.1763.0053

it weren't for his best friend, Richard Price. Price, no slouch in the science department himself, found Bayes' unpublished manuscript in a drawer after Bayes died, realized its importance, spent two years fixing it up, and sent it to the Royal Society of London for publication in 1763.[19]

In the manuscript, Bayes (with Price) describes a thought experiment to illustrate his hypothesis. Bayes asks the reader to imagine a billiard table and two people, the guesser and the assistant. The guesser turns away from the table, and the assistant rolls the cue ball onto the table and lets it settle somewhere. The guesser's job is to forecast where the cue ball is located on the flat surface. She has a piece of paper and a pencil and draws a rectangle to represent the level platform. The assistant then rolls a second ball and tells the guesser only if it settled to the right or to the left of the original cue ball. The guesser makes an initial estimate on the paper as to which side of the table the cue ball resides. The assistant then rolls a third ball and tells the guesser on which side of the original cue ball it landed. Based on that information, the guesser adjusts her initial estimate. The more balls the assistant rolls, the more precise the guesser gets with her forecast. The guesser will never know exactly where the cue ball is but can get fairly close. The important fact is, there's no change in the quality of each measurement. They're all exactly the same (right or left). What matters is repeated measurements. That's what improves the accuracy of the forecast.

This, in essence, is Bayes' thesis. We can have an initial estimate of the answer no matter how broad that might be (somewhere on the billiard table) and gradually collect new evidence, right or left of the cue ball, that allows us to adjust that initial estimate to get closer to the real answer.

---

[19]McGrayne, Sharon Bertsch, 2011. The Theory That Would Not Die: How Bayes' Rule Cracked the Enigma Code, Hunted Down Russian Submarines, & Emerged Triumphant from Two Centuries of C. Yale University Press.

According to Sharon McGrayne, author of the 2011 book *The Theory That Would Not Die: How Bayes' Rule Cracked the Enigma Code, Hunted Down Russian Submarines, and Emerged Triumphant from Two Centuries of Controversy*, "By updating our initial beliefs with objective new information, we get a new and improved belief."[18] She says that "Bayes is a measure of belief. And it says that we can learn even from missing and inadequate data, from approximations, and from ignorance."

Even though Bayes was a mathematician, he didn't work out the actual probabilistic formula called Bayes' rule (see Figure 6.3) that is used today. That didn't come until Pierre-Simon Laplace, the French mathematician, astronomer, and physicist who was best known for his investigations into the stability of the solar system and his discovery of the Central Limit Theorem, identified independently, in 1774, the same notion that Bayes did and spent the next 40 years working out the math. Today, we attribute Bayes' theorem to Thomas Bayes because of scientific convention (he was the first to come up with the idea). But in reality, we should call it the Bayes-Price-Laplace algorithm. Without Price and Laplace, the Bayes theorem would never have seen the light of day.

> Pierre-Simon Laplace was also the inventor of the Laplace transform, a foundation of control theory.[20] It's what makes the math and software that controls big physical processes actually work. It's used today in most industrial environments. So, you could argue that Laplace was also a founding father of industrial control systems and operational technology, another critical domain in cybersecurity.

[20]Staff, 1998. Laplace transform. Encyclopedia Britannica.

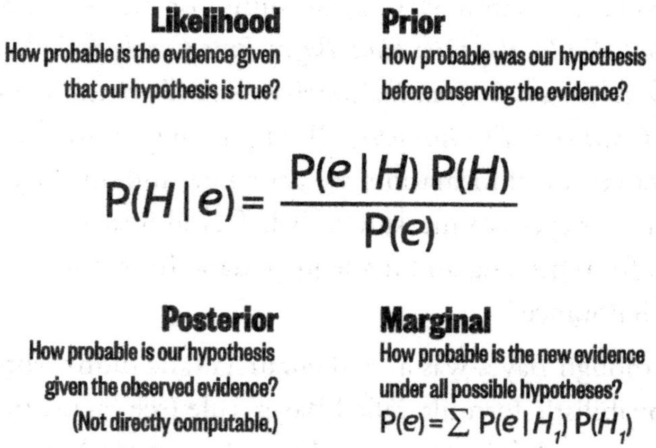

Likelihood
How probable is the evidence given that our hypothesis is true?
Prior
How probable was our hypothesis before observing the evidence?
$P(H \mid e) = \frac{P(e \mid H)\,P(H)}{P(e)}$
Posterior
How probable is our hypothesis given the observed evidence? (Not directly computable.)
Marginal
How probable is the new evidence under all possible hypotheses?
$P(e) = \sum P(e \mid H_i)\,P(H_i)$

Figure 6.3 Bayes' rule[21]

Modern Bayesian scientists use words like the *prior* to represent the initial estimate (the cue ball by itself on the table), the *likelihood* to represent the probability of the new information we are receiving (where is the cue ball in relation to the second ball), and the *posterior* to represent the new estimate after we combine the prior and the likelihood in the Bayes theorem. According to McGrayne, "Each time the system is recalculated, the posterior becomes the prior of the new iteration."

That is an elegant idea, but the scientific community completely rejected the thesis after the Royal Society published Bayes' manuscript. You have to remember that, at the time, science was moving away from religious dogma as a way to describe the world. These new scientist-statisticians, called the *frequentists*, were basing everything on observable facts. They had to count things like the number of cards in a deck before they would feel comfortable predicting the odds of an ace showing up on the flop. The idea that you could brand Bayes' fuzzy estimates as science without observable

[21]Action, I. (2012). Psychology In Action. [online] Psychology In Action. www.psychologyinaction.org/psychology-in-action-1/2012/10/22/bayes-rule-and-bomb-threats (accessed 10/30/22).

facts was anathema, and leading statisticians attacked it at every opportunity for the next 150 years.

To them, modern science required both objectivity and past knowledge. According to Hubbard and Siersen in their book *How to Measure Anything in Cybersecurity Risk*, Gottfried Achenwall introduced the word *statistics* in 1749 derived from the Latin word *statisticum*, meaning "pertaining to the state." Statistics was literally the quantitative study of the state. According to McGrayne, the frequentist thought that the crazy Bayesian philosophy requires a measure of "...belief and approximations. It is subjectivity run amok, ignorance coined into science."

But the real world has problems where the data is scant. Leaders worry about potential events that have never happened but are possible (like a future ransomware attack). Bayesian philosophy was a way to estimate answers that were useful in the real world. Outsiders to the statistics community began experimenting with the method to attain real results.

Amazingly, after 280 years, the Bayes rule still meets with friction in the scientific community. There still seems to be an attitude in some circles of one or the other; either you're a frequentist or a Bayesian. That's a shame because, like Euclid's first principle math rules, the Bayesian rule is true because it works. I'm a pragmatist, a firm believer in using the tools that fit best to the task at hand. If the frequentist's tools fit, use those. If the Bayesian tools are a better choice, use those. The great thing about the Bayes rule is that you can use both. At this point, the Bayesian math tool set has so many examples of solving real-world problems that it seems ludicrous to argue against it. And it's clear at this point in the cybersecurity evolution that frequentist's tool sets have not helped in predicting cybersecurity risk. What I'm advocating here is that it's time for the security community to try a new set of tools. It's time we adopted the Bayes approach.

Using Bayes to Defeat the Germans in WWII

I mentioned McGrayne's book, *The Theory That Would Not Die.* It's a delightful history of the Bayes theory's evolution from creation to modern day, its successes and failures, and blood feuds between mathematicians over the years. I highly recommend it if this subject intrigues you, and it should. The author gave a Google Talk about the book in 2011 if you're looking for a *Reader's Digest* version.[22] In the book, she outlines more than 20 success stories, tales where scientists used the Bayes rule to solve complex problems over the years. But my favorite Bayes success story is how Alan Turing used it to crack the German code machine, Enigma, in WWII.

Turing is my all-time favorite computer science hero. In his short and tragic life, he accomplished so many impressive things. In the 1930s, he mathematically proved that computers were possible (with the Turing machine) some 10 years before we were actually able to make them.[23] Today, every single computer you use, from your smartphone to your laptop to your workloads in the cloud, are all Turing machines. In 1950, he published the first test for artificial intelligence (the Turing test) that leaders in the field are still debating today.[24] And during WWII, his six years of work at Bletchley Park breaking German encrypted messages made by the Enigma machine, according to some historians, probably saved 20 million lives and

[22]McGrayne, Sharon Bertsch , 2011. The Theory That Would Not Die [WWW Document]. Google. www.youtube.com/watch?v=8oD6eBkjF9o (accessed 11/9/22).

[23]Turing, A., 1936. On Computable Numbers with an Application to the ENTSCHEIDUNGSPROBLEM. Proceedings of the London Mathematical Society.

[24]Turing, A., 1950. Computing Machinery and Intelligence: The Imitation Game. Mind 49, 433–460.

shortened the war by 4 years.[25] And he used the Bayes hypothesis to do it.[22]

There were many versions of the Enigma machine before, during, and after the war, but in general, the encryption machinery consisted of four mechanical parts (see Figure 6.4).

Keyboard Coders would type the plaintext message, one letter at a time, on something that looked like a typewriter. When they pressed the plaintext letter on the keyboard, the transformed encrypted letter would light up. The coder would write that letter down in an encrypted message for transmission later via Morse Code radio.

Plugboard Using 26 sockets, one socket for each letter in the alphabet, coders would use "steckers" to plug one letter into another one, say F to Z. This had the effect of swapping the values. If the coder pressed F on the keyboard, Z would go through the system.

Rotors Each rotor, a ring with a unique arrangement of 26 letters, had a starting position that coders changed on a regular basis. In a three-rotor system, the machine came with five rotors to choose from. Each rotor performs a simple substitution cipher. For example, the pin corresponding to the letter *R* might be wired to the contact for letter *T*. When the coder pressed a key on the keyboard, the right rotor would move forward one letter. This ensured that even if the coder typed the same letter twice, the encrypted letters would be different. Once the right rotor clicked more than 26 times, the middle rotor would click to the next letter. Once the middle rotor

---

[25]Copeland, P.J., 2012b. Alan Turing: The codebreaker who saved "millions of lives" [WWW Document]. BBC News. www.bbc.com/news/technology-18419691 (accessed 12/18/22).

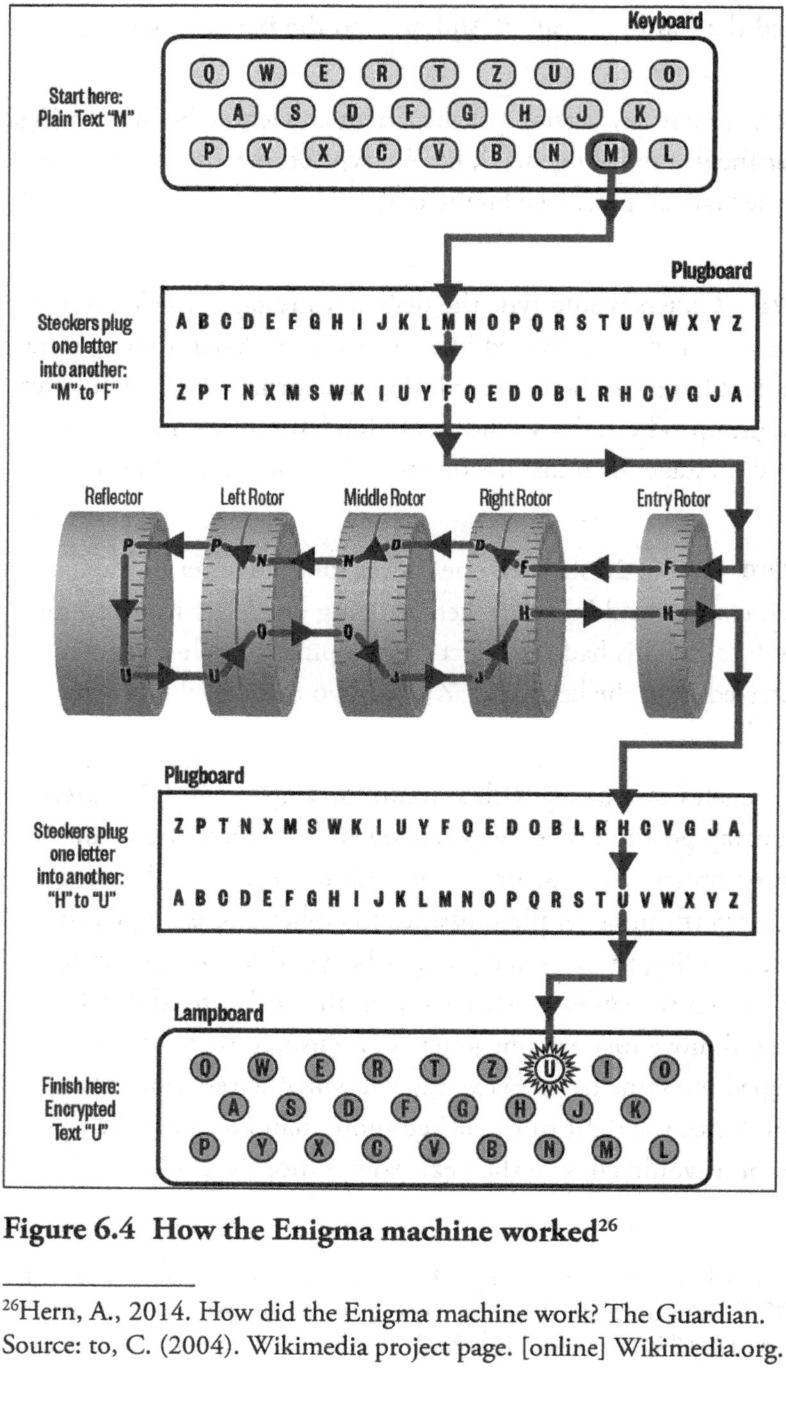

Figure 6.4 How the Enigma machine worked[26]

[26]Hern, A., 2014. How did the Enigma machine work? The Guardian. Source: to, C. (2004). Wikimedia project page. [online] Wikimedia.org.

clicked 26 times, the left rotor would click to the next letter. The result was more than 17,000 different combinations before the system repeated itself.

Reflector Once the signal passed through the plugboard and through the three rotors, it passed through the reflector that redirected the signal back through the rotors, this time left to right; and then back through the plugboard; and finally, back to the keyboard to light up the encrypted letter.

All in all, each individual unencrypted letter went through eight transformations: plugboard, three rotors right to left, three rotors left to right, plugboard. With this system, the number of ways the Germans could scramble a message was nearly 159 quintillion; that's 159 followed by 10 zeros.

According to McGrayne, Turing, with the help of mathematician Gordon Welchman and engineer Harold "Doc" Keen, designed a "high-speed electromechanical machine for testing every possible wheel arrangement in an Enigma." Turing called the machine the Bombe. His radical Bayesian design "tested hunches, 15-letter tidbits suspected of being in the original message. Because it was faster to toss out possibilities than to find one that fit, Turing's Bombe simultaneously tested for wheel combinations that could not produce the hunch." He also invented the manual Bayes system called Banburismus that "let him guess a stretch of letters in an Enigma message, hedge his bets, measure his belief in their validity by using Bayesian methods to assess their probabilities, and add more clues as they arrived." This system could "identify the settings for 2 of Enigma's 3 wheels and reduce the number of wheel settings to be tested on the Bombes from 336 to as few as 18."

Breaking Enigma codes was time sensitive. The Germans changed their Enigma settings (plugboard and rotor configurations) routinely, most times daily but sometimes every eight hours. Turing needed a way to measure his priors, his hunches from Banburismus. He invented the "ban" (short from Banburismus), which according to Irving John (Jack) Good (one of Turing's closest associates at Bletchley), "measured the smallest weight of evidence perceptible to the intuition." The way that McGrayne describes it, "One ban represented odds of 10 to 1 in favor of a guess, but Turing normally dealt with much smaller quantities, decibans, and even centibans." When the bans added up to 50 to 1, cryptanalysts were almost certain that their 15-letter tidbits were correct. According to McGrayne, "Each ban made a hypothesis 10 times more likely." Remember, Turing was trying to find ways to discard hunches quickly, not find the exact answer. When he got to 50-1, he could stop the process.

If you think Turing's "bans" sound eerily similar to Claude Shannon's "bits," you'd be right. Shannon published his groundbreaking paper, "A Mathematical Theory of Communication," in 1948 and according to the science site hrf, he "defines the smallest units of information that cannot be divided any further. These units are called *bits*, which stand for binary digits. Strings of bits can be used to encode any message. Digital coding is based around bits and has just two values: 0 or 1."[27, 28] Shannon introduced the idea of information entropy. According to Jane Stewart Adams in a fabulous essay called "The Ban and the Bit: Alan Turing, Claude Shannon, and the Entropy Measure," information wasn't contained in the bits themselves but how disordered they were when they arrived.[29]

---

[27]Shannon, C.E., 1948. A Mathematical Theory of Communication. System Technical Journal 27, 379–423.

[28]Staff, 2017. Claude Shannon's Information Theory Explained [WWW Document]. HRF. URL https://healthresearchfunding.org/claude-shannons-information-theory-explained/ ((accessed 11.9.2211/9/22).

[29]Adams, J.S., 2014. The Ban and the Bit: Alan Turing, Claude Shannon, and the Entropy Measure [WWW Document]. thejunglejane. thejunglejane.com/writing/the-ban-and-the-bit-alan-turing-claude-shannon-and-the-entropy-measure (accessed 11/9/22).

According to James Gleick, author of "The Information: A History, a Theory, a Flood," a Shannon bit "was a fulcrum around which the world began to turn. . .. The bit now joined the inch, the pound, the quart, and the minute as a determinate quantity—a fundamental unit of measure. But measuring what? 'A unit for measuring information,' Shannon wrote, as though there were such a thing, measurable and quantifiable, as information."[30]

According to Good, Turing independently invented bans in 1941, seven years before the Shannon paper.[31] The interesting thing is that Turing actually spent several days with Shannon in the United States in 1943.[28] The intriguing question is did these two men talk about bans and bits when they met? In other words, did Turing give Shannon the idea? Shannon emphatically says no, and I believe him. Turing was still working under Britain's Secrecy Act. Only a handful of Allies actually knew what was going on at Bletchley Park at the time. Turing was one of them, but he never talked about Enigma outside of those circles even when he was arrested and threatened with prison later in life. It's a weird coincidence, though, and makes you wonder.

At the height of the war, Bletchley Park was a code-breaking factory with as many as 200 bombes running at any given time supported by some 9,000 analysts. Turing, and all the codebreakers at Bletchley Park, made it possible for Allied leaders to see Hitler's orders most times before the German commanders in the field saw them. Turing's life tragedy resulted from two facts: he was gay (illegal in the United Kingdom at the time), and the British were implacable about the need to keep their code-breaking capabilities secret. Many Bletchley Park workers went to their graves without anybody in their families knowing the significance of what they did during the war.

---

[30]Gleick, J., 2012. The Information: A History, A Theory, A Flood. Vintage.
[31]Good, I.J., 2011. A List of Properties of Bayes-Turing Factors. NSA FOIA Case #58820.

After, British Prime Minister Winston Churchill gave the order to destroy all the Bombes except for a handful to keep the secret safe. He used the remaining Bombes and its successors, like the Colossus, to spy on the Russians after the war, and he didn't want anybody to know that he could do it.

Code breaking was so secret that after the war nobody outside the small and cleared code-breaker community knew who Turing was or what he accomplished, or even that the Bayes rule was a good method to use in cryptanalysis. And then, according to McGrayne, paranoia captured the West's imagination. The Soviets detonated their first atomic bomb. China became a communist country. We found spies everywhere: Alger Hiss, Klaus Fuchs, and Julius and Ethel Rosenberg. Senator Joseph McCarthy accused prominent U.S. citizens of being communist. Two openly gay English spies, Guy Burgess and Donald Maclean, escaped to the USSR. American intelligence warned the British about another homosexual spy: Anthony Blunt. Leaders on both sides of the pond were worried about an international homosexual spy ring. The Americans banned gays from entering the country, and the British started arresting homosexuals in droves.

And that's what happened to Turing. He got arrested for being gay, and since nobody knew who he was and his work was so secret, no government official stepped up to vouch for him or to protect him. According to McGrayne, "As the world lionized the Manhattan Project physicists who engineered the atomic and hydrogen bombs, as Nazi war criminals went free, and as the United States recruited German rocket experts, Turing was found guilty. Less than a decade after England fought a war against Nazis who had conducted medical experiments on their prisoners, an English judge forced Turing to choose between prison and chemical castration." Turing chose castration, a series of estrogen injections designed (with no scientific credence) to curb his sexual preference. He grew breasts, and the drugs messed with his mind. On June 7, 1954, two years after he was arrested, he committed suicide at the age of 42.

I first learned about Turing in the early 2000s after I read Neal Stephenson's novel, *Cryptonomicon*.[32] Over the years since, I kept picking up pieces of Turing's story. The stark tragedy of this is hard to take, even for me, and I've reread this story many times. For me, it's like going through the grieving process. One of our greatest minds, one of our most brilliant mathematicians, and one who almost single-handedly saved 20 million lives, was cut down in his prime at the age of 42, alone, with no friends or colleagues, with nobody seeing who he really was at a time when it mattered most. I just want to raise my fist to the skies and rage. And the mind boggles just thinking about the could-have-beens. What would Turing have done with artificial intelligence if left to himself after the war? What computers would he have helped build? What would he and Shannon have done together to advance information theory? What progress could we have made in the Bayes theorem?

Consider the Bayes Rule for Cybersecurity Risk Forecasting

As I said, the Bayes rule is the third leg to our risk forecasting stool alongside some superforecasting techniques and Fermi estimates. The idea that you can make a broad estimate about your risk with nothing more than an educated guess (the initial cue ball) and then refine that guess over time with new information as it becomes available (rolling many more balls on the table) is genius. You don't need to have years and years of actuarial data before you can calculate the risk. You don't have to count all the things first. Most important, it's not just a good idea either. It's a great idea that's supported by 250 years of math evolution from Thomas Bayes to Pierre Simon Laplace to Alan Turing and to Bill Gates.

[32]Stephenson, N., 2002. Cryptonomicon. Harper Collins.

For years, I've been trying to get my head around how to calculate cyber risk for my organization with enough precision to make good decisions. With superforecasting, Fermi estimates, and the Bayes rule, the path ahead is clear. In the next section, I will demonstrate how to do it. I'm going to go through an example of how to calculate our first prior using some Fermi estimates to forecast cyber risk.

Risk Forecasting with the Bayes Rule: A Practical Example

To calculate our first estimate of the probability of material impact to our organization this year, the first question (the prior) we should probably answer is, what is the probability that any company would get hit with a material impact cyberattack? This is our first Fermi estimate. In this analysis, I'm going to restrict my calculations to U.S. organizations mostly because there is a lot of research data available for the United States that isn't available worldwide. We can use the answers we get with this data to extrapolate internationally in a typical Fermi estimate kind of way. But even so, there will be both hard facts and assumptions to keep track of. Let's start with the FBI's Internet Crime Report of 2021.[33]

In that study, the FBI's Internet Crime Complaint Center (IC3) said that they received just under a million complaints (847,376) in 2021. Let's assume that all of those represent material losses. That's probably not true, but that's our first assumption to note. But the IC3 also estimated (their assumption) that only 15 percent of organizations actually report their incidents. So, how many total should there be? Doing the math (see Figure 6.5), that means that more than five and a half million (5,649,173) U.S. organizations should have reported complaints to the IC3 in 2021.

[33]Staff, 2021. Internet Crime Report, Internet Crime Complaint Center. FBI.

Assumptions	Math Problem 2	Facts
All 847,376 complaints are material. IC3: 15% of organizations report their attacks.	X = The IC3 estimate of U.S. complaints that should have been reported in 2021. $\frac{15}{100} = \frac{847,376}{X}$	847,376 complaints received by IC3 in 2021.

$$X = 100 * \frac{847,376}{15}$$

$$X = 5,649,173$$

Figure 6.5 Math problem 2: the IC3 estimate of U.S. complaints that should have been reported in 2021

That said, my assumption is that there are many reasons why organizations don't report their cyber incidents to the FBI, and the main one might be that the incident didn't turn out to be material. As a conservative estimate then, let's assume that only 25 percent of the potential unreported incidents were material. That number is probably way smaller, but it is good enough for now (see Figure 6.6).

The number of unreported material complaints is equal to what the total number of incidents IC3 expected occurred in 2021 (5,649,173) minus the known reported complaints (847,376). Doing the subtraction, that number is just over four and half million (Z = 4,801,797).

With my assumption that only 25 percent of the unreported complaints were material, 25 percent of just over four and half million (4,801,747) is an estimated 1.2 million (Y = 1,200,449).

So, the total number of material complaints is the known reported complaints from IC3 (847,376) plus the estimated

Assumptions	Math Problem 3	Facts
5,649,173 is the estimated number of all U.S. cyber incidents (complaints) in 2021.	Z = The number of unreported complaints.	847,376 complaints received by IC3 in 2021.
25% of the unreported complaints are material incidents.	Y = The estimated number of material unreported complaints.	
	Z = 5,649,173 − 847,376	
	Z = 4,801,797	
	Y = 4,801,797 * 25%	
	Y = 1,200,449	

Figure 6.6 Math problem 3: the IC3 estimate of U.S. unreported material complaints in 2021

Assumptions	Math Problem 4	Facts
All 847,376 complaints are material.	X = The estimated total number of material complaints.	847,376 complaints received by IC3 in 2021.
1,200,449 is the number of unreported material complaints.	X = 847,376 + 1,200,449	
	X = 2,047,825	

Figure 6.7 Math problem 4: the estimated total number of material complaints in 2021

unreported material complaints (1,200,449) for a total of just over 2 million (2,047,825). See Figure 6.7.

In other words, the FBI IC3 estimates that the number of material cyber events in the United States in 2021 is just over 2 million (2,047,825). Hold that number in your head for a second.

I'm also assuming that no organization gets hit twice in the same year. That's probably not true, but for now, let's roll with it. Let's also assume that any nation-state attacks that caused material damage will be included in the IC3 stats.

The question then arises, "How many organizations exist in the United States that could potentially report to the IC3?" To do that, we need numbers on private companies, educational institutions, and public institutions. We know from stats published by the U.S. Census Bureau in 2019 that the United States had 6.1 million (6,102,412) registered companies.[34] Employee sizes for that group range from 5 to more than 500. For the moment, we'll assume that employee size doesn't matter in our forecast. We know that's probably not true either, but we will list it as an assumption and look for data later that will inform the assumption one way or the other. We will also assume that the number includes nongovernmental organizations (NGOs).

Further, according to the National Center for Education Statistics, in 2020, there were 128,961 total schools for public and private prekindergarten, elementary, middle, secondary, postsecondary, and other schools.[35] For the postsecondary schools, that's a mix of 4-year and 2-year programs of various student sizes. It also represents a mix of student sizes for the elementary schools. We will also assume that student body size doesn't matter for this forecast either.

Interestingly, we don't have an official number of sanctioned federal government entities. According to Clyde Wayne Crews at Forbes in 2021, there is no official, authoritative list maintained by

[34]Staff, 2022. 2019 SUSB Annual Data Tables by Establishment Industry [WWW Document]. Census.gov. www.census.gov/data/tables/2019/econ/susb/2019-susb-annual.html (accessed 11/9/22).
[35]Staff, 2019. The NCES Fast Facts Tool provides quick answers to many education questions (National Center for Education Statistics) [WWW Document]. nces.ed.gov/FastFacts/display.asp?id=84 (accessed 11/9/22).

any one of them.[36] No one U.S. federal government entity is officially tasked with keeping track of all the other federal agencies. I know that sounds crazy, but apparently it's so. He lists eight different reports, from the Administrative Conference of the United States to the Federal Register Agency List, that estimate the number range of government agencies from 61 to 443 depending on how they count it. Let's take the average, 252, as a starting point.

Finally, from the U.S. Census Bureau in 2017, 90,126 local governments existed in the United States.[37] Assume that the size of the local government doesn't matter for this forecast either.

To summarize then, within the United States, there are

- 6,102,412 registered companies
- 128,961 schools
- 252 federal government agencies
- 90,126 local government organizations (state, city, county, etc.)
- 6,321,751 U.S. organizations

All of these could register a material report to the FBI's IC3. With our assumption that 2,047,825 organizations should have reported to the IC3 in 2021, the first prior in our Bayesian analysis is that there is roughly a 32 percent chance (2 million reported breaches divided by 6.3 million total organizations) that any recognized organization in the United States could have had a material cyberattack that year. See Figure 6.8.

[36]Crews, C.W., Jr., 2017b. How Many Federal Agencies Exist? We Can't Drain The Swamp Until We Know. Forbes.
[37]Staff, 2020. From Municipalities to Special Districts, Official Count of Every Type of Local Government in 2017 Census of Governments [WWW Document]. Census.gov. www.census.gov/library/publications/2019/econ/from_municipalities_to_special_districts.html (accessed 11/9/22).

Assumptions	Math Problem 5	Facts
2,047,825 total material complaints should have been reported to the IC3 in 2021.	$$\text{First Prior} = \frac{2{,}047{,}825}{6{,}321{,}751}$$	N/A
6,321,751 total official organizations in the U.S.	$$\text{First Prior} = 32\%$$	

Figure 6.8 Math problem 5: the first prior that any officially recognized organization in the United States could have had a material cyberattack in 2021

Before we call that our official Bayesian prior, though, let's check our assumptions.

- All of the just under a million complaints (847,376) to the IC3 were material.
- Only 25 percent of the estimated unreported incidents to the IC3 were material.
- Any nation-state attacks that caused material damage will be included in the IC3 stats.
- No company gets hit more than once in a given year.
- The number of employees or students of an organization doesn't matter for the forecast.
- The total number of companies listed by the US Census Bureau includes NGOs.
- The average (252) of existing federal organizations taken from eight different reports is close enough.

Those are some big assumptions. But for this first estimate, this first Bayesian prior, it's good enough. This is us rolling the cue ball onto the billiard table and making a first guess as to where it is. Using Fermi's outside-in forecast, a technique used by Dr. Tetlock's superforecasters described in his book of the same name, for any organization in the United States, the probability of material impact due to a cyber incident in 2021 was 32 percent, about a one and three chance.

Let me say that again. Extrapolating for every year, for any United States organization, there is a 1 in 3 chance of experiencing a material cyber event every year.

But Wait, What About Me?

As you read that 32 percent number, you're likely saying to yourself, "That's all great and fine, but I'm special. I work for a small startup making concrete. There is no way that there's a 32 percent chance that the company will be materially impacted by a cyber event this year. It must be way lower than that." Or, "I work for a Fortune 1000 company. There is no way that there is only a 32 percent chance. It has to be much bigger than that. This 32 percent chance has no meaning to me. It doesn't help me at all."

But remember, the first prior is just the assistant rolling the cue ball onto the table and asking us to make the first estimate about its placement. The next thing we need to do is to check our assumptions and make additional measurements. We'll be looking to collect new evidence about those assumptions and adjust our 32 percent forecast up or down depending on where the evidence leads us. For example, if we found sometime in the future that my assumption about unreported material events in the IC3 report was closer to 10 percent than 25 percent, we would adjust the probability down. On the other hand, if we found that the actual number of federal organizations was really 80 versus the average 252 that we used, then we would adjust the probability up. Just like Tetlock's superforecasters do on a regular basis, keep your eye on your assumptions and be ready to adjust when new evidence is available.

The next step is to continue to collect new evidence. We're going to roll more balls onto the billiard table. Two research reports published by the Cyentia Institute will help us in this round.

- "Information Risk Insights Study: A Clearer Vision for Assessing the Risk of Cyber Incidents"[38]
- "IRIS Risk Retina: Data for Cyber Risk Quantification"[39]

These two Cyentia reports are the closest things I found that match my thinking around superforecasters, Bayesian philosophy, and Fermi estimates. In the first paper, Cyentia partnered with Advizen (a Zywave company), which provided the breach data set for Fortune 1000 companies in the past decade. I have high confidence in the data set since it's public knowledge who all the Fortune 1000 companies are and, because of compliance reasons, the data breach reporting is robust.

The first finding that is important to our study is that for the past 5 years, just under one in four Fortune 1000 companies get hit each year by a material cyber event. That number is slightly lower than our first Bayesian prior of 1 in 3. But Cyentia pulled its analysis apart by looking at the odds of ranked quartiles. It looked at the odds for the top 250 firms, then the next 250, etc. It turns out that if your company is in the Fortune 250, you are 5 times as likely to have a material breach than if you are in the bottom 250. From their report:

- *Fortune 250*: A 1 in 2 chance
- *Fortune 251 to 500*: A 1 in 3 chance
- *Fortune 501 to 750*: A 1 in 5 chance
- *Fortune 751 to 1000*: A 1 in 10 chance

---

[38]Staff, 2020. Information Risk Insights Study: A Clearer Vision for Assessing the Risk of Cyber Incidents. The Cyentia Institute.
[39]Staff, 2021. IRIS Risk Retina - Data for Cyber Risk Quantification. Cyentia Institute.

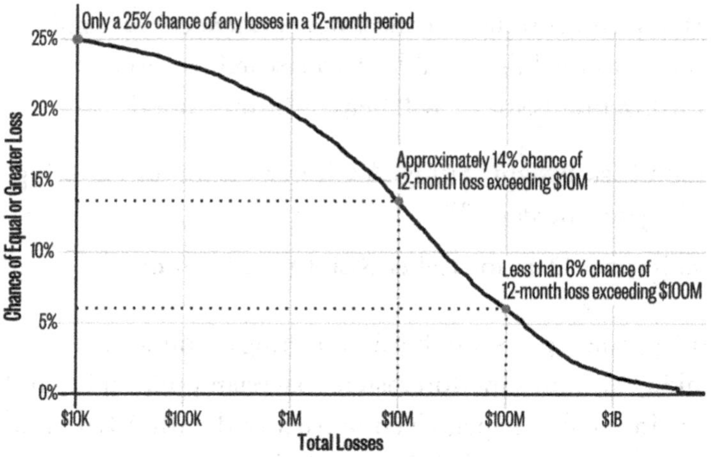

Figure 6.9 Example loss exceedance curve[39]

It did a similar analysis for calculating the chances of a Fortune 1000 company experiencing multiple attacks in the same year. This goes to answer one of our Bayesian assumptions.

- *Fortune 250*: A 1 in 3 chance
- *Fortune 251 to 500*: A 1 in 7 chance
- *Fortune 501 to 750*: A 1 in 12 chance
- *Fortune 751 to 1000*: A 1 in 24 chance

The last thing from their report to consider is that they calculated different probabilities for different loss scenarios. They use a graph called a Loss Exceedance Curve (see Figure 6.9), which according to Bryan Smith at the Fair Institute, "...is a way to visualize the probability of the loss exceeding a certain amount. . . . The x-axis plots the annualized loss exposure for the given risk scenario considered in the analysis. The y-axis plots the probability of a loss being greater than the intersection with the x-axis, from 0 to 100 percent." What that means is that there is a different probability for different values of loss. From the Cyentia report:

- 25 percent for any loss whatsoever
- 14 percent chance of losing $10 million or more
- 6 percent chance of losing $100 million or more

This is important when it comes to risk tolerance. For some Fortune 1000 companies, a 14 percent chance of losing $10 million is an acceptable risk. For a handful of them, that's just couch cushion money. For others, that 14 percent chance of losing $10 million might be too much to bear compared to all the other risks their leadership team is trying to avoid. The reason to use loss exceedance curves is to give the leadership the option to choose. When we were using qualitative heat maps with our high, medium, and low assessments, there was no way for company leadership to evaluate whether the risk was within their tolerance. Loss exceedance curves give them a visual reference of where their tolerance falls. See Figure 6.9.

Cyentia then combined three data sets from Advizen, Dun & Bradstreet, and the U.S. Census Bureau for breaches reported for all companies in the United States, not just Fortune 1000. It admits in the report that compared to the Fortune 1000 data set, it's not as robust, but Cyentia still has high confidence in it being the best available. The report has a section where it forecasts the probability of a material breach for each commercial sector (Construction, Agriculture, Trade, etc.). They conclude that there is a less than 1 in 100 chance for any company regardless of sector to have a material breach this year but with caveats. In an email conversation with Wade Baker, the co-founder of the Cyentia Institute, he said that "Since each sector is composed of mostly smaller firms, it pulls the typical probability down dramatically."

The contrast between Cyentia's 1 percent compared to my IC3 forecast of 32 percent is quite large. But Wade says that the more accurate forecast comes from the size of the organization, not the sector. In the report, they show quite the large probability gap among revenue groupings.

- *Less than $1 billion in annual revenues (where most organizations live)*: < 2 percent
- *Between $1 billion and $10 billion*: 9.6 percent
- *Between $10 billion and $100 billion*: 22.6 percent
- *Greater than $100 billion*: 75 percent

But they also point out that larger organizations are more likely to report a breach, more than 1,000 times more likely compared to small (<$10 million) businesses, so the probabilities are probably skewed in that direction as well.

How Do You Incorporate This New Data?

That begs the question, how do you incorporate this data into your forecast? How do you use the prior forecast, 32 percent, with this report? First things first, if you're working for a Fortune 1000 company, I would throw out the generic forecast that I just did from the FBI's reporting. Cyentia's report on Fortune 1000 companies is way more precise for that group, and the data set is so robust, that I feel confident those forecasts are more accurate for Fortune 1000 companies than my generic forecast for any and all companies using FBI data. Also, the second report I listed, "IRIS Risk Retina - Data for Cyber Risk Quantification," is all about nonprofits. If I was working for a nonprofit, I would use that report to establish my prior.

But, if you don't work for a Fortune 1000 company or a nonprofit, say you're Marvel Studios, how do you absorb this new data about revenue size into your forecast? If we were inclined to throw this into Bayes' algorithm and do the math, we could. But we're doing Fermi estimates here. That will likely be good enough.

According to Zippia (a company that tracks analytics about companies), Marvel Studios made almost $116 million (115.7) in revenue in 2021.[40] That puts it in the "less than $1 billion" in annual revenues category (where most of us live). According to Cyentia, that type of company has less than a 2 in 100 chance of having a material breach. That's a big gap compared to my IC3 prior of 32 percent.

Does that make you want to reduce the prior or increase it? Since Cyentia's forecast is lower than my IC3 forecast, logic says that I would lower it. But by how much? Do you lower it all the way down to 2 percent? You could if you feel that the Cyentia report is so strong that it overwhelms the IC3 analysis like it did for the Fortune 1000 companies or the nonprofits. You could absolutely do that. But, the authors of this analysis say in the report that the data is not as robust as the Fortune 1000 data. And I feel confident in my IC3 analysis.

Remember, the concept behind Bayes is that it's a measure of your belief, your personal confidence. For me then, it's not a complete replacement. I would adjust the IC3 prior down some, say to 15 percent, and start looking for more evidence to help support the change.

One technique used by Tetlock's superforecasters when making these adjustments is asking themselves how confident they are in the change. In their minds, they want to be at least 95 percent confident that the adjustment is correct, not 100 percent, but almost. I know that's an abstract way to think about it. How can you be 95 percent confident about something? How would you rate the difference

---

[40]Staff, 2021. Marvel Entertainment Revenue: Annual, Historic, And Financials [WWW Document]. Zippia. www.zippia.com/marvel-entertainment-careers-63407/revenue (accessed 11/9/22).

between 95 percent and 85 percent? I know I can't do that. One trick they use is asking themselves to make a bet. Would they bet $100 of their own money that this adjustment was correct? A bet implies some risk and commitment. You may be totally sure about something when you make a bet but you're not 100 percent sure. So, if you are so positive about your adjustment that you're willing to bet $100 on it, that's a good approximation for being 95 percent confident. If not, back the adjustment off a point or two. With my new prior, 15 percent, I wouldn't bet $100 of my own money that 15 percent is the correct number. What about 17 percent? OK, I would bet $100 on that.

To recap, I used two different frequentist data sets. I used the FBI IC3 data and some Fermi estimations to find the initial prior. I then used the Cyentia report to make an adjustment to that initial forecast. The bottom line is that, for Marvel Studios, I'm forecasting the probability of material impact this year as 17 percent, or just under a 1 in 5 chance. Remember, as you discover new evidence about our assumptions or new facts become available, adjust the estimate up or down based on the new information. But for now, we have a new prior of 17 percent.

It's a gut call. Remember, though, that this is still just an outside-in analysis, a Fermi prediction. This forecast has nothing to do with the Marvel Studios actual defensive posture (inside-out). It doesn't take into consideration any defensive measures that Marvel Studios has deployed to strengthen its posture in terms of cybersecurity first principles. We'll look at that next.

An Inside-Out Analysis: The First Principles

With outside-in analysis, I have demonstrated how network defenders can take an initial estimate and adjust it as new evidence comes in. We took the IC3 prior and adjusted it with the Cyentia data. We can repeat the process now with inside-out analysis. In other words, we can use our outside-in forecast as the new prior and then estimate how well we have deployed our first principle strategies in turn and adjust the prior up or down based on that new evidence. That means we have to assume some things.

Let's assume that if we fully deploy each of our first principle strategies, then the impact is a reduction in risk probability to our organization by some amount. Let's assume these values:

- *Zero trust*: 10 percent
- *Intrusion kill chain prevention*: 10 percent
- *Resilience*: 15 percent
- *Automation*: 5 percent

These are best guesses on my part, and that's why they're assumptions. You might use different numbers, and that's perfectly fine. Over time, the superforecaster in me will look for new evidence that will validate or invalidate those values. But for now, the Fermi analyst in me says they are close enough. And remember, in this model, you only get the full probability reduction if you have completely deployed each strategy. Most network defenders, even those that work for robust security organizations, don't have any of these strategies fully deployed.

An Inside-Out Analysis: The Contoso Corporation

To see how this works, let's analyze a company through this first principle lens: the Contoso Corporation. The Contoso Corporation is an imaginary company that Microsoft uses to explain to potential customers about how to deploy its set of products.[41] Microsoft

[41]Staff, 2022. Microsoft 365 for enterprise for the Contoso Corporation - Microsoft 365 Enterprise [WWW Document]. Microsoft Learn. learn.microsoft.com/en-us/microsoft-365/enterprise/contoso-case-study?view=o365-worldwide (accessed 11/9/22).

explains that the company "is a fictional but representative global manufacturing conglomerate with its headquarters in Paris." Think Fujitsu, but French. Since Microsoft analysts have put a lot of work into the backstory of how the Contoso Corporation is architecturally deployed, I don't have to make one myself that has enough detail to be useful. Further, I don't have to pick on a real company like Marvel Studios for this analysis.

Here's a summary of the Contoso Corporation.

For the Contoso General View of the Business

- The Paris office has 25,000 employees; each regional office has 2,000 employees.
- It has a large sales and support organization for more than 100,000 products.
- It has an annual revenue of $35 billion (similar to Fujitsu).
- It's not a Fortune 1000 company or a nonprofit organization.

For the Contoso Technical Architecture

- Uses Microsoft 365 for office applications (email, word processing, spreadsheets, etc.).
- Is currently transitioning from data center operations to cloud-based operations, but it's years away from completing the transition.
- Customers use their Microsoft, Facebook, or Google Mail accounts to sign in to the company's public website.
- Vendors and partners use their LinkedIn, Salesforce, or Google Mail accounts to sign in to the company's partner extranet.

- Has deployed an SD-WAN to optimize its connectivity to Microsoft services in the cloud.
- Has deployed regional application servers that synchronize with the centralized Paris campus data centers.

For the Contoso Zero Trust Deployment

- Uses on-premise Active Directory Domain Services (AD DS) forest for authentication to Microsoft 365 cloud resources with password hash synchronization (PHS), but it also uses third-party tools in the cloud for federation services.
- Has deployed special rules for senior leadership, executive staff, and specific users in the finance, legal, and research departments who have access to highly regulated data.
- Collects system, application, and driver data from devices for analysis and can automatically block access or patch with suggested fixes.
- Requires multifactor authentication (MFA) for their sensitive data.
- Categorizes data into three levels of access.
- Deploys data loss protection (DLP) services for Exchange Online, SharePoint, and OneDrive.
- Designated people execute global system administrator changes and receive only time-based temporary passwords with their AD DS Privileged Identity Management (PIM) system.

For the Contoso Resilience Deployment

- Data is encrypted at rest and available only to authenticated users.

For the Contoso Intrusion Kill Chain Deployment

- Contoso uses Microsoft Defender Antivirus on the endpoint.

Since the Contoso Corporation is a global manufacturing conglomerate and not an entertainment company like Marvel, we need to start over with our outside-in Fermi estimate using the FBI's IC3 data. Our first prior is 32 percent. But, according to Cyentia, there is a 22 percent chance that Contoso (annual revenue of $35 billion) will be impacted by a material breach this year; just over a 1 in 5 chance.

The question is then, how far down do you adjust the 32 percent prior with this new information? I still have high confidence in my own IC3 outside-in analysis. I have less confidence in the Cyentia data with the caveats I have already explained, but it's still a good forecast. I would bet $100 of my own money that the actual probability of material impact is about 5 points below my generic prior. So, let's set the prior to 27 percent.

Using 27 percent as our current prior, the next step of incorporating new evidence (more balls on the billiard table) is to assess how well the Contoso Corporation is doing in implementing our cybersecurity first principle strategies. Based on how well or poorly they are deployed will impact our forecast up or down.

An Inside-Out Analysis: First Principle Strategies

Zero Trust 8 percent out of a possible 10 percent reduction adjustment. The Contoso Corporation as described has a strong identity access management (IAM) program that consists of information governance and administration (IGA), privileged identity management (PIM), and privileged access management (PAM). They provide their customers, contractors, and employees with single sign-on capability and MFA for sensitive data. For vulnerability management, they have a strong program for Microsoft products, but it's a lot weaker for any third-party applications. There is no mention of a software bill of material (SBOM) program, but they do track devices, applications, and operating system patch levels for Microsoft products. There is no discussion of a software-defined perimeter. With all of that, the Contoso Corporation is well along its zero trust journey. They still have a ways to go, but it's mature.

Intrusion Kill Chain Prevention 1 percent out of a possible 10 percent reduction adjustment. The Contoso Corporation doesn't really think about specific adversary tactics. It has a security stack of mostly Microsoft security products, and it has the capability to deliver telemetry from that stack to a security operations center (SOC), but there is no mention that Contoso has a SOC, an intelligence group, a red/blue/purple team, or a desire to share adversary playbook intelligence with its peers. I'm giving them a 1 percent reduction since Contoso uses Microsoft Defender Antivirus for automatic endpoint protection from malware, but really, they have no intrusion kill chain prevention program to speak of.

Resilience 1 percent out of a possible 15 percent reduction adjustment. The Contoso Corporation does have a healthy encryption program that works with its multilevel zero trust program. That said, I found no mention of any crisis planning, backup programs, incident response capability, or even the incipient beginnings of a chaos engineering capability. The Contoso Corporation might well deflect an inexperienced ransomware crew, but any attack from a professional crew will likely cause a material impact.

Automation 0 percent out of a possible 5 percent reduction adjustment. The Contoso Corporation doesn't mention anything about its site reliability engineering (SRE), its DevSecOps, or even its Agile development program. It mentions nothing about securing its own code or even trying to track the components it's using from open source. They are getting no benefit from automation that I can see. The Contoso architecture documents also don't mention anything about its compliance systems. In Chapter 7, I talk about how to forecast the risk of noncompliance into your risk forecast.

With all of those reduction adjustments (8 percent for zero trust, 1 percent for intrusion kill chain prevention, 1 percent for resilience, and 0 percent for automation), I would bet $100 that the Contoso Corporation has a 17 percent chance of being materially impacted by a cyberattack this year: just under a 1 in 5 chance. This is the Contoso Corporation's new prior. See Figure 6.10.

What Now? Are We Within the Risk Tolerance of the Business?

If I was the Contoso CSO, there are several next steps to consider and assumptions to validate. The first thing to do is to confirm the dollar amount of what is material for the company. With annual revenues of $35 billion, is a $10 million loss material? $100 million? Something bigger? Something smaller? And how do you determine that number? That would be several one-on-one conversations with the CFO, the CEO, and members of the board. And, by the way, that number will likely change over time as the fortunes of the company go up and down. Make sure you're checking in with senior leadership annually to confirm the number.

I would definitely take the Cyentia loss exceedance curve for Fortune 1000 companies as a baseline, find the value on the curve, and adjust my forecast up or down depending. For example, Cyentia says that for Fortune 1000 companies, there is a 14 percent chance of

Assumptions	Math Problem 6	Facts
32%: Initial outside-in first prior estimate for all U.S. organizations based on IC3 Data. 27%: Adjusted Contoso outside-in prior based on downward adjustment from the Cyentia report on revenue size. 8%: Zero Trust deployment downward adjustment. 1%: Intrusion Kill Chain deployment downward adjustment. 1%: Resilience deployment downward adjustment. 0%: Automation deployment downward adjustment.	X = The Contoso Corporation's next prior using inside-out analysis. X = Adjusted Contoso outside-in prior – zero trust adjustment – intrusion kill chain adjustment – resilience adjustment – automation adjustment. X = 27% – 8% – 1% – 1% – 0% X = 17%	N/A

Figure 6.10 Math problem 6: the Contoso Corporation's next prior using inside-out analysis

losing $10 million or more. If $10 million is the Contoso indicator for materiality, that 14 percent chance would drag the current prior of 17 percent down one or two points to, say, 15 percent, a 3 in 20 chance.

The next step is to determine if the current forecast is in the tolerance of the leadership chain. If it is, if they think that a 3 in 20 chance is an acceptable risk to the business, then nothing needs to be done here in terms of significant new investment in people, process, and technology. The infosec team needs to maintain and perhaps become more efficient in executing its zero trust, intrusion kill chain, resilience, and automation tactics, but we're not going to roll out some new initiative. On the other hand, if senior leadership is uncomfortable with the 3 in 20 chance and demands that I get it under 10 percent, or a 1 in 10 chance, I have some planning to do.

I would look at resilience first. Contoso's resilience plan is weak, and some improvements in basic meat-and-potatoes IT functionality (such as automated backups, practice restorations, crisis planning, and incident response) could significantly reduce its risk compared to the other first principal strategies that might cost a lot more to implement. After all, getting good at intrusion kill chain prevention is not cheap. That said, let's not forget to keep track of the cost for reducing risk to less than 10 percent. If the spend to accomplish that task is greater than the $10 million loss we were trying to prevent, perhaps we should go back to the drawing board and come up with a less costly plan. This is security risk forecasting in practice.

Conclusion

I have been thinking about finding a better way to convey cyber risk to the board for a long time. I kept struggling with my lack of knowledge about statistics and kept trying to rely on the frequentist view that I needed more data, that I needed to count all the things. But I knew deep down that this wasn't the path; there had to be a better way.

Dr. Tetlock's book on superforecasting opened my mind to the idea that infosec professionals didn't need precision answers to make resource decisions about security improvements. We could make good enough estimates, Fermi estimates, and back-of-the-envelope estimates that would take less time and the answers would be close enough to be impactful. And then I learned that the Bayes rule was the mathematical foundation that explained why superforecasting techniques worked.

Working through the examples in this essay for Marvel Studios and the Contoso Corporation, you may feel queasy that I am basing cyber risk forecasts for multimillion-dollar companies on Kentucky windage. I get it. It's tough to let go of the frequentist mindset. But I will just remind you that people way smarter than you and me, like Alan Turing, used these techniques to solve more complex problems than calculating cyber risk. Maybe you should try it. Besides, the old way of collecting all the data and using qualitative heat maps hasn't really worked since we started doing it some 20 years ago. It's time to consider a change.

7 Automation

It is not the strongest of the species that survives, nor the most intelligent that survives. It is the one that is the most adaptable to change.

—Charles Darwin

Currently, DevOps is more like a philosophical movement, not yet a precise collection of practices, descriptive or prescriptive.

—Gene Kim

Overview

In this chapter, we turn our attention to automation. Traditionally, the infosec community doesn't consider automation to be in the purview of the security professional. That has been a giant mistake in first principle thinking. Because of that error, the IT community has sprinted away from the security community in pursuing advanced software development methods. In this chapter, I will explain why it's time to catch up. I will talk about why automation in general is important to eradicate mundane and error-prone manual tasks. I will then show how the software development community evolved their thinking from Gantt charts in the early 1900s all the way to DevOps today and that DevSecOps is the logical next step. I will then tackle the tricky subject of automating the compliance systems across our deployed first principle architecture. It's tricky because compliance doesn't have a major impact on reducing the probability of material impact, but depending on the industry you're in, you will likely have to plug the telemetry from your deployed first principle tactics into the compliance system. Finally, I will explain the relatively new concept of chaos engineering and how it's an advanced automated resilience tactic that today is reserved for large organizations that deliver global services that can never go down.

Why Security Automation Is Essential

In 2022, IT and security professionals use terms such as *DevOps*, *DevSecOps*, and *site reliability engineering* to describe philosophies and best practices around rapid software development and infrastructure as code. But it was a long and incremental journey from the 1960s to the beginning of these movements in the early 2000s. By the 2010s, it was clear that startups could use these strategies against their more conservative and slow-moving competitors and that Silicon Valley giants like AWS, Google, and Netflix could use them to establish their dominance in the industry. And yet, the infosec community has been slow to adopt the ideas. In an Internet world where data is king, security practitioners still rely on tools and semimanual processes to get the work done. Some of the tools like security orchestration, automation and response (SOAR) and security information and event management (SIEM) are quite good, but they are half measures. They haven't allowed the infosec community to embrace the infrastructure-as-code models. It's one thing to collect telemetry from the security stack and to automatically parse the data to remove the noise from the signal. It's quite another to build a DevSecOps first principle system of systems that does the following:

- Monitors and updates the zero trust program: software bill of materials (SBOM) maintenance, vulnerability management, and identity and access management

- Searches for known adversary behavior across the intrusion kill chain within all data islands
- Instantly updates the security stack on those same data islands with the latest countermeasures from newly acquired kill chain intelligence
- Automatically shares and collects threat intelligence with peers
- Monitors and manages the continuous backup and encryption systems on all material data
- Regularly tests the restore process for that material data
- Probes the resilience of the system to continuously deliver service in case of catastrophe
- Collects the telemetry from all the first principle strategy systems to support the compliance program
- Collects the system stats and Fermi assumptions that allow the calculation of the organization's risk forecast, the next Bayes' prior

The same benefits that these modern coding best practices gave to the IT community could greatly reduce the probability of material impact to our organizations if the security community adopted them. It's a big ask. Automating all of that functionality is not something that will get done overnight. The point is to start. Every step in the direction of automating those systems will greatly improve your situation. If I have not convinced you, let me explain how the IT community got there.

Early History of Software Development Philosophies

Back in the dinosaur days (1960s) when computers were bigger than houses, large software development projects didn't have a standard methodology yet. We were still figuring out what to do with these things called *mainframes*. Computer scientists leaned on established general-purpose project management theory to do software development, like the original Gantt charts from the 1910s and the critical path method made popular in the 1950s.[1]

In 1956, Herbert Benington invented the first version of the Waterfall software development model.[2] Interestingly, Benington didn't get credit for his work early on. Dr. Winston Royce (1970) got the credit when he published a criticism of the model that didn't even mention it by name.[3] But his paper had nice diagrams that showed the process (requirements, analysis, design, implementation, testing, and operations) all flowing from top to bottom, just like a waterfall. In 1976, Bell and Taylor referred to the Royce diagrams as the Waterfall model and the name stuck to Dr. Royce for a bit.[4]

By the time the personal computing revolution began in the 1980s, software development was in a full-blown and acknowledged crisis. In the 1960s, software engineers were already unable to build the systems they were asked to build and organizations couldn't hire enough programmers to get the job done. In the 1970s, complexity was going through the roof. Computer science's founding father, Edsger Dijkstra, said this about the problem in an ACM Turing Lecture in 1972: "The major cause [of the software crisis] is that the machines have become several orders of magnitude more powerful! . . . As long as there were no machines, programming was

---

[1]Krutikov, A., 2021. Back to School: History of Software Development Methodologies [WWW Document]. Qulix. www.qulix.com/about/blog/history-of-software-development-methodologies (accessed 12/18/22).
[2]Benington, H.D., 1983. Production of Large Computer Programs. Annals of the History of Computing 5, 350–361. https://doi.org/10.1109/MAHC.1983.10102
[3]Mkrtchyan, R., 2017. All You Need to Know About the Waterfall Model. LinkedIn.
[4]Hartson, R., Pyla, P.S., 2018. The UX Book: Designing a Quality User Experience. Morgan Kaufmann.

no problem at all.... And now [that] we have gigantic computers, programming has become an equally gigantic problem."[5]

That is eerily similar to the security situation today. Our security environments have exploded in complexity, and for years there has been a recognized industry shortage of qualified security professionals.

In 1985, to address the software crisis issue, the U.S. Department of Defense (DoD) adopted the Waterfall model as a requirement for all contractors, despite Royce's criticism, and started a period of ponderous, iceberg-like progress in producing software.[6] According to Alexey Krutikov, "Although Royce himself believed that Waterfall should be iterative, advocated pilots and micro models, Waterfall was and continues to be wrongly considered as a sequential methodology." It was sequential because developers weren't allowed to proceed to the next Waterfall level until the current level was complete.[7] If developers made changes in the implementation stage, the team had to go all the way back to the beginning and start over. The impact was that many programming projects took years to finish and the teams spent as much time documenting the requirements as they did writing code. Contrast that to today's DevOps environments where the goal is to deploy at least 10 changes to the code base a day.[8]

---

[5]E. W. Dijkstra Archive, 1972. The Humble Programmer [WWW Document]. University of Texas at Austin, Computer Science, College of Natural Resources. www.cs.utexas.edu/~EWD/transcriptions/EWD03xx/EWD340.html (accessed 02/06/23).

[6]Staff, 1985. DEFENSE SYSTEM SOFTWARE DEVELOPMENT: DOD-STD-2167A. DEPARTMENT OF DEFENSE.

[7]Staff, 2021. A Brief History of Software Development Methodologies [WWW Document]. growin. www.growin.com/blog/history-of-software-development-methodologies (accessed 12/18/22).

[8]Allspaw, J., Hammond, P., 2009. Velocity 09: 10+ Deploys Pe. YouTube.

Agile Becomes the Challenger

In the 1990s, some rebel developers started experimenting with ways to improve the process. They began toying with the Rational Unified Process (1994), Scrum (1995), and Extreme Programming (1996).[1] But in February 2001, 17 programmers traveled to Utah for a long weekend of skiing and discussions about building software. The result was the Agile Manifesto: a rejection of the Waterfall model and an embracement of the idea of producing real, working code as a milestone of progress.[9]

Up to this point, software development was mainly concerned with general-purpose coding. In other words, software projects built applications to solve specific problems in business, in the government space, and in academia. There wasn't a lot of talk about using software to run the IT infrastructure, and there wasn't much discussion about how to write secure software. This is the point where it all started to change. As a community, we started to see parallel development in improving security in all software as well as deploying code as infrastructure.

When Do We Start Thinking About Security?

In 2000, the desktop computer operating system that dominated the market was Windows. Consumers had deployed it on at least 75 percent of the desktops worldwide.[10, 11] In May of that year, hackers

[9]Lynn, R., 2018. The History of Agile [WWW Document]. Planview. www.planview.com/resources/guide/agile-methodologies-a-beginners-guide/history-of-agile (accessed 12/18/22).

[10]Eylenburg, A., n.d. Operating Systems: Market Shares since the 1970s [WWW Document]. eylenburg. eylenburg.github.io/os_marketshare.htm (accessed 12/18/22).

[11]Staff, n.d. Desktop Operating System Market Share Worldwide [WWW Document]. StatCounter Global Stats. gs.statcounter.com/os-market-share/desktop/worldwide#monthly-201901-202012 (accessed 11/26/22).

released the ILoveYou Worm that began a string of global impactful worms[12] that targeted Microsoft Windows products (operating systems and browsers) throughout 2001.

- *July 2001*: Code Red Worm
- *August 2001*: Code Red II Worm
- *September 2001*: Nimda Worm
- *October 2001*: Klez Worm
- Others

By February 2002, Bill Gates (chairman and chief software architect at Microsoft) turned the company on a dime to implement "Trustworthy Computing." He shut down future deployments of the Windows operating system to redirect development focus on security. The result was the creation of the first Microsoft Security Development Lifecycle (SDLC).[13, 14]

In 2003, Dave Wickers and Jeff Williams, working for Aspect Security, a software consultancy company, published an education piece on the top software security coding issues of the day. That eventually turned into the the Open Web Application Security

---

[12]Spencer, S., 2012. Timeline of Computer Viruses [WWW Document]. Mapcon Technologies, Inc. www.mapcon.com/us-en/timeline-of-computer-viruses (accessed 12/18/22).

[13]Goodwin, L., 2022. Celebrating 20 Years of Trustworthy Computing [WWW Document]. Microsoft Security Blog. www.microsoft.com/en-us/security/blog/2022/01/21/celebrating-20-years-of-trustworthy-computing (accessed 12/18/22).

[14]Trent, R., 2014. The Story Behind the Microsoft Security Development Lifecycle [WWW Document]. ITPro Today: IT News, How-Tos, Trends, Case Studies, Career Tips, More. www.itprotoday.com/strategy/story-behind-microsoft-security-development-lifecycle (accessed 12/18/22).

Project (OWASP) Top 10, a reference document describing the most critical security concerns for web applications.[15]

To be clear, it wasn't that software developers weren't thinking about building secure systems. It's just that there weren't any formal examples that they could point to for inspiration, and there weren't any accepted best practices by the community. Frankly, business leaders and product managers weren't asking for it. The early 2000s saw the first movements in the community to change those situations.

Coding the Infrastructure

In 1994, Amazon began work on an e-commerce service called Merchant.com to help third-party merchants like Target or Marks & Spencer build online shopping sites on top of Amazon's e-commerce engine.[16] This effort eventually led to AWS ten years later. In 2003, Amazon began building infrastructure-as-code projects internally (the beginnings of DevOps); a set of common infrastructure services everyone could access without reinventing the wheel every time. Amazon business leaders soon realized that they could build the operating system for the Internet from these services. This revelation fast tracked the development of AWS.

In 2004, when Google was nothing more than a search engine and not the Internet giant that it is today, company leaders made an extraordinary decision. Instead of assigning the responsibility of network management to an IT team as was the standard best practice of the day, they handed the task off to the development team.

---

[15]Curphey, M., 2014. The Start of OWASP – A True Story [WWW Document]. Veracode. www.veracode.com/blog/intro-appsec/start-owasp-true-story (accessed 12/18/22).

[16]Miller, R., 2016. How AWS came to be • TechCrunch [WWW Document]. TechCrunch. techcrunch.com/2016/07/02/andy-jassys-brief-history-of-the-genesis-of-aws/?guccounter=1 (accessed 12/18/22).

This group of site reliability engineers (SREs) got busy automating all the infrastructure tasks that were repetitive, error-prone, and provided little value to the future for the company. They called those tasks *toil* and contributed to the movement that wouldn't have a name for another six years: DevOps.[17]

Dr. Gary McGraw published the first Building Security In Maturity Model (BSIMM) report in March 2008; it was a survey of some 30+ companies that collated initiatives and activities around software security.[18] The BSIMM is not prescriptive. It is merely a collection of software security best practices that participating organizations adhere to. The purpose is to let organizations review what their peers are doing in the industry in terms of developing secure software. In 2009, Pravir Chandra published the first Software Assurance Maturity Model (SAMM), a prescriptive security best practice security model.[19] It's prescriptive because the model advises what organizations should be doing with respect to building secure software systems. With these two models, the security community started to have a way to measure its progress against its peers in the industry (BSIMM) and against what security experts recommend (SAMM).

Amazon started the cloud revolution when it rolled out AWS in 2006.[15] Microsoft followed suit with a competing service in 2010 with Azure.[20] Google started to compete in the space with

---

[17]Murphy, N.R., Beyer, B., Jones, C., Petoff, J., 2016. Site Reliability Engineering: How Google Runs Production Systems. O'Reilly Media, Inc.
[18]Staff, n.d. About the Building Security In Maturity Model [WWW Document]. BSIMM. www.bsimm.com/about.html (accessed 12/18/22).
[19]Staff, n.d. SAMM model overview [WWW Document]. OWASPSAMM. owaspsamm.org/model (accessed 12/18/22).
[20]Roosevelt_Abandy, 2022. The History of Microsoft Azure [WWW Document]. TECHCOMMUNITY.MICROSOFT.COM. techcommunity .microsoft.com/t5/educator-developer-blog/the-history-of-microsoft-azure/ ba-p/3574204 (accessed 12/18/22).

Google Cloud Platform (GCP) in 2012.[21] And there are other smaller cloud service providers. But, when AWS rolled out, the cloud became the impetus for everyone in the IT community to consider infrastructure as code. But even as Agile replaced the Waterfall model as the standard software development framework, it was still agonizingly slow. Startups born in the cloud realized that they could do better by using software to create a competitive edge against their brick-and-mortar competitors. With software, they could upgrade their products and services over the Internet. They could run circles around their competition that still had to ship hardware. They could beat their competition to market for software applications if they could just streamline the process.

DevSecOps: An Essential Tactic for Automation

In 2009, DevOps began to emerge as an industry best practice out of three converging ideas.

- The 2009 Velocity Conference talk called "10+ Deploys per Day" by John Allspaw and Paul Hammond[7]
- The previously described Agile development method[8]
- The Eric Ries' book *Lean Startup*, which influenced many Silicon Valley companies between 2007 and 2010[22]

DevOps is the idea that there needs to be a much tighter integration between software developers and information technology operations (ITOps); it's the idea that once the developers, the quality

[21]Meier, R., 2017. An Annotated History of Google's Cloud Platform - Reto Meier [WWW Document]. Medium. medium.com/@retomeier/an-annotated-history-of-googles-cloud-platform-90b90f948920 (accessed 12/18/22).
[22]Ries, E., 2011. The Lean Startup: How Today's Entrepreneurs Use Continuous Innovation to Create Radically Successful Businesses. Currency.

assurance teams, and the security analysts pass any new code or maintenance updates to ITOps for deployment, their jobs aren't done. Before DevOps, developers would toss their "working" code over the wall to operations and wouldn't have to attend the late-night operations phone bridge dealing with the deployed code not working properly or breaking some other part of the system. Instead of creating artificial black boxes within each team where updates come in, get worked on, and then are passed to the next black box, DevOps is the recognition that update creation, deployment, and maintenance are one big system of systems and need to be managed that way. It is the idea that organizations would use the same Agile methodology they use today with their software development teams but expand it across all organizations in the deployment cycle: product managers, marketing professionals, developers, quality assurance practitioners, systems engineers, system administrators, operations staff, database administrators, network engineers, and security professionals. DevOps uses the Agile philosophy across the entire life cycle of deployed systems from design to development to testing to deployment to maintenance and finally to end of life.

In 2013, Gene Kim, Kevin Behr, and George Spafford published the Cybersecurity Canon Hall of Fame book *The Phoenix Project: A Novel about IT, DevOps, and Helping Your Business Win.*[23] It captures the essence of the DevOps movement in a novel because the authors wanted it to be accessible to more people, not just the tech nerds but also to general-purpose business leaders. In the story, there is an Obi-Wan-like board member that helps the CIO transform the business. He is a parts manufacturing guru and, throughout the story, imparts DevOps wisdom by explaining that ITOps should be similar to streamlining plant manufacturing similar to how the Toyota Car Company does it. Toyota leaders instituted the Toyota Production

---

[23] Kim, G., Behr, K., Spafford, G., 2014. The Phoenix Project: A Novel about IT, DevOps, and Helping Your Business Win. It Revolution Press.

System (TPS) immediately after World War II, and the basic idea was to eliminate waste in every nook and cranny within the company. Researchers and business leaders have studied the TPS for more than 50 years, and Kim et al., believe that software development should be similar to how the TPS builds cars. The Phoenix Project borrows heavily from Mike Rother's book *Toyota Kata*,[24] and the idea of continuous improvement is a key concept that our Obi-Wan-like board member imparts to our interim CIO.

By 2014 or so, the big Internet giants like Facebook, Amazon, Apple, Netflix, and Google (FAANG) had become who they were, stand-alone leaders in their industry, due in no small part to their adoption of the DevOps philosophy. Their competitors who traditionally used the old Waterfall software development method might take years to deploy a new service for their customers. The DevOps companies were deploying disruptive services on the fly and incrementally improving them with 10 deployment updates a day.

What Happened to Security?

At this point, you might be saying to yourself, this is all well and good, but security seems to have fallen off the map. With OWASP, BSIMM, and SAMM, we were at least in the discussion. But in the years between 2008 and say 2017, it seemed that the IT community and their new and fancy DevOps model sprinted away from the security community. Even in the novel *The Phoenix Project*, the security leaders weren't part of the DevOps movement. They were outsiders not convinced about the new direction. They eventually came around, but it took the entire novel.

John Willis, one of the authors of *The DevOps Handbook*, said in an interview in March 2021, that everybody involved in the DevOps

[24]Rother, M., 2009a. Toyota Kata: Managing People for Improvement, Adaptiveness and Superior Results. McGraw Hill Professional.

movement was patting themselves on the back for creating this great thing, but we almost completely forgot about security for eight years or so. People were talking about DevOps and security but not with any detail.[25, 26] Around 2017, Shannon Lietz, then working for Intuit, staked a claim for the DevSecOps phrase.[27] She created a foundation and website dedicated to the purpose of putting security into DevOps. There was some controversy there because many in the movement thought that they had invented the idea, but according to Willis, none of that matters. By creating the foundation, she got the idea front and center again in both the IT and security communities, and DevSecOps started to gain traction.

DevSecOps on Track

In 2021, Gartner placed DevSecOps on its Hype Chart as on the "slope of Enlightenment" with about 2–5 years away from reaching the Plateau of Productivity.[28] The same year, the U.S. Department of Defense formalized their own process by publishing version 1 of their DevSecOps Reference Design document.[29]

If your organization has adopted some form of the DevOps model, then you most likely have a version of the continuous integration/continuous delivery pipeline (CI/CD). The CI/CD

---

[25]Kim, G., Debois, P., Humble, J., Willis, J., Forsgren, N., 2021. The Devops Handbook: How to Create World-Class Agility, Reliability, & Security in Technology Organizations. IT Revolution Press.
[26]Willis, J., 2012. The Convergence of DevOps [WWW Document]. IT Revolution. itrevolution.com/articles/the-convergence-of-devops (accessed 12.6.22).
[27]Staff, n.d. Shannon Lietz [WWW Document]. DevSecOps. www.devsecops.org/shannon-lietz (accessed 12/18/22).
[28]Herschmann, J., 2021. Hype Cycle for Agile and DevOps, 2021. Linked In .
[29]Dod, 2021. DOD Enterprise DevSecOps - Pathway to a Reference Design, DOD Cyber Exchange. Department of Defense.

pipeline is the DevOps best practice in which, according to Synopsys, "incremental code changes are made frequently and reliably. Automated build-and-test steps triggered by CI ensure that code changes being merged into the repository are reliable. The code is then delivered quickly and seamlessly as a part of the CD process."

These pipelines are complex infrastructure-as-code software projects that, according to Teri Radichel (an AWS DevSecOps expert), "require appropriate architecture and design by the right people, not just technology. The CI/CD pipeline is part of a larger security architecture that must be well thought-out. Otherwise your security strategy will either be eternally talking about cloud but never getting there, or akin to herding cats."[30] But Teri's cat herding description is purely about the development community's integration of general-purpose security practices into their already existing DevOps systems. According to IBM, DevSecOps is the "integration of security at every phase of the software development."[31] It's great that this kind of thinking and deployment is so mature and the security community should embrace the progress. But it has nothing to do with automating our first principle architecture that I outlined at the top of the chapter. Some organizations have bits and pieces of that infrastructure deployed but nobody has a comprehensive system or even an intention to build one.

This is just another reason to think in terms of first principles. If our intent is to reduce the probability of material impact, then it absolutely follows that as our environments get more complex every day and we continue to not have enough people on hand to manage everything, automating the manual work, the toil as the Google SREs would say, is just one more lever that security leadership can pull that will have an impact.

---

[30]Radichel, T., 2022. My History of DevSecOps – Cloud Security – Medium. Cloud Security.

[31]Staff, 2020. What is DevSecOps? [WWW Document]. IBM. www.ibm.com/cloud/learn/devsecops (accessed 11/22/22).

DevSecOps As a First Principle Strategy

I have advocated for five first principle strategies in this book: zero trust, intrusion kill chain prevention, resilience, risk forecasting, and automation. Underneath the first four are a number of tactics that support them. For example, for the zero trust strategy, one tactic required is a robust identity and authorization program. For the intrusion kill chain prevention strategy, you need the ability to build adversary playbooks. For resilience, the company requires a good material data backup and recovery program. For risk forecasting, security practitioners must master the discipline of outside-in and inside-out risk assessments. And those are just a small sampling of things required by first principle thinking that could help to reduce the probability of material impact.

But, security teams can't, or shouldn't, do this in a vacuum or in parallel to what the IT side of the house is already doing. Why reinvent the wheel? After all, the entire mantra of the DevOps movement is to move development and operations onto the same team, not keep them in black-box silos that never talk to each other. The security community has to attach ourselves to the existing CI/CD pipeline process. In other words, we have to become part of the internal DevOps program, not resist it or build our own. Specifically, we have to find ways of inserting code into the pipeline that supports each of our strategies.

Final Thoughts About Automation As a Strategy

And all of it is a big lift for the infosec professional. These are big disruptive ideas. But it's time to make the change, to shift left, as they say, and get this done. The immediate impact to the security leader is that some portion of your team, maybe the biggest portion, will become part of the internal DevOps movement, maybe as developers but most definitely as product managers for each of these elements of your first principle strategy. That's something to consider when budgeting season comes around and you are considering the skillsets of your team.

The truth of the matter is that if the security community has any hope of making progress in deploying our first principle strategies, we have to automate the toil, the manual and repetitive security work that has to be done in order to build and maintain the tactics that support these strategies. Consider this automation effort as the glue that binds everything together, that makes the entire effort a system of systems that has feedback loops into the various pieces and parts.

We've been wrestling with the idea of software development methodologies (Waterfall, Agile), infrastructure-as-code projects (cloud deployments, DevOps, DevSecOps), and coding best practices (OWASP, BSIMMS, SAMM) going on for two decades now. These are not independent systems. They overlap and interact. Up to this point, at least for the security side, they have been manual tasks, toil, that are prone to mistakes. We all know that automation can reduce the impact, can at least be consistent with mistakes we make, and can offer a uniform fix across the enterprise once we have decided what to do. Automation has to be the fifth first principle strategy that we are all pursuing. DevSecOps has to be the tactic we implement.

Compliance: A First Principle Tactic That Cuts Across All Strategies

The idea of compliance is used by many kinds of organizations and industries. Government entities pass laws, like the European Parliament's General Data Protection Regulation (GDPR), to enforce the cyber behavior their citizens expect.[32] Vendor groups, like the Payment Card Industry (PCI) Security Standards Council, develop

---

[32]Nadeau, M., 2020. What is the GDPR, its requirements and facts? [WWW Document]. CSO Online. www.csoonline.com/article/3202771/general-data-protection-regulation-gdpr-requirements-deadlines-and-facts.html?nsdr=true&page=2 (accessed 12/4/22).

compliance standards to avoid government regulation.[33] Compliance can also be used by neutral third-party standards developers like the International Organization for Standardization (ISO) as a revenue-generating business model (the ISO charges for its standards products).[34] It can also be used by government entities establishing a baseline for their own internal IT infrastructure, like the U.S.'s National Institute of Standards and Technology (NIST).[35] NIST standards products have expanded out of the U.S. federal government and into the commercial sector too because they're free, vendor agnostic, and normally of the highest quality.

By definition, compliance is the act of conforming to a set of rules. If they come from government legislators, they manifest as laws. From vendor groups, they emerge as the price of doing business so that an entire vertical sector can thrive. From standards bodies, both governmental and nongovernmental, they represent neutral third-party agreements that other interested parties can point to. Compliant organizations can say they are following generally accepted international best practices.

Compliance Industry

An entire consulting industry provides services to organizations that need help navigating the complex legal web of compliance law. They generally offer services to help organizations with compliance alerts, calendars, and customized compliance reports.

---

[33]Fruhlinger, J., 2022. PCI DSS explained: Requirements, fines, and steps to compliance [WWW Document]. CSO Online. www.csoonline.com/article/3566072/pci-dss-explained-requirements-fines-and-steps-to-compliance.html (accessed 12/4/22).

[34]Kenton, W., 2022. What Is the International Organization for Standardization (ISO)? Investopedia.

[35]Staff, 2008. NIST General Information [WWW Document]. NIST. www.nist.gov/director/pao/nist-general-information (accessed 12/18/22).

There are software platforms too, called governance, risk, and compliance (GRC) software, that are used by companies to control the accessibility of data and manage those IT operations that are subject to regulation. According to TrustRadius, "Some financial and publicly traded companies are required by federal statute to complete elements of enterprise risk management (ERM). In addition, a company's ERM score will impact their S&P credit rating." GRC platforms help them do that by offering compliance services like automated management and audits and inspection management.

They focus on two business goals: loss of data and workloads and ensuring regulatory compliance. TrustRadius says, "Most GRC tools can serve both goals, but they may be more specialized in one area over the other."[36] According to Nick Inman at Kroll Consulting, about a third of his clients forecast that they will spend greater than 5 percent of revenue to satisfy compliance requirements.[37] To be clear, "to satisfy compliance requirements" means an investment to build resources (people, process, and technology) that can prove to auditors that the company is compliant. It's not an investment in building a comprehensive cybersecurity first principle program. Compliance programs can help identify security gaps in the architecture with a checklist framework, but notice that in the discussion of what first principles are (see Chapter 1), compliance doesn't show up. To reduce the probability of material impact, compliance isn't essential. There are plenty of examples where compliant organizations experienced a material event. In a 2017 ISACA report, "Compliant, Yet Breached,"

---

[36]Staff, n.d. Top Governance, Risk & Compliance Platforms 2022 [WWW Document]. TrustRadius. www.trustradius.com/governance-risk-compliance-grc (accessed 12/4/22).

[37]Inman, N., n.d. Global Regulatory Outlook 2021: The Future of Global Financial Regulation [WWW Document]. Kroll. www.kroll.com/en/insights/publications/financial-compliance-regulation/global-regulatory-outlook-2021 (accessed 12/4/22).

the author, Tony Chandola, highlights more than a dozen.[38] There are other reasons to build compliance programs, but improving an organization's security posture isn't one of them.

Two Compliance Categories: Ticket to Ride, Penalties, and Fines

The impact of compliance rules on the day-to-day security practitioner usually falls into two categories. The first category is a ticket to proceed. For example, to sell cloud services to the U.S. government, vendors have to demonstrate that they meet a set of minimum requirements in their security configuration established by the Federal Risk and Authorization Management Program (FEDRAMP). Building and maintaining a security program that complies with FEDRAMP standards and demonstrating that you have achieved that minimum bar becomes an essential task to doing business with the U.S. government. Another example is that business leaders might insist that their contractors and supply chain vendors meet the ISO 27000 standards before contracts can be approved. In both cases, compliance with those standards is your ticket to do business. You have to have the ticket or nothing will happen.

The second category is the potential range of fines and other penalties your organization might have to pay for cybersecurity noncompliance. For example, Google paid a $170 million fine in 2019 for failure to comply with the Children's Online Privacy Protection Act (COPPA).[39] The European Parliament fined Amazon in 2021 $877 million for failure to comply with GDPR.[40] The U.S.

---

[38]Chandola, T., 2017. Compliant, Yet Breached. ISACA Journal 5.
[39]Kelly, M., 2019. Google will pay $170 million for YouTube's child privacy violations. The Verge.
[40]Lawler, R., 2021. Amazon fined record $887 million over EU privacy violations. The Verge.

Office of Civil Rights (OCR) fined Anthem $16 million for Health Insurance Portability and Accountability Act (HIPAA) noncompliance.[41]

To be clear, I'm not talking about fines levied against companies for noncompliance in areas unrelated to cybersecurity. Those numbers are astronomical and most often hit financial institutions. For example, the 2020 Finbold Bank Fines Report listed the Goldman Sachs settlement of $3.9 billion to the Malaysian government for money laundering and fraud as the most expensive penalty of that year.[42] But that wasn't an isolated event. There were 12 such fines levied against U.S. organizations alone for a total of $10.9 billion. To fill out the top 20 country totals, fines range from $959 million to $.62 million.

I'm not talking about those kinds of fraud noncompliance. I'm interested in cybersecurity compliance. In terms of first principles, what's the probability that a failure-to-comply penalty will be material to the business in the next three years? And, if the senior leadership thinks that probability is too high, what's the cost to reduce it?

The Probability of Material Impact Due to Noncompliance

For this second category, to forecast this probability, I will follow the same basic steps I outlined in Chapter 6. The thing with compliance, though, is that there are so many permutations and combinations of compliance laws that may impact your specific organization that there is no one generic forecast that you can make for the category of

[41]Staff, 2018. Anthem pays OCR $16 Million in record HIPAA settlement following largest health data breach in history - October 15, 2018 [WWW Document]. HHS.gov. www.hhs.gov/hipaa/for-professionals/compliance-enforcement/agreements/anthem/index.html (accessed 12/18/22).
[42]Staff, 2020. The Bank Fines 2020 report [WWW Document]. Finbold. finbold.com/bank-fines-2020 (accessed 12/4/22).

compliance risk. It depends on how big the organization is, what part of the world it operates in, and which industry it belongs to.

Reviewing reports by CSO Online[43] and DLA Piper,[44] a conservative estimate as to the total number of cybersecurity compliance laws that exist in the world in 2021 is north of 50, and that's an estimate that is skewed toward western countries. There are likely many more in smaller developing countries. There will absolutely be many more in the years to come for everybody. Network defenders will have to do their own specific risk forecast analysis based on their circumstances.

To provide an example, though, I will focus on healthcare and the U.S. 1996 HIPAA.[45] I will look at the risk forecast for one of the companies that the Department of Health and Human Services' Office for Civil Rights (OCR) fined in 2022: ACM Podiatry.[46]

According to Smiljanic Stasha, staff writer for the PolicyAdvice website, there are 784,626 healthcare companies in the United States as of 2022.[47] Assume that all of them are impacted by HIPAA. Also assume that they are all equally likely to get a HIPPA fine. That's probably not true. In the same way that hackers target larger organizations because that's where the money is (see Chapter 6),

[43]Staff, 2022. Security and privacy laws, regulations, and compliance: The complete guide [WWW Document]. CSO Online. www.csoonline.com/article/3604334/csos-ultimate-guide-to-security-and-privacy-laws-regulations-and-compliance.html?upd=1633550065086#FISMA (accessed 12/4/22).
[44]Staff, 2022. Data Protection Laws of the World. DLA Piper.
[45]Archer, Bill , 1996. Health Insurance Portability and Accountability Act.
[46]Staff, 2022. ACPM Podiatry HIPAA Enforcement Action [WWW Document]. HHS.gov. www.hhs.gov/hipaa/for-professionals/compliance-enforcement/agreements/acpm/index.html (accessed 12/18/22).
[47]Stasha, Smiljanic , 2022. Healthcare statistics for 2021 [WWW Document]. Policy Advice. policyadvice.net/insurance/insights/healthcare-statistics (accessed 11/23/22).

compliance enforcement agencies are more likely to target larger organizations for fines too. But for now, let's assume that it's all equal.

According to the HIPAA Journal website, OCR issued 17 HIPPA fines in 2022. The chances then that any one healthcare organization in the United States will have to pay a HIPPA fine is quite small. It might as well be a 0 percent chance. For the 17 companies that did get fined, this was a potential black swan event for them. ACM Podiatry was one of those companies, and it paid a $100,000 fine.

ZoomInfo, a company that provides B2B intelligence for sales and marketing customers, estimates that ACM Podiatry brings in an average of $15 million in revenue each year.[48] If we use the Kroll Consulting estimate that many organizations will spend the equivalent of 5 percent of their revenue on compliance programs, ACM Podiatry could have spent $750,000 to avoid a $100,000 fine. Or, they could have not gone through the trouble of establishing the program, rolled the dice, and reasonably expected not to be fined at all. The latter is what it appears the company did. It just happened to get caught in a black swan event.

The $100,000 fine puts ACM Podiatry in one of two possible tiers of HIPPA fines.[49] Tier 2 means that the company should have known about the violation and done something to correct it. Tier 3 means that the company knew about the issues and decided, on purpose, not to fix it. If ACM Podiatry was in Tier 3, HIPPA says that it has 30 days to fix the identified issues. If the company doesn't,

[48]Staff, n.d. Who is ACPM Podiatry Group [WWW Document]. ZoomInfo. www.zoominfo.com/c/acpm-podiatry-group-ltd/1101297340

[49]Staff, 2022. HIPAA Violation Fines - Updated for 2022 [WWW Document]. HIPAA Journal. www.hipaajournal.com/hipaa-violation-fines (accessed 12/18/22).

it moves into Tier 4 and could be fined $1.5 million a year until the issues are corrected.

Like Marvel Studios from Chapter 6, ACM Podiatry is in the same Cyentia risk class based on revenue (less than $1 billion). With an outside-in Fermi estimate, not looking at how well ACM Podiatry adheres to our first principles (a Fermi inside-out analysis), it has the same probability of material impact due to a cyber event: 17 percent. In this case, I'm now considering new evidence about the risk of noncompliance and will adjust the 17 percent prior up or down accordingly. But, since there is almost a 0 percent chance of receiving a HIPPA fine, there is no adjustment. The new prior is the same prior: 17 percent.

For compliance specifically, the ACM Podiatry's CSO might recommend to the leadership team that it's not worth the $750,000 to build the system that will help demonstrate compliance to auditors when a fine is not likely to happen. Even if it does, the fine will cost significantly less ($100,000) than what it would cost to build the compliance system. This is not willful neglect. Not building the auditing infrastructure isn't the same as not building a better security posture. The CSO should recommend continued investment in the first principle strategies, and it's likely that if those programs are in place, a HIPPA auditor won't find a violation anyway. That said, if the senior leadership's risk tolerance is conservative and they insist on a strategy to mitigate the fine, the CSO might look into insurance to cover the cost.

This is tricky because those 50+ laws that I mentioned earlier in the chapter all have different provisions. Your mileage may vary, and it's best to consult your company's own legal department to get their take. But in general, there is no specific prohibition in most compliance law against using insurance to cover the cost of fines. Still, according to Jones Day, a long-established legal firm, insurance claims against compliance penalties based on willful misconduct will likely get challenged by the insurer.[50] In the ACM Podiatry case, it's best to stay in the HIPPA Tier 2 category—a mistake but not willful misconduct.

Another potential reason to build a compliance program is the threat of class-action lawsuits. According to Hagens Berman, an international law firm that specializes in this type of legal action, lawyers build these kinds of cases "on behalf of a group of people or business entities who have suffered common injuries as a result of the defendants' conduct."[51] For a cybersecurity example, in 2019, ZenDesk investors initiated a class action lawsuit alleging that ZenDesk had been subject to a data breach in 2016 among other things.[52]

In general, to mitigate the threat of this kind of lawsuit, company lawyers could use a mature compliance program to demonstrate to the court that leadership took reasonable measures to prevent a breach. Similar to compliance fines, though, the numbers of cybersecurity class-action lawsuits are quite small. An exact number is difficult to pin down but is likely in the range between 30 to 2,000 depending on how you count them. The chances that any one company in the United States out of the more than six million in existence (see Chapter 6) will experience one of these lawsuits is quite small. For ACM Podiatry, It would be difficult to justify the three-quarters of a million dollars it would take to build a compliance program for a risk that is almost negligible.

---

[50]Emmerig, J., 2019. Data Breach Class Actions in Australia. Jones Day.
[51]Staff, n.d. What is a Class Action Lawsuit? [WWW Document]. Hagens Berman. www.hbsslaw.com/about/what-is-a-class-action-lawsuit (accessed 11/25/22).
[52]Staff, 2019. Levi & Korsinsky Announces Zendesk Class Action Investigation; ZEN Lawsuit - Levi & Korsinsky, LLP [WWW Document]. Levi & Korsinsky LLP. www.zlk.com/press/levi-korsinsky-announces-zendesk-class-action-investigation-zen-lawsuit (accessed 11/25/22).

The last reason to build a compliance program is to protect brand reputation. If you're trying to convince potential customers to buy your services, you could roll out the compliance results for your industry for the last five years to prove that your company can be trusted. But this is a marketing decision. It's akin to buying a commercial for a popular TV show. It also may be an "unofficial" ticket to do business for certain industries. If every competitor in your space has a mature compliance program, establishing one may just be the cost of being in that specific business.

Is Compliance a First Principle Tactic?

Compliance is an odd duck. If you look at the first principle road map (see the introduction chapter, you will notice that I have it as a tactic that cuts across all first principle strategies the same as the DevSecOps tactic. There are two reasons for this. First, if you're building a compliance program, you will want to tap into all of the deployed first principle tactics to gather the intelligence telemetry that will satisfy the auditors. Second, it's best to plug into the continuous integration/continuous delivery (CI/CD) parts of the organization to reduce the volume of manual toil it takes to build those same reports.

For our first principle strategy, though, compliance is just another tactic that we might use in the same way we might use SBOMs, purple teams, or encryption. In terms of pure impact, though, it's probably not high in the priority list. The reason I list it as a tactic, though, is that, for certain industries like finance and healthcare, security professionals will likely be involved in the company's compliance program in some fashion because the organization's leadership has decided that it's a business requirement. That might be true, but adhering to compliance rules and spending resources proving that you do so will likely not reduce the probability of material impact by much.

Chaos Engineering for Automation and Resilience

Chaos engineering is the resilience discipline of controlled stress test experimentation in CI/CD environments to uncover systemic weaknesses. Chaos engineers build hypotheses around expected software behavior, design small footprint (tiny blast radius) experiments that vary steady state behavior (like bandwidth and CPU use), and run those experiments in production systems to learn about unknown system weaknesses. Admittedly, this is an advanced tactic for the first principle strategy and is not for the small, medium, and even some larger companies. But, if your organization provides global digital services that can have zero downtime, then you likely have a team of chaos engineers somewhere performing these experiments.

To understand why chaos engineering is required by these global service providers, you must first accept the fact that we no longer live in a linear, digital world. When the Internet emerged as a useful business tool (1990s), things were pretty simple. We didn't think so at the time, but compared to today, that world was kindergarten. If you changed one thing in that world, you pretty much knew what was going to happen. But today's IT environments are systems of systems. We're in PhD land here. They are complicated, and most of us have no idea how they actually work and what the real dependencies are between all the software modules deployed on all of our data islands.

According to Rosenthal, Jones, and Aschbacher in their book *Chaos Engineering: System Resiliency in Practice*,[53] "A change to input of a linear system produces a corresponding change to the output of the system. Nonlinear systems have output that varies wildly based on changes to the constituent parts." It's like that old chestnut that when a butterfly flaps its wings in China, you might end up with a hurricane in the Gulf of Mexico. When the hard drive of a system

---

[53]Rosenthal, C., Jones, N., 2020. Chaos Engineering: System Resiliency in Practice. O'Reilly Media.

running a nonessential monitoring app in an AWS region in North America fails but somehow causes a system wide failure, this is what I'm talking about.

These systems are complicated, and humans can't possibly understand all the permutations in their head. Software engineers think they know, and DevOps and SRE teams write linear regression tests for things they assume to be true. But those teams don't learn anything new by doing so. They test properties of the system that are already known, like previously corrected defects and boundary conditions of the main features of a product.

Rosenthal, Jones, and Aschbacher say that these kinds of linear regression tests, "...require that the engineer writing the test knows specific properties about the system that they are looking for." Chaos engineering, in contrast, is the pursuit of the unknown. They don't replace linear regression tests; they are trying to solve a different problem by uncovering unknown and, as yet, undiscovered design faults.

Chaos engineering is built on the scientific method. DevOps teams develop a hypothesis around steady-state behavior and run experiments in production to see if the hypothesis holds. If they discover a difference in steady state between the control group and the experimental group on production systems, then they have learned something new. If not, they have gained more confidence in their hypothesis. They use techniques to minimize the blast radius on the production system and monitor the entire experiment carefully to ensure no catastrophic effect, but they have to be on the production system to do it.

In Chapter 5, I pointed to Netflix as the poster child for this new tactic. I said that Netflix routinely runs an app, like Chaos Money, that randomly destroys pieces of their customer-facing infrastructure, on purpose, so that their network architects understand resilience engineering down deep in their core.

When I first learned about this technique, I was stunned by the audacity, and seemingly recklessness, of the approach. In my past career, I would never destroy parts of my production system on purpose for an experiment. I may do it by mistake, but never on purpose. In hindsight, as I have learned more about the subject, that's not exactly how chaos engineering works. It's audacious for sure, but the Netflix chaos engineering system is mature, and its DevOps teams have been developing the practice since 2008. The teams learned how to do this, and their experts wouldn't recommend that newbies to the idea start by destroying parts of their production system. You have to ease into it.

History of Chaos Engineering

Chaos engineering began in 2008 with a couple of delivery failures at Netflix.[54] The company was transitioning from a DVD-mailing company to a streaming company. The Netflix leadership team very publicly announced its commitment to adopt AWS cloud services and abandon its own data centers. This was a big idea since Amazon just rolled out the service two years before and it wasn't what anybody would claim as mature yet.

The Netflix precipitating event was a database failure that prevented the company from delivering DVDs to its customers for three days. That obviously wasn't resilient (see Chapter 5). Further, that Christmas in 2008, AWS suffered a major outage that prevented Netflix customers from using the new streaming service. In response, Netflix engineers developed their first chaos engineering product in 2010, called Chaos Monkey, that helped them counter the vanishing instance problem caused by the AWS outage. With that success, Netflix began building its own chaos engineering team and wondered if it could scale. If the team could fix the small scale vanishing instances problem, could they do the same at the vanishing region scale?

In fairness, Netflix wasn't the only company thinking along these lines. In 2006, Google SREs established their own disaster recovery testing (DiRT) program to intentionally insert failures into their internal systems to discover unknown risks. But their cool name for it (DiRT) wasn't as hip as the Netflix name (Chaos Monkey), and it didn't catch on. The idea was similar, though.[55]

By 2011, Netflix began adding new failure modules that provided a more complete suite of resilience features. Those modules eventually became known as the Netflix Simian Army and include colorful names like Latency Monkey, Conformity Monkey, and Doctor Monkey, just to name three. There are many more.

Netflix shared the source code for Chaos Monkey on GitHub in 2012, and by 2013, other organizations started playing with the idea. By 2014, Netflix created a new employee role (chaos engineer) and began working on ideas of reducing the blast radius of planned injected failures. By 2016, Netflix had an entire team of chaos engineers working on the Simian Army. By this time, there was a small but growing contingent of companies experimenting with the idea too (like Capital One, Google, Slack, Microsoft, and LinkedIn).

What Does Chaos Engineering Have to Do with Automation and Resilience?

Traditionally, linear regression tests, SRE and DevOps teams, and IT resilience have generally been the purview of the CIO. There are definite divisions of labor for resilience, though. The CIO is handling the DevOps piece, and the CSO needs to be part of the team. But I'm making the case that chaos engineering is something that should be

---

[54]Staff, 2018. Chaos Monkey at Netflix: the Origin of Chaos Engineering [WWW Document]. Gremlin. www.gremlin.com/chaos-monkey/the-origin-of-chaos-monkey (accessed 12/6/22).
[55]Bort, J., 2016. Meet Kripa Krishnan, Google's queen of chaos. Insider.

owned by the CSO. Who better to discover potential unknown systemic failures that might impact production or the ability to recover from an event quickly? The CIO handles the known stuff. In terms of first principles, the CSO's job description should be to discover unknown faults in the system that will cause material damage.

According to Rinehart and Shortridge in their book *Security Chaos Engineering*, traditional security programs orbit around failure avoidance.[56] Infosec teams design and implement people, process, and technology policy designed to prevent the organization from getting anywhere near a disaster. In contrast, they say that failure is where an infosec team learns the most. I agree. If you can build these small experiments that uncover potential systematic failure, that might be the most valuable thing an infosec team does.

Rinehart and Shortridge say that this mindset changes the infosec team's focus away from building a purely defensive posture and toward something that is adaptive. Instead of seeking defensive perfection, pursue the ability to handle failure gracefully. And that's as close to the resilience definition described in Chapter 5 as you're going to get. It also implies that, especially at this scale, this graceful handling of failure will be handled at the infrastructure-as-code level.

They recommend that the infosec community move away from security theater (a concept made famous by one of cybersecurity's thought leaders, Bruce Schneier).[57] This is the idea that infosec teams perform work that creates the perception of improved security but, in reality, doesn't add much. One example of this could be the purchase of an antiphishing product that delivers approved phishing email messages to employees to train them not to click bad URLs. Or another is building an insider threat program designed to prevent

[56]Shortridge, K., Rhinehart, A., 2023. Security Chaos Engineering.
[57]Glaskowsky, P., 2008. Bruce Schneier's new view on Security Theater. CNET.

employees from taking their old PowerPoint slides with them to their next job. In the big scheme of things, are those kinds of security theater programs as impactful as discovering a previously unknown fault in the organization's system design that could cause catastrophic failure? The notion is worth considering.

Specifically with respect to traditional security, however, Rinehart and Shortridge suggest that you could apply the chaos engineering idea to things like red teaming (see Chapter 4). Instead of turning loose the red team to find some hole in the defensive posture, we could instead develop a hypothesis around how the organization should react to a specific attack sequence, for example, Wicked Panda. If we treat red-teaming exercises as a science experiment with a hypothesis that defines how we think the organization will react to a Wicked Panda attack, we might learn something new. If that's true, we could expand this kind of thinking to all sorts of traditional security tasks such as container security, CI/CD pipeline security, security monitoring, incident response, and so forth. You might say you're already doing those things. But what I'm suggesting is a subtle shift away from rudimentary tests of the system with things we already know about and toward the more advanced scientific method designed to uncover the things we don't already know.

That said, chaos engineering is not for everybody. It's another tactic that we might use to reduce the probability of material impact because of a cyber event. It's another arrow in our quiver to build our resilience program alongside the other arrows like crisis planning, incident response, backups, and encryption. The concept is probably a bridge too far for most small- to medium-sized organizations that struggle to find resources just to keep the lights on. But, for big Silicon Valley companies that deliver services from around the world (the Netflixes, the Googles, the LinkedIns, etc.) and for most Fortune 500 companies, chaos engineering is something to consider. Indeed, many of these companies may already be on this path.

Conclusion

Since the beginning of the computer era, security professionals have left the automation strategy largely to the IT community. In contrast, developers have evolved their philosophical thinking from the Waterfall method in the 1950s to the Agile Manifesto in the 2000s to the DevOps tactic in the 2010s. In that same time, though, the evolution of security has advanced in parallel with concepts such as zero trust, intrusion kill chain prevention, resilience, and risk forecasting, but not in an integrated way with their IT counterparts. Interestingly, security professionals have turned to vendors and platforms to automate pieces and parts of the security infrastructure never realizing that their systems are as important as their organization's IT systems and should be managed in a similar DevOps manner too. There are best practices for developing secure code in the CI/CD pipeline (OWASP, BSIMM, and SAMM), but those ideas don't cover the automation of the first principle strategies and tactics explained in this book. In this chapter, I advocated for the idea that the infosec community must pursue this strategy.

Further, I addressed how the idea of compliance is an odd duck in the security community. The practice doesn't really impact the probability of material impact due to a cyber event, but it might be required to conduct business with another organization (ticket to proceed). I further looked at the probability that a compliance fine or class-action lawsuit might warrant an investment of resources to build a compliance program. The number of compliance laws is vast and ever-changing, and there is no one general-purpose rule to forecast the risk. Using the Fermi estimate outside-in technique, I demonstrated how a healthcare security professional might calculate the potential risk, but those calculations are very much dependent on the size of the organization, where it conducts business in the world, and the industry it services.

Finally, I concluded with a relatively new and advanced automation resilience technique called chaos engineering that will likely only be used by mature and well-resourced organizations. Still, the ideas around developing hypotheses and testing systems to verify those hypotheses could be used in other first principle tactics like red teaming.

Automation is a key and essential strategy for our first principle philosophy. Looking at the road map (Introduction), there is a reason that it touches all the others. As security professionals, we may not implement all of the tactics for each first principle strategy, but for the ones that we do, we need to automate as much as possible to eliminate the toil and errors inherent in the manual process.

8 Summation

If you don't like peas, it is probably because you have not had them fresh. It is the difference between reading a great book and reading the summary on the back.

—Lemony Snicket

To summarize the summary of the summary: people are a problem.

—Douglas Adams

Writing long books is a laborious and impoverishing act of foolishness: expanding in 500 pages an idea that could be perfectly explained in a few minutes. A better procedure is to pretend that those books already exist and to offer a summary, a commentary.

—Jorge Luis Borges

Overview

This book is the culmination of roughly 30 years of my experience working in the cybersecurity community. I arrived on the scene just as the Internet began to be useful to business, to academia, and to general-purpose government functions. You could say that I was there from the beginning. The current state of cybersecurity thinking is largely due to me and my peers in the industry trying to figure it out on the fly. We have made some great progress. We have also made some big mistakes, which is par for the course in any great adventure. Most of the mistakes get corrected over time with the people, process, and technology triad as we find new and better ways to accomplish certain tasks or realize that the method we were using to accomplish something wasn't really working. The one mistake we haven't corrected, though, is coming to some consensus about what all this effort is really about. It's a common meme in the community that if you ask any one security professional in a room of 100 about what it is they are trying to do with their infosec programs, you will likely get 100 different answers. Boiling it down, those answers are some version or combination of these ideas:

- Implement the CIA triad.
- Patch all of your software.
- Prevent malware installations.
- Implement incident response.
- Adhere to some security frameworks.
- Commit to mandatory compliance regulations.

All of those are worthy concepts, tactics that you might pursue, but they don't really answer the most important question. When the senior executive team or the board asks you, "What's your cybersecurity strategy for the organization and why?" responding with any of them will likely not get you invited to the next board meeting. They have nothing to do with business specifically, and the description of them is not in the standard vernacular that leaders are used to dealing with. More important, they don't get to the root of the matter.

For each of them, you can hear the seasoned infosec professional say, "But what about. . .?" For example, the CIA triad is great, but what about the cafeteria's online menu? Is that so important that we have to protect it with CIA? Patching is useful, but what about malware? Preventing malware installation is desirable, but what about lateral movement? Responding to incidents is important, but what about preventing the breach in the first place? Frameworks are good checklists, but what about compliance? Compliance is necessary, but what about the CIA triad, patching, anti-malware, and incident response? Clearly, there needs to be a more fundamental strategy, something that captures the essence of why we do security. We should get back to first principles.

The idea of scientific first principles has been around since the age of Aristotle. To solve any thorny problem set, big thinkers like Euclid, Descartes, Whitehead and Russell, and Elon Musk all realized that they had to reduce it down to its primary essence. Euclid boiled geometry down to simple postulates. Descartes condensed the Principles of Philosophy down to "I think, therefore I am." Whitehead and Russel wrote 80 pages to mathematically prove that 1 + 1 = 2. Musk rethought the very nature of orbital space flight. If these scientific leaders could do it for their respective fields, isn't it reasonable to assume that the infosec community should do it too?

And so here it is. The absolute cybersecurity first principle is this:

Reduce the probability of material impact due to a cyber event over the next three years. When you read that purpose statement, it's irreducible. You don't hear infosec practitioners say, "But what about. . .?" The CIA triad, patching, anti-malware, incident response, security frameworks and compliance all fit nicely underneath that umbrella. It's the overarching universal strategy for what we are all trying to do regardless of the organizational size and purpose.

Of course, as in other fields, the cybersecurity atomic first principle is an all-encompassing strategy. Even though the "what" is clear, the "how" we go about it will involve multiple smaller strategies that flow logically from it.

- **Zero trust**
  Reduce the digital attack surface by limiting access and permissions to only the people, devices, and software that absolutely need them to keep the business functioning as desired by the leadership, and nothing else.
- **Intrusion kill chain prevention**
  Design and deploy detection and prevention controls for all known adversary attack campaigns.
- **Resilience**
  During and after some catastrophic event, continue to deliver the organization's purpose as if nothing happened.
- **Risk forecasting**
  Forecast the probability of material impact due to a cyber event with just enough precision that enables leaders to make reasonable cybersecurity resource decisions.
- **Automation**
  Reduce the manual and repetitive security work (the toil) inherent in all of our first principle strategies.

These first principle strategies are clear. When we all agree that the ultimate first principle is to reduce the probability of material impact, they each logically follow as the next steps. This is problem solving. We are breaking the big ultimate first problem into smaller more manageable problems. The choice of tactics for how to accomplish each strategy are many.

Zero Trust

- **Meat-and-potatoes zero trust**
  Zero trust is a journey, and you can start by using the systems you already have in place.

- **Logical and microsegmentation**
  Create access rules tied to people, devices, and software applications.
- **Vulnerability management**
  Continuously monitor all software assets (version control, open source packages nested libraries, current configuration, access history, and exposure to newly discovered vulnerabilities and exploits).
- **Software bill of materials (SBOMs)**
  Maintain a formal record containing the details and supply chain relationships of various components used in building software.
- **Identity and authorization management (IAM)**
  Deploy identity governance and administration (IGA), privileged identity management (PIM), and privileged access management (PAM).
- **Single sign-on**
  Enable users and applications to assert their identity once to a trusted source and never have to remember or send passwords again.
- **Multifactor authentication**
  Enforce two or three forms of identity verification: something they have, like a smartphone; something they are, like a fingerprint; or something they know, like a password.
- **Software-defined perimeter**
  Move the IAM function away from the material systems you are trying to protect.

Intrusion Kill Chain Prevention

- **The adversary model trifecta**
  Use the Lockheed Martin Kill Chain model as an overarching strategic template, the MITRE ATT&CK® Framework for

operational intelligence, and the DOD's Diamond model for your intelligence teams.

- **Cyberthreat intelligence**
  Use the intelligence life cycle to collect raw information on material information requirements and transform that information into intelligence products for decision-making and the detection of known adversary attack behavior.
- **Intelligence sharing**
  Build sharing relationships with peers in like-minded verticals (ISACs and ISAOs).
- **Orchestrating the security stack**
  Automate the collection of adversary activity across the intrusion kill chain and the deployment of detection and prevention controls to the deployed security stack.
- **Security operations centers**
  As your organization grows in capability, build or hire an SOC to manage the workflow and status of the various groups and functions in order to coordinate actions among them.
- **Red/blue/purple team operations**
  Exercise adversary emulation teams (red team) against your data islands and monitor and improve how the SOC (blue team) responds.

Resilience

- **Crisis handling**
  Design plans with outcomes in mind. Use scenarios to train decision-makers regularly. When the plan goes south during an actual event, which it will, focus on outcomes.

- **Backups and restores**
  Make a copy of all material data. More important, regularly practice restoring that data into production.
- **Encryption**
  Encode all material data at rest and in motion.
- **Resilience systems are themselves material**
  Backups, restores, and encryption, because of data they protect, must be protected with the same first principle strategies and tactics as other material systems.
- **Incident response**
  Monitor, investigate, and develop cyber "events" within the SOC until it is clear that they are actual cyber "incidents." At that milestone, trigger the organization's crisis handling plan that will start bringing in other organizational resources.

Risk Forecasting

- **Bayes rule**
  Make an initial probability estimate of a material impact due to a cyber event with information you have on hand. As you collect more evidence, adjust the estimate up or down accordingly.
- **Superforecasting**
  Probability is a measure of your certainty. Use outside-in analysis to make a prediction in the general case. Adjust that initial forecast down appropriately using inside-out analysis regarding how well your specific organization adheres to first principle strategies.
- **Fermi estimates**
  For cybersecurity resourcing decisions, back-of-the-envelope calculations based on superforecasting techniques are good enough.

Automation

- **DevSecOps**
  Catch up to our brothers and sisters on the DevOps side and adopt their methods to automate our first principle tactics.
- **Compliance**
  If your organization requires a ticket to ride to conduct business or could be exposed to hefty penalties and fines for noncompliance, it's likely that it has built an entire system to track progress and report. These systems don't improve the organization's security posture per se, but whatever they are should tie into the deployed first principle tactics.
- **Chaos engineering**
  Mostly reserved for large companies in terms of revenue, it is the use of the scientific method to discover unknown systemic weaknesses that will prevent the organization from being resilient in the face of a catastrophic failure.

Conclusion

I want to reiterate here that I'm not advocating that all network defenders should deploy all of these first principle strategies and tactics in equal measure. Every organization is different. What will have the greatest impact for your organization, within the resource constraints of the people, process, and technology triad at your disposal, will vary greatly depending on how big your organization is. The fact is that implementing many of these strategies is not cheap. You have to weigh the potential probability reduction against your organization's own risk tolerance and the potential cost to deploy and maintain it. For example, when you work at a big Fortune 500 company, zero trust, intrusion kill chain prevention, and automation are possible. But when you work at an early-stage startup, resilience is most likely the strategy that will cost the least and have the greatest impact on reducing the probability of material impact to your organization.

The point is that there are reasons to pursue these strategies in total and in part. Every one of them has the potential to reduce the probability of material impact due to a cyber event. Being able to measure that impact (risk forecasting) is an essential skill for all infosec practitioners but especially for senior cybersecurity leaders. Using that skill will allow those leaders to pick the most impactful first principle strategies and tactics that are appropriate for their organization.

And that's it. Those are all the tools you need to design, build, and improve a cybersecurity program based on first principle thinking. Now go reduce the probability of material impact to your organization due to a cyber event. While you're at it, reach out to me every once in a while and let me know how it's going (`rick.howard@theCyberWire.com`).

INDEX

B

C

D

E

H

I

J

K

N

O

P

V